BLACK BRITANNIA

BLACK BRITANNIA

A History of Blacks in Britain

by
Edward Scobie

Johnson Publishing Company Inc.
Chicago, 1972

*ISBN No. 0–87485–056–8
Library of Congress Catalog Card No. 72–82184*

*Published 1972
Printed in the United States of America*

Designed by John Carafoli

Black Britannia *has been set in
various faces of linotype Palatino by the Typoservice
Corporation, Indianapolis, Indiana.*

*We are grateful to the editor of the former
"independent labour weekly" for permission
to quote the extract from* Tribune *on pages 220-223*

To my homeland, Dominica,
and its people—
both I love dearly.

FOREWORD

One of the best-known and most stirring of patriotic songs was written by the celebrated English musical scholar and composer Thomas Arne in 1740. It was introduced in Mallet's *Masque of Alfred.* This song "Rule Britannia," although not the British national anthem, is a worthy competitor which has been known to move Britons to make colonial conquests for king and country; to commit acts of superhuman bravery, again for king and country; and to sing with lusty fervor its patriotic words. This second, or alternative, national anthem says in part, "Rule Britannia, Britannia rule the waves, Britons never never never shall be slaves."

But Dr. Thomas Arne was wrong. For he should have known only too well that certain Britons were slaves. They were slaves in the British colonies of the Caribbean and in British North America; but more important, at least as far as this work is concerned, these Britons were slaves in Britain—Dr. Arne's Britannia. These Britons were black. Dr. Arne must have seen them walking in the London streets behind their masters. And it is with them that much of *Black Britannia* deals. After their emancipation by the English courts in 1772 black Britons were no longer slaves in Britain in the legal sense, but they were still slaves in the social and economic fabric of British life. This legacy, though improving constantly, has survived and today blacks in Britain find themselves slaves to the same prejudices which once kept them in chains. The latter part of *Black Britannia* is concerned with these present day black Britons who have to live in a racial straight jacket, with the weight of social and economic strictures still bearing heavily on them; even today, almost into its last quarter, the twentieth century is still painfully at war, with many lessons still to learn as it moves into the pages of history.

Even before the reign of Queen Elizabeth I, which began in 1558, people in England had the experience of living with many blacks in their midst. This is an aspect of the African Slave Trade which concerns Britain as it does other European countries like Portugal and Spain.

This work sets out to examine when, how, and why slaves started finding themselves in Britain. It will do this by discussing the findings of anthropologists, analyzing facts from contemporary sources, such as letters, diaries, newspaper reports, journals, court and official documents and books. But this examination, covering also the conditions under which these early migrants lived, constitutes only a part of this work. The rest covers the latter part of the nineteenth century when seamen and others came to Britain, and continues through this century up to the present time. Particular emphasis will be laid on the period after World War II when migration of black people into Britain reached staggering proportions, causing racial tension to mount and culminate in race riots and the Commonwealth Immigrants Act which tried to stem the flood of migration.

There are many authorities and friends whom I want to thank for their suggestions in respect of material for this book. Especial thanks to Professor Liebert of Yale University who gave me access to letters which passed between James Boswell and Francis Barber while work on the *Life of Johnson* was in progress. Then comes Mrs. Rowell, the Custodian of Dr. Johnson's house on Gough Square, Fleet Street, who, during the countless conversations we had about "dear Frank" and Dr. Johnson, gave me many personal and interesting tit-bits about the relationship between the two of them. Nor can I forget my friends: poet and BBC producer Terence Tiller for initial encouragement, and writers Jan Carew and Andrew Salkey for valuable discussions on British racial attitudes which we experienced while struggling to carve out a living on the fringes of writing and broadcasting in Britain. My thanks, too, to the officials in the Reading Room of the British Museum for their patience in advising me and helping me to get the books I needed for research.

I must single out Commander T. S. L. Fox-Pitt, O.B.E. secretary of the Anti-Slavery Society, with whom I discussed the work several times and who made suggestions and always managed to give me that extra piece of vital information. Not only that, he allowed me free use of the books in the library of the society. I am deeply grateful to him.

I want to thank the original proprietor of the Chalton Publishing Company in London for allowing me to use material which appeared in *Flamingo* magazine while I was editor-in-chief during the years 1961–63; and Mr. Michael Foot, editor of the former "Independent Labour Weekly," *Tribune* for permission to use the long extract from an article by Mervyn Jones in the issue of September 15, 1958, quoted in Chapter XIV. My grateful appreciation to Mr. Ralph Casimir, Dominican poet and friend for the loan of his files and his abiding interest in the book. Typing the last five chapters, which constitute the bulk of the work, was undertaken by my secretary, Miss Hildreth Jno Charles, of Mahaut, Dominica, who had to wade through the often illegible jig-saw of my longhand. She was first-class. To Mrs. Molly Scobie, I am thankful. She not only typed the first six chapters of the manuscript several times in its early stages, and made corrections, but some years ago gave me much needed encouragement when my spirits were low. I owe a debt of gratitude to Mrs. Doris E. Saunders for her valuable suggestion that I should extend the work to include the years before, between, and after the two world wars, up to the present time. Book Division editor Mrs. Brenda M. Biram was wonderful and it was her painstaking revision, patience and great interest in the manuscript which helped to end the long years of frustration by getting it into print. I must offer sincere thanks to Dr. C. L. R. James, who read the manuscript and made important suggestions, which were incorporated.

The writing of this work was a labor of love. Any imperfections which may be found in it are the author's responsibility.

Edward Scobie
March, 1972
Livingston College,
Rutgers University.

CONTENTS

BLACK BRITANNIA

a
b
c
h
i
n
OLAUDAH EQUIANO;
OR,
GUSTAVUS VASSA,
THE
African.

PART ONE

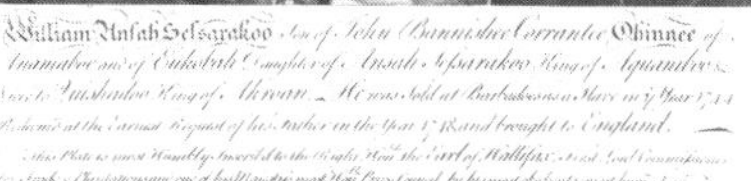

SLAVES ON THE LIVERPOOL QUAY-SIDE

A MUNGO MACARONI.

Key to Illustrations

a) George Augustus Polgreen Bridgtower, composer

b) Francis Barber, servant and friend to Dr. Samuel Johnson

c) Bill Richmond, pugilist

d) Chevalier Georges de St. Georges, son of Marquis de Langley and a black slave.

e) Duchess of Portsmouth with her blackamoor

f) African Prince Sessarakoo (Barbados Museum and Historical Society).

g) Slaves on the Liverpool quayside.

h) Francis Williams (Institute of Jamaica photograph).

i) Olaudah Equiano, or Gustavus Vassa

j) Tom Molineaux, prize fighter

k) Dr. Samual Johnson (H. Zinram, London, W.l.)

l) Hogarth's "Taste in High Life" British Museum).

m) Julius Soubise, the Mungo Macaroni

n) Richard Hill (Institute of Jamaica Photograph).

o) Jacobus Eliza Capitein, scholar.

p) A social gathering (John R. Freeman (Photographers) Ltd. London, W.l.).

q) Ira Aldridge, the African Roscius.

CHAPTER I

COURTESANS AND BLACKAMOORS

The Gray's Inn Revels were different that Christmas of 1594. But the idea was still the same: entertainments to parody the affairs and ceremonies of the English court. The Revels would start on Hallowe'en and last until Candlemass. A Prince of Purpool was installed on December 20th. He was two characters in one—Purpool and the Lord of Misrule. By the 28th there were so many spectators that Gray's Inn Hall became too packed for anyone to enter. That evening the actors put on *The Comedy of Errors.* Six days later the Revels were in full swing. Among those present were Lord Burleigh, the Earl of Essex, the Lord Keeper, Sir Robert Cecil and the Earls of Shrewsbury, Cumberland, Northumberland, and Southampton. The amusements began with a symbolic piece of the restoration of amity between Graius and Templarius. After that the Prince of Purpool held court. To pay homage to him came the Abbess of Clerkenwell, holder of the Nunnery and Lands and Privileges of Clerkenwell, "with a choir of Nuns, with burning lamps, to chaunt Placebo to the gentlemen of the Prince's Privy-Chamber, on the Day of His Excellency's Coronation."

It was the Abbess who made the difference in that year's Revels. For she was not a lady of court but a courtesan from Clerkenwell. She was tall, statuesque, and haughty. Her name was Lucy Negro and she was in fact black and an African.

This Lucy Negro was not the only black courtesan around Clerkenwell. There were several in the district at the time especially around "The Swan, a Dane's beershop in Turnbull Street." Here, fashionable young gentlemen of the Inns of Court used to frolic. Dr. George Bagshawe Harrison, authority on Shakespeare, claims that the Bard of Avon fell in love with Lucy Negro, the most famous courtesan of them all, only to lose her later on to the Earl of Southampton. Dr. Harrison makes a further more startling statement: "This Lucy Negro I would identify as the Dark Lady of the Sonnets."

Dr. Leslie Hotson, a man of brilliant and unorthodox scholarship and an expert on Shakespeare, after exhaustive research throws further light on Lucy Negro:

> We arrive at a beautiful harlot, black as hell, notorious in 1588 or 1589, named Lucy or Luce. . . . This at once takes our mind five or six years onwards to the Gesta Grayorum—the chronicle of Henry Prince of Purpoole's reign in 1594–95, and to the unsavoury list of the Prince's feodaries, in which we read that a bawd named Lucy Negro "Abbess de Clerkenwell, holdeth the nunnery of Clerkenwell . . ."
>
> By this time, then, some five or six years after the Sonnets Black Lucy or Luce has set up as the "madam" of a house in Clerkenwell. Her name was Morgan . . . I have been at some pains to collect facts and reports about Luce Morgan. My reward is the discovery of a series of documents indicating that some years before she charmed Shakespeare she had first charmed Queen Elizabeth.

It was quite common for Africans to take part in masques and pageants during that time—like the one called *The Masque of Blackness*, a pageant of Ethiopia staged by Ben Johnson in 1605, in which Queen Anne, wife of James I, played, and for which the ladies of the Court blackened their faces.

In Shakespeare's lifetime and after, blacks were very much in evidence in a particular show—London's colorful Lord Mayor's Show. One black known as "King of the Moors," mounted on a "lion" and preceded by other blacks bearing bars of gold, would lead the show. In 1680 a historian wrote: "On the Lion is mounted a young Negro Prince attired in a very right habit . . . with a fold hilt in scarf of gold by his side. With one hand he holds a golden bridle; in the other St. George's Banner and representeth power."

However, some anthropologists believe that black courtesans were not the first blacks to set foot in Britain. About the first arrivals there have been different claims. The late J. A. Rogers, the Jamaica-born historian, basing his claims on the writings of Tacitus who mentions "the dark complexion of the Silures, or Black Celts and the unusually curly hair" maintains that a black aboriginal race lived side by side with a white one in the British Isles in pre-Roman times. Another claim comes from the British archaeologist and writer David McRichie. He declared that the Moors dominated Scotland as late as the time of the Saxon kings. He goes on to say:

> So late as the tenth century three of these provinces [of Scotland] were wholly black and the supreme ruler of these became for a time the paramount King of Transmarine Scotland. We see one of the black people—the Moors of the Romans—in the person of a King of Alban of the tenth century. History knows him as Kenneth, sometimes as Dubh and as Niger. . . . We know as a historic fact that a Niger Val Dubh has lived and reigned over certain black divisions of our islands—and probably white divisions also—and that a race known as the "Sons of the Black" succeeded him in history.

These blacks, McRitchie contends, were bred out until the black man finally disappeared by mating with whites only, so that

> . . . no ethnologist could detect the presence of other blood . . . and yet, in both cases, the male descendants would bear the surname first given to their remote ancestors—a surname signifying "the black man. . ." You may see faces of a distinctly Mongolian and even of a Negroid cast in families whose pedigree may be traced for many generations without disclosing the slightest hint of extra-British blood. . . . So far as complexion goes there can be no doubt as to the presence of a vast infusion of "coloured" blood. There are, of course, no living Britons who are as black as Negroes but some are as dark as mulattoes and many darker than Chinese. To regard ourselves in the mass as a "white people" except in a comparative degree, is quite a mistake.

McRitchie's findings, like those of the other two British archaeologists, Gerald Massey and Godfrey Higgins, who unearthed data on the Negro in ancient Britain—are not supported by evidence of skeletal remains approximating to the black man in the ancient records of Britain. However, anthropologist Kenneth Little stated:

> Lack of skeletal remains does not, of course, rule out the possibility of well pigmented skins having been an aboriginal feature, but passing over the question of "swarthiness" of the Romans themselves and the possibility of Negroid elements amongst their auxiliaries and camp followers, it seems safest to start the British history of the Negro about the middle of the sixteenth century. . . .

It is possible to go further back than the middle of the sixteenth century and find historical documents to prove that even as early as 1501 there were blacks at court in Scotland. That year one of the King's minstrels was "Peter the Moryen or Moor," and three years later two blackamoor girls arrived and were educated at court where they waited on the queen. They were baptized Elen and Margaret, and in June, 1507, a tournament was held in honor of the Queen's black lady, Elen Moore "which was conducted with great splendour."

One of the first recorded instances of blacks living south of the border was the return, in 1554, of the London trader John Lok from a voyage to the West Coast of Africa, bringing with him a cargo of five African slaves, "whereof some were tall and strong men." They were taught the language in order that they might be used by merchants plying the slave trade. The blacks seem to have taken quickly to English food and life. But, Lok said, "the colde and moist aire doth somewhat offend them."

From the time that such English merchants began taking part in the African Slave Trade, the presence of blacks in England began to increase slowly. To add to their number, black musicians like those associated with the commedia dell'arte and the courts of Italian princes performed in Elizabethan entertainments. But these, as a rule, did not remain in the country.

Even at this early stage the government began to show concern over the number of blacks in England. On August 11, 1596, the Acts of Privy Council stated:

> Her Majestie understanding that there are of late divers blackamoors brought to this realm, of which kinde of people there are already too manie, considering how God hath blessed this land with great increase of people of our own nation . . . those kinde of people should be sent forth of the land. . . .

By the time of the Restoration in 1660, when Britain had been in the Slave Trade for forty years, there was a steady flow of black men and women into England, although the number was not recorded. One of the earliest items to appear in a newspaper about a black boy was in the *Mecurius Politicus* of August 11, 1659:

> A negro-boy, about nine years of age, in a grey serge suit, his hair cut close to his head, was lost on Tuesday last, August 9th at night, in St.

> Nicholas Lane, London. If anyone can give notice of him to Mr. Thomas Barker at the Sugar Loaf in that lane, they shall be rewarded for their pains.

At about this time it became the vogue for titled and eminent persons to keep blackamoors as pets. "In Bath's heyday," wrote Elspeth Huxley, "to see a Negro page in hose and doublet carrying the fan of a pomaded lady stepping forth from a sedan chair was a sight as commonplace as gouty gentlemen. Sometimes the pages wore silver collars and were pampered like pet dogs." They belonged to the first sizeable colored community in Britain, slaves brought over in the eighteenth century."

Samuel Pepys noted that when Lord Sandwich travelled to England from Portugal in 1662 with Catherine of Braganza, who was to marry Charles II, he took as a present to the young ladies of his family "a little Turke and a negroe."

There was a good reason for the popularity of these plump-faced little boys whom society women dressed exotically in eastern rather than African dress. A black-skinned attendant showed off the whiteness of his mistress's skin to great advantage. But blackamoors were kept for other reasons, too. They had to perform certain trivial chores, chiefly waiting on their mistresses while they were in the boudoir titivating themselves. They waited, also, at the tea-table, carried m'lady's train as she moved about the place, held her fan and smelling salts, fed her parrots and combed her lap dogs. Silver or copper collars were riveted round the necks of these black boys and in the reign of Queen Anne it was the custom for ladies and gentlemen to inscribe their coats of arms and ciphers on these collars and to give the blackamoors the same fancy names they gave their lap dogs. For example, "My Lady Bromfield's black in Lincoln's Inn Fields." When these blackamoors ran away they could easily be identified by the collar-inscriptions and taken back to their mistresses.

The men who owned slaves were just as apt to poke fun at the blacks and treat them as comic creatures. They gave them classical names like Plato, Nero, Socrates, and Pluto.

The Earl of Suffolk and Brandon chose the name Scipio Africanus for his servant. And when the youth died the Earl had an epitaph inscribed on his tomb:

Here
Lieth the Body of
Scipio Africanus,
NEGRO SERVANT TO YE RIGHT
HONOURABLE CHARLES WILLIAM
EARL OF SUFFOLK AND BRANDON,
who died ye 21 December,
1720, aged 18 years.

As the years passed and these chubby, cuddly black playthings lost their puppy fat and became awkward adolescents and later reached manhood, trouble started—trouble for them. M'lady could not have a youth who had reached the age of puberty sitting on her lap in the boudoir where she dressed and undressed! She threw him out into the pantry or the stable at the mercy of the butler, the pantryman and the groom—not caring what happened to him. Where once he had been a pampered favorite, treated with more fondness than the rest of the servants, now the blackamoor found himself being bullied by them. Some blackamoors then fell on evil days. Others contracted diseases like tuberculosis and died. But many of them became absorbed into English life, marrying, raising families and becoming permanent residents in Britain. A small, very talented handful even gained fame and prominence and were accepted in the highest circles in the land.

Meanwhile, by the beginning of the eighteenth century, other blacks were entering Britain from the colonies in increasing numbers. The mass migration had begun. African slaves were becoming a familiar sight, especially around the cobblestoned and muddy streets of Bristol, Liverpool, and London.

BIBLIOGRAPHY TO CHAPTER ONE

Burton, Elizabeth and Kelly, Felix. *The Elizabethans at Home.* London: 1958.

Dickens, Charles, ed. "The Black Man" *All the Year Round,* Vol. 13, new series (1875).

Duke, H. E. and Campion, Bernard. *The Story of Gray's Inn* (published with the approval of the Bench of the Ancient and Honourable Society of Gray's Inn). London: 1950.

Harrison, G. B. *Shakespeare at Work (1592–1603).* London: 1933.

Hotson, Leslie. *Mr. W. H.* London: 1964.

Huxley, Elspeth. "Blacks Next Door" from "Settlers in Britain." *Punch* (29 January, 1964).

MacInnes, C. W. *England and Slavery.* London: 1934.

Mackenzie-Grieve, Averil. *The Last Years of the English Slave Trade. Liverpool 1750-1807.* London: 1941.

McRitchie, David. *Ancient and Modern Britons.* Vols. 1 and 2. London: 1884.

Rogers, J. A. *Sex and Race.* Vol. 1. New York: 1952.

Sayle, R. T. D. *Lord Mayor Pageants (Show of 1680).* London: 1931.

CHAPTER II

"BREAD AND LIBERTY IN OLD ENGLAND"

The rapid growth of the black population in Britain took place during the Georgian era—primarily when the first three Hanoverian monarchs ruled England. The first Hanoverian George to occupy the English throne brought two black favorites with him from Germany, Mustapha and Mahomet. He had such a high regard for them that some of the English nobility were jealous.

The history of these two royal favorites is an interesting one. Both of them were taken prisoner by the Imperialists in Hungary and entered the service of George I as a reward for having saved his life during the siege of Vienna in 1685. So when the king left Hanover and ascended the British throne they came with him. George I valued their services highly and kept them constantly at his side ministering to his wants. Mahomet became a Christian. He died of dropsy on November 1, 1726, leaving a family by a Hanoverian wife who survived him. Alexander Pope saw fit to extol his worth in these couplets:

From peer or Bishop 'tis no easy thing
To draw a man who loves his God or King.
Alas! I copy (or my draught would fail),
From honest Mah'met or plain Parson Hale.

After the death of George I Mustapha entered the service of George II.

The fact that Mustapha and Mahomet were the darlings of royalty seemed to create a favorable climate for the thousands of blacks who were coming to London. Their numbers reached such proportions that by October, 1764, *The Gentleman's Magazine* reported: "The number in this metropolis [London] only, is supposed to be near 20,000"; Gilbert Francklyn, writing about slavery and the treatment of slaves declared that in the six years after the War of American Independence ended in 1783 the number had risen to forty thousand—and the figure did not include those who lived in Liverpool, Bristol, and elsewhere.

The sight of blacks in London and several other parts of England was as commonplace an affair as it is today, judging from numerous contemporary reports. In 1788, for instance, Phillip Thicknesse, a former governor of the West Indies, could write:

> London abounds with an incredible number of these black men, who have clubs to support those who are out of a place; and in every country town, nay in almost every village, are to be seen a little race of mulattoes, mischievous as monkeys and infinitely more dangerous.

The forty thousand blacks were quite a high proportion (5%) of the population of London, which, in the latter part of the eighteenth century was 800,000.

To examine this migration in detail it is necessary to get a clear picture of Britain's position in the slave trade.

It was during the period of the first three Georges that slavery flourished in America and the West Indies. Slave owners were reaping rich harvests from the slaves who worked on their cotton, rice, tobacco, and sugar plantations. Of the two thousand sea-going vessels that left the Pool of London yearly (not to mention the fifteen hundred which sailed away from Liverpool and Bristol) hundreds were engaged in the slave trade carrying from thirty-five thousand to one hundred thousand slaves annually across the Atlantic to North America and the West Indies.

As far back as 1662 slavery had already been given royal blessing. Charles II had granted a monopoly to one company and by 1700 this company—known as the Royal African Company—had sent forty thousand African slaves to the colonies to add to the one hundred and sixty thousand shipped by private traders. The slave trade had been accepted as necessary for the economic prosperity of Britain. By an Act of Parliament in 1669 the Royal African Company's monopoly was rescinded and the slave trade opened to all subjects of the Crown. However, the Royal

African Company continued to trade on a large scale, receiving parliamentary grants from time to time. There were also a number of Acts of Parliament encouraging the trade. One of them ruled that: "The trade to and from Africa is very advantageous to Great Britain, and necessary for supplying the plantations and colonies with a sufficient number of negroes at reasonable rates."

The eighteenth century brought with it no appreciable change of public opinion on the economic necessity of the slave trade. In fact, in 1713, by the Treaty of Utrecht—the Asiento—slave trading increased when Queen Anne entered into an agreement with Philip V, the Catholic monarch of Spain, to supply, in the space of thirty years, 144,000 slaves at the rate of 4,800 yearly. The price per head was as high as £23.10s. Apart from this figure, which was part of a contractual agreement between Queen Anne and Philip V, slaves fetched prices ranging from £28 to £50 per head. Prices for female slaves were quite high, especially if they were attractive. White plantation owners were prepared to pay from £20 to £80 per head for healthy black women.

The case of an attractive octoroon, Eliza, who was sold in Lexington, Kentucky and described by Dr. Schulte Nordholt, the Dutch historian, from contemporary sources, illustrates how highly buyers were prepared to pay for female slaves:

There were 2,000 people there to see the scene. The auctioneer, an old man, began by recommending the poor girl as a perfect mistress, using insinuating jokes. The bidding started at $250 but soon went up to $1,200. Then there were only two buyers left, who went on bidding carefully, reaching $1,450.

The bidding continued up to $1,475 and then suddenly the old man lifted the girl's skirts and "laid bare her beautiful, symmetrical body, from her feet to her waist. 'Ah, gentlemen!' he exclaimed, slapping her naked thigh with his rough hands, 'who is going to be the winner of this prize?' " The price went up by another $10 and then it was over.

Slaves were an economic necessity to Britain, since without them the sugar plantations in the Caribbean could not be worked. Plantation owners were determined to hang on to them even if they had to beat them into submission. But slave merchants in the City of London, Liverpool, and Bristol, ships' captains and plantation owners in the Caribbean were not the only ones to gain by this traffic.

According to a correspondent of *The Gentleman's Magazine,*

> Forty or more Members of Parliament in 1766 were the owners of West Indian plantations, the descendants of planters or had other ties and interests in the West Indies. In the single month of July 1757, one hundred and seventy-five ships arrived in British ports with cargoes from the West Indies valued at £2,000,000. Sugar was so profitable and fitted so well into the mercantilist economy that the British government actually toyed with the idea of trading Canada back to the French after its capitulation, in exchange for Guadeloupe.

Because of this great value placed on sugar, punishments for absconding plantation slaves were severe to the point of brutality and even death.

England was viewed as a haven by these thousands of slaves in the colonies. As a contemporary observer put it, they preferred "a crust of bread and liberty in Old England to slavery in the West Indies," which carried with it manacles, whips, attack by fierce dogs, beatings, and death. Although it was against the law to murder slaves, they had no legal status in the English colonies and could not give evidence in court, and acts of murder by planters were therefore not regarded as serious. From the *Slavery Papers* annotated by Edgell Rickword, one need recount only a few of the thousands of cases of cruelty to slaves to show the wisdom of the migration.

A female slave in St. George's, Grenada, had her fingers cut off because she had committed some trivial offence. Her master suspended her by her hands, flogged her brutally causing cuts on her back, stomach, breast and thighs. Another house servant in Jamaica broke a plate and spilt a cup of tea. Her master, a doctor, nailed her by the ear to a post and then retired to bed, leaving the slave there. Next morning he found that she had run away having torn the head of the nail through her ear. She was eventually captured and the doctor whipped her, clipped off both ears with a large pair of scissors and then sent her out to work picking cotton seeds. A clergyman's wife in Port Royal, Jamaica, was so cruel that she used to pour hot sealing wax on her slaves after flogging them. She once tied up a woman slave by the hands and rubbed hot cayenne pepper in the private parts of her body causing the woman to scream all night in agony.

Slaves began slipping quietly away from every vessel and hiding themselves in England where, as was not the case in the colonies, masters could be brought before the court for beating them. Other slaves were brought over by planters or hid themselves on board ship or were smuggled in by seamen who sold them. Some came to attend sick persons or children during the voyage.

Although at first blacks were imported to satisfy the fashion they also carried prestige for the retiring planters. These planters had left England poor and returned rich—and to prove it they had several black servants. It was also quite usual for a planter to import slaves for resale in England.

In turn other middle-class aspirants to respectability and gentility followed suit and took on black servants. The commanders of slaving vessels, too, were allowed to take a few slaves in each cargo for their personal profit. Ships' captains then were well rewarded and loved to display their good fortune by dressing in gaudily-laced coats and cocked hats, with silver or sometimes gold buttons on their coats. A special mark of distinction was the black slave attending them in the streets.

African slaves who found themselves in London congregated and settled in the eastern and riverside parishes. It was from there that the industrial districts began to spread. The area towards Shadwell, Limehouse, Whitechapel, and Wapping consisted of numerous workshops and small dingy houses. It was the centre of the seafaring world and slaves who slipped into London usually settled in these parts. These eastern parishes offered better hiding places than the western section of London with its noble squares—Bedford, Russell, Berkeley, Cavendish, Gordon, and Hanover—where moved the eminent and genteel citizens. Runaway slaves found friends and sympathizers among the lower classes and fitted easily into the crowded London streets which still bustled with Hogarthian life. There, lawlessness was rampant, streets reeked of sewage and offal, and cobbles were slippery with mud. Iron-sheathed posts guarded the jostling pedestrians from the wheels of carriages. Shop signs hid the sky and creaked in the wind. And traitors' heads hung on Temple Bar for all to see.

In fact, London life from the time of Queen Anne and George I, was vigorous and fraught with danger. Ned Ward, who was described as "that garrulous combative master of vernacular rhyming," painted a vivid picture of the metropolis in his "Hudibras Redivivus":

Young drunkards reeling, bayliffs dogging,
Old strumpets plying, mumpers progging, beggars scrounging,
Fat dray-men squabbling, chair-men ambling,

Oyster-whores fighting, school-boys scrambling,
Street porters running, rascals batt'ling,
Pick-pockets crowding, coaches rattling,
News bawling, ballad-wenches singing,
Guns roaring, and the church-bells ringing.

To that could be added "blackamoors preening" and "runaway slaves hiding"; and in 1744 footpads bludgeoning their victims in broad daylight in Fleet Street and the Strand and by night lurking in the Covent Garden piazzas to waylay playgoers coming out of the theatres. For rarely a week passed when there was not at least one violent crime among the London population. But Londoners like New Yorkers today looked upon murders and riots as mere nuisances incidental to life in so robust a city.

There was another side to life in London—one which appealed to liberal-minded men and women—for it was a place where a man could live according to his own mind and whim. There was much social injustice but at the same time one could find there friends of religious liberty, the of slaves caused no uneasiness in their minds and that afternoon in ecclesiastical tyrants. It was a place where slaves could escape from their cruel masters. Nevertheless, they were still regarded as slaves, and merchants in London, Liverpool, and Bristol as well as the prosperous rising middle class of those cities were outbidding each other at public auctions where slaves were sold with other "cargo" like flour or wine. Newspapers of the time were full of advertisements of those auctions and of private offers of slaves for sale. In 1763 *The Gentleman's Magazine* reported the first slave auction in England: "At the sale of Rice the broker's effects, a Negro boy was put up for auction and sold for £32."

Advertisements of private sales followed the same pattern. The condition of the slave to be sold, the kind of work he could do and details of where the sales would take place were listed.

Other advertisements, dealing with the treatment of slaves, also appeared. These showed quite definitely that in the eyes of the English merchants and planters, slaves were no different from the beasts of the field. To prevent escape, slaves were padlocked like dogs, and this advertisement, which appeared in the *London Advertiser* of 1756 was not unusual: "Silver Padlocks for Blacks or Dogs, collars etc." The man who inserted this item in the paper was Matthew Dyer, a goldsmith who worked at the Crown in Duck Lane, Orchard Street, Westminster. He was very popular with titled ladies who patronised his shop when they wanted silver or gold collars for their slaves.

By the time George III came to the throne, the trade in slaves was certainly flourishing in England, especially in Liverpool. At one time, this city imported seven-eighths of the blacks of the whole European trade to build docks and later the grandiose municipal buildings. The rich merchants and their bejeweled wives, who were carried around in sedan-chairs by blue-frocked bearers, lived in luxury in or near Castle Street. The auctioning philosophers and the men who sought freedom from political and 1766 was like many others: eight slaves—leftovers from the slave ship *Thomas*—were put up for sale at the Customs House together with twelve pipes of raisin wine, two boxes of bottled cider, and six sacks of flour. A Liverpool chronicler of the nineteenth century who styled himself "A Genuine Dicky Sam" described what took place:

> Just picture to yourself after the auctioneer has disposed of the first lots, he comes to the more important, namely, the selling of the slaves. The crowd has greatly increased, many have heard that blacks were to be sold, and therefore, they have come to satisfy their curiosity. The auctioneer stands on a chair, one of the slaves is brought out of the shed close by; the crowd now jostle one against the other, in order to get a good look at a man to be sold to anyone who will buy him. The auctioneer commences with:
>
> "Now, gentlemen, here is a fine negro, just imported from Old Calabar, aged about 28, finely proportioned, healthy, and good looking; he would make a good general servant or cook. What shall I say for him? I can give you a clean title with him; you see he is branded DD on the forehead, so you have no fear of losing him. Come gentlemen, what shall I say for him?"
>
> A voice in the crowd says £5. The auctioneer replies, "Why, he is worth £50, and only £5 offered. Hold up your hand, Caesar."
>
> At this juncture, a merchant hints to the auctioneer that a drop of rum handed around might help the bidders; the hint is taken, the rum handed round, and the bidding recommences. The prices generally advance to £15. "Any advance?" says the auctioneer. "Going for £15. Going, gone!" at which sum he is knocked down and delivered to the buyer.

Young black girls, too, were auctioned publicly in London, Bristol and Liverpool—as can be seen from a report in Williamson's *Advertiser* of that period:

> A young negress is pushed forward. She has the quality of a statue uncouthly dressed. . . . A cluster of seamen start bawdy joking among

> themselves, and a shopkeeper with his young wife on his arm draws away in disfavour. The woman watches the negress. She has passed through streets where slave collars, branding-irons, thumb-screws and mouthpieces are displayed for sale. She knows their use, but they are so remote from her experience, that their significance has hitherto remained unreal . . . but the slave girl raises fleeting doubt, compassion. . . . She would like to have her as a maidservant and treat her well—teach her Christian virtues and good housewifery. . . .

Liverpool's wealth, though dependent on the proceeds of its trade in human beings, did not cause much heartsearching among its rather vulgar nouveaux riches. Occasionally, however, there was adverse and biting comment from outspoken individuals; as in the case of the famous tragedian, George Frederick Cooke.

One night at the Liverpool Theatre Cooke staggered on the stage drunk, as was his custom. As soon as the audience noticed this, they began to hiss and boo him. A rising surge of anger brought Cooke to his senses and sobered him somewhat. Then he shouted back at them in his most professional and declamatory voice: "I have not come here to be insulted by a set of wretches, of which every brick in your infernal town is cemented with an African's blood."

The history of Bristol, too, is written with the blood of Africa. Its buildings were built on capital accumulated from the sweat and labor of slaves. Its slave merchants became wealthy trading in the traffic. Bristol as a slaving port stood on equal ground with London until 1750. Nearly a thousand slave ships left the port every year to make the journey to the West Coast of Africa and thence to the Caribbean. As was bound to happen, thousands of slaves managed, by various ways to settle in Bristol—some as stowaways, others as servants and maidservants and butlers, the pattern following that of Liverpool and London. Bristol's population was estimated at 43,275 in 1750, of which approximately 5,000 were blacks. In Bristol, as in Liverpool and London, the auctioneering of slaves in the coffee houses and taverns was a common occurrence. A dozen or more slaves would be auctioned off. Young bloods would congregate for amusement and for the distinction of buying a black servant, and if there was a young female in the group the bidding always became fast and furious. Slave captains, too, would swagger around Bristol with their own slaves in attendance. Child slaves were, as usual, viewed as toys for amusement, like parrots or monkeys. Adults were trained for house service and could be disposed of like property if they displeased their masters for there was a constant demand for black servants.

It was in such a climate that the thousands of slaves in England moved; in Bristol, Liverpool, London or wherever else they settled, the pattern of life for them was the same. Several more years were to pass before they could walk the streets of English cities as free men.

BIBLIOGRAPHY TO CHAPTER TWO

Clunn, Harold P. *The Face of London*. London: 1951.

Cunard, Nancy, ed. "Slavery Papers" (annoted by Edgell Rickword) in *Negro Anthology*, 1931–1933. London: 1934.

The Gentleman's Magazine. (London: October, 1764).

A Genuine "Dicky Sam." *Liverpool and Slavery*. Liverpool: 1884.

Greenidge, C. W. W. *Slavery*. London: 1958.

Humphreys, A. R. *The Augustan World*. London: 1954.

Klingberg, Frank J. *The Anti-Slavery Movement in England*. New Haven: 1924.

Latimer, John. *The Annals of Bristol*. Bristol: 1893.

Mackenzie-Grieve, Averil. *The Last Years of the English Slave Trade*. London: 1941.

Nordholt, J. W. Schulte, *The People that Walk in Darkness*. London: 1960.

Ward, Ned. *Hudibras Redivivus* (Canto VII 20-7) London: 1705-7.

CHAPTER III

SERVANTS AND SCHOLARS

Before 1772, earning a living in England was by no means easy for the thousands of black slaves. By law they were not entitled to wages unless a court had ordered it, and when they did receive any it was due either to the kindness of their masters or a court order compelling a master to pay his slave—as happened when John Caesar's wife petitioned the sessions in 1717 claiming that her husband had served Benjamin and John Wood, printers and embossers in Whitechapel as a slave without wages for fourteen years. His masters had treated him cruelly and had even imprisoned him in their house. Caesar's wife told the court that she herself was very poor and that she would become chargeable to the parish if her husband was not freed from his imprisonment at the Woods' house and allowed to work for wages. The court not only ruled that the masters should give Caesar a reasonable wage but they fixed the amount themselves. This was not an isolated case. In fact slave masters then hit upon the ruse of getting slaves to enter into indentures with them in order to avoid having to give them wages.

Jobs for blacks were limited and many were of a menial kind. Slaves were mainly servants, stable-boys, grooms, valets or butlers in the houses of titled people and the eminent, like Dr. Johnson, Sir Joshua Reynolds, George, Lord Brudenell, and the Duke of Montagu. There was Johnson's Francis Barber; Reynolds had Bob White, and Ignatius Sancho was personal attendant to the Duke of Montagu for several years. Their masters, being liberal-minded men, paid them wages.

Manservants got as much as seven shillings a week. Black women could average five shillings weekly as laundrymaids, parlormaids, housemaids, or cooks. As far back as 1613 there were several instances of blacks working as domestics. Lady Anne Clifford, the Countess of Dorset, numbered two black servants, John Morocco and Grace Robinson, among her household of Knole. Judging from historian V. Sackville West's description of Knole at the end of the eighteenth century, blacks were a permanent fixture there until an unfortunate incident: "The black page at Knole, of which there had always been one and who had always been called John Morocco regardless of what his true name might be, had been replaced by a Chinaman ever since the house steward had killed the John Morocco of the moment in a fight in Black Boy Passage."

A slave's working life—for males as well as females—started in very early childhood and continued until the slave was too old or too feeble to work.

Mistresses not only used girl slaves to wait on them but taught them how to sew, knit, read, and write. One girl even learned to speak French fluently. Female servants, not unnaturally, fared better than men. Mary, housemaid to Roubiliac, the sculptor, received wages and remained with him for six years. He was very fond of her. Joseph Nollekens' Elisabeth Rosina Clements seemed to have been quite a favorite too. She had a great sense of humor which appealed to Nollekens. Of a chestnut brown color tinctured with olive, she was nicknamed "Black Bet" by shopkeepers. Artist friends who visited Nollekens preferred to call her "Bronze." When she and her master were very old, it used to give him much pleasure to watch Bronze making the cat "Jenny Dawdle" dance round the studio. Nollekens would laugh so much that he would get a fit of coughing, with tears trickling down his cheeks on to his bib. When he died he left Bronze nineteen guineas. Other masters like Johnson and the Duke of Montagu were more liberal to their servants in their will, but then Joseph Nollekens, apart from being a celebrated sculptor, was known as one of the greatest misers of his day.

Not all black people in England in the eighteenth century were domestic servants. Some youths became apprentices. By 1731 there were so many of them that the Lord Mayor and Aldermen of London passed an ordinance making it an offense to teach blacks a trade. Others, like Francis Barber when he got tired of "washing bottles and making pills" for Mr.

Diamond, the apothecary to whom he was apprenticed, joined the navy. Many were taken on in the British army and several regiments had a certain number of black trumpeters and drummers on their strength. The idea was to display the growth and might of the British Empire. Black trumpeters in the Life Guards were chosen especially for their great height and they were an impressive sight in their resplendent uniforms, marching side by side with the shorter British soldiers. Another novelty in the British army was the Jingling Johnnie, who showed great skill and agility in handling the cymbals. Dressed in peacock-colored Eastern style costume, the Jingling Johnnies leapt about in rhythm while accompanying themselves energetically on the cymbals. English crowds were always delighted with these colorful performances, and regiments like the Coldstream Guards and the Connaught Rangers were great favorites with Londoners for that reason. The Jingling Johnnies did not have it all to themselves, however, because black tambourine players and drummers in the Twenty-fourth Foot and the Royal Artillery were also big attractions.

By the last quarter of the eighteenth century when there were thousands more blacks in London, hundreds became crossing sweepers, sellers of tracts, fruit vendors, entertainers, and beggars. Several black crossing sweepers appear to have been disabled—like one-legged Billy Waters who was immortalized by Pierce Egan. A small percentage managed to scrape a tidy fortune. One West Indian returned to the Caribbean carrying with him over £1,500. Another black crossing sweeper believed to have died in poverty left behind £8,000!

Most black beggars did well. English passers-by seemed so much intrigued by them that white beggars tried to assume a black disguise by covering themselves with lampblack. Three black beggars, Charlie M'Gee, Joseph Johnson, and Toby were familiar sights in the city of London from the latter part of the eighteenth century until well into the nineteenth.

Charles M'Gee was born in Ribon, Jamaica, in 1744. He made his home in London, and used to stand and ply his trade near a spot which thousands of people passed in the course of a day—an obelisk at the foot of Ludgate Hill. He was of striking appearance, smooth blue-black in color. He had lost an eye and the shock of white hair that heightened his blackness was tied up behind in a tail. At the back of the head his hair was quite thick and rested in a large tuft on the cape of his coat. With his hair dressed in such a manner M'Gee looked as though he was wearing a wig. By the time he was seventy-three his begging had made him a wealthy man.

Joseph Johnson, a notably resourceful beggar, had been invalided out of the merchant service and since no London parish would give him assistance, took to begging. He started on Tower Hill where he amused Londoners by singing George Alexander Stevens' "Storm." Later, he ventured into the busy streets and became what was called a "Regular Chaunter." With a little ingenuity Johnson increased his daily takings considerably. All he did was to build a model of the ship "Nelson," which he attached to his cap. When he bowed to thank his audience the movement would make the model ship seem as though it was tossing on the ocean waves. He was always sure of a good collection after that. Johnson did not limit his begging to the metropolis. He visited market places in Staines, Rumford, and St. Albans, where he never failed to get the farmer's penny either by singing "The British Seaman's Praise" or Green's more popular song, "The Wooden Walls of Old England."

Making up this trio of resourceful beggars was Toby, a character well-known to Londoners. He had no toes and his head was always tied with a white handkerchief. He bent himself almost double so as to walk with hand-crutches. In that position he took up the entire width of the pavement. Toby's trick was to pretend to be exhausted whenever he approached a house where he knew gin was in plentiful supply. Of all the denizens of Church Lane, St. Giles, Toby spent "the most money on that national cordial."

Like all black beggars and blind persons Toby "seldom failed to excite compassion." Begging was such good business that more and more blacks were attracted to the streets as beggars and street entertainers. With the various pitches overcrowded some beggars fell on hard times and became destitute.

London was not the only city with black beggars and street entertainers. Well known in the Liverpool streets around 1791 was a West Indian tenor named J. Alexander. He used to promenade around the city carrying a small black bag in one hand and a music book in the other. When asked about himself, Alexander would reply: "I came to England on a Welsh ship and now I can read, I can write and I can sing in Welsh as well as in

English. Some people can only do hard work. I live by my talents. I have a good voice. Of course I have trained it. I take lessons in singing. In the winter time I sing at concerts, and then my name is put on the bill."

Alexander's lack of modesty did not make him unpopular with the crowds who listened to his singing in the Liverpool streets. At the end of a day's singing he sometimes collected as much as ten shillings, which in those days was quite a tidy sum.

Out of the thousands of blacks who lived in Britain during the eighteenth century, a few had jobs that were not menial. There were the protégés, the darlings of royalty, the favored, talented few who made their mark on the Georgian society of England; and there were those who came, or better, were sent, primarily to be educated.

Students came mainly from West Africa and were the sons of chiefs and notables of African tribes in the neighborhood of British mercantile settlements on the coast. Among the first was Robert Davies who was described as "a person of mixed blood," and had been baptized a Christian and given the appropriate names. He went to England in 1710. After studying English he was employed for five years by the African Company as an interpreter. Then, there were three students from the Gold Coast who were sent to a school in Islington. One of these youths, named Quaque, studied for holy orders, and after ordination at Oxford returned to be chaplain at Cape Coast Castle. He remained in that post for fifty years.

A slave in the West Indies had little or no chance to get even an elementary education; those who owned slaves knew only too well that to teach a slave how to read and write would intensify his dissatisfaction. No educated slave could be content to remain manacled in chains as the property of another man. That was why in the West Indies and North America the penalties for educating slaves were very severe. Special legislation was passed in the State of Virginia preventing slaves from learning how to read. Slaves have, in fact, been executed only because they were able to read and write.

Yet there were times when slave merchants and plantation owners found it necessary to make their slaves literate. The first slaves whom the London trader, John Lok, brought over from West Africa in 1554 were taken to England to learn the language and get a general education so that they could be used as interpreters and assistants by the slave merchants. They were the first blacks to be educated in England.

There was also the belief during the years of slavery that blacks were not capable of absorbing the education of the white man; that they were his intellectual inferiors. Colonists were always quick to compare slaves to apes. It was for this reason that a Jamaican, Francis Williams, was chosen as a guinea pig in a most unusual experiment: to prove that a black man had the same intellectual faculties as a white man.

The man who decided to try this experiment was the Duke of Montagu, who lived in Jamaica in the very early years of the eighteenth century. He chose Francis Williams because he noticed that the boy had a quick, lively intelligence.

Francis Williams was born in Kingston, Jamaica in 1702, the youngest of three sons of John and Dorothy Williams, who were free blacks. The duke sent him to England where he began his studies in private schools. Afterwards he entered Cambridge University. There he specialised in mathematics, literature and Latin, finally graduating with a bachelor's degree. When Williams left Cambridge he went to London where he was accepted in the literary and fashionable Georgian society, becoming quite famous, too, for a ballad which he composed called "Welcome, welcome, brother debtor." It was so much in vogue in London that some minor composers, irritated to see a black doing so well, attempted, without success, to claim it as their own.

The pleasures of Georgian society were not enough to keep Francis Williams in England. He longed to return to Jamaica even though he knew he would be treated with much less tolerance. So, with unwarranted optimism, he set sail for Jamaica, hoping that his education would help him in securing a good position with the government. His hopes were not entirely groundless because his guardian angel, the Duke of Montagu, tried to obtain a place for him in the council of government. This appointment, although put forward and backed by the Duke himself, was turned down by white officials. To have a black sitting in council with white members was unheard of in those days. Slavery was at its height and the bigoted historian Edward Long could write: "Their natural baseness of mind seems to afford least hope of their being—except by miraculous interposition of Divine Providence—so far refined as to think as well as act like men." Yet this same man admitted that Francis Williams was an able scholar.

By 1735 Francis Williams was living the cultivated life of a scholar in Spanish Town, Jamaica. An unknown artist of the period painted a caricature portrait (in oils) of Williams in his library which is tastefully set up with a scholar's books and furniture of the style of the first half of the eighteenth century. On a three-legged table with carved and turned baluster legs are *Newton's Philosophy,* a celestial globe, a pewter ink-stand, a box and compasses. Behind are book-shelves with works by Newton, Locke, Cowley, Boyle, Bacon, Sherlock, and Rapin. On the left is a walnut armchair with tall back and shaped splat carved above with a shell, and having cabriole legs. On the floor is another globe inscribed "The Western or Atlantick Ocean."

When Williams was refused a government post he decided to set up school at Spanish Town, where he taught reading, writing, Latin, and what Long described as "the elements of mathematics." The white officials and plantation owners on the island did not think him good enough to sit side by side with them in council but nevertheless sent their children to his school . . . . . placing their youngsters' early education in the hands of a black man who, in their eyes, was not far removed from "an orang outang."

But it is not only as a scholar—the first Jamaican to achieve this distinction—that Francis Williams is remembered. Neither is it because he was a "guinea pig" upon whom the intellectual and moral capabilities of all African slaves depended. Francis Williams was a poet of some merit who specialized in writing Latin verse. He reveled in composing Latin odes to every new governor of Jamaica. One of his best pieces, "An Ode to George Haldane," was translated from the Latin by Edward Long. At the time it was written Haldane was taking over the post of Governor of Jamaica; it is couched within the rigid confines of the heroic couplet made popular by Alexander Pope and characteristic of the period, as the following stanza will show:

Rash councils now, with each malignant plan,
Each faction, that in evil hour began,
At your approach are in confusion fled,
Nor while you rule, shall raise their dastard head.

Alike the master and the slave shall see
Their neck reliv'd, the yoke unbound by thee.

When the Reverend Robert Boucher Nicholls, Dean of Middleham, saw the ode a feeling of indignation against the colonists for comparing blacks to apes was so strong in him that he exclaimed: "I have never heard that an orang outang has composed an Ode. Among the defenders of slavery we do not find one half of the literary merit of Francis Williams." Even Edward Long said "it flowed from the polished pen of one who had received an academic education." On this occasion Long unaccountably allowed his reason to take control and his bigotry to recede, even, as he put it, to the extent of forgetting that the writer was black.

Francis Williams thought himself several cuts above the illiterate slaves on the island, but Jamaican whites said that Williams was haughty, opinionated, entertained the highest opinion of himself and of his own knowledge, treated his parents with much disdain, and behaved towards his children with severity bordering on cruelty. Long, of course, exaggerated these characteristics and claimed that Williams was also fond of having great deference paid to him—that he sported odd clothes and walked about with a grave countenance to give the impression of wisdom and learning and, to heighten this view, he wore a huge wig, a sword, and a ruffled shirt that made him look a very fearsome figure.

Edward Long did, however, admit that as a poet and scholar Francis Williams had merit. In other words, the Duke of Montagu's experiment had been successful—Francis Williams the "guinea pig" had become a scholar. Grudgingly, white colonists agreed that it was not only white men who could benefit from education. It hurt men like Long and that other proslavery writer Samuel Estwick to think that, given opportunities, African slaves could after all become literate and sophisticated even in the Anglo-Saxon syndrome, which is of minor relevance, if any, in the black man's struggle for total liberation. The African already had a past which had been distorted in the writings of white historians with half-truths and outright lies. Frantz Fanon, the Martiniquan psychiatrist and a major spokesman in the black revolution up until his death in 1961, was amazed when he uncovered the truths about Africa which white historians had concealed. He wrote about this discovery with the wonder and passion of a man who has freed himself of the sub-cultural chains of colonialism which had imposed a cloud of inferiority on him and made him less than a man. Fanon had freed his mind from a lifetime of deception and, like other black men and women, gloried in this new-found truth, which caused him to write ecstatically:

> I rummaged frenetically through all the antiquity of the black man. What I found there took away my breath. . . . Ségou, Djenne, cities of more than a hundred thousand people: accounts of learned blacks (doctors of theology who went to Mecca to interpret the Koran). All of that exhumed from the past, spread with its insides out, made it possible for me to find a valid historic place. I was not primitive, not even a half-man. I belonged to a race that had already been working in gold and silver two thousand years ago.

Professor Jan Carew of Princeton University, a distinguished scholar and writer from Guyana, has destroyed the myth that Africans were civilized by slavery—a myth that has gone unchallenged for four centuries by generations of Anglo-Saxon and even certain black historians. Carew's denunciation was the result of careful study and profound understanding of the African diaspora. He states in "The African and the American Indian," (unpublished):

> The fiction that both the African and the Indian were civilized by slavery and colonial oppression, itself a fantastic contradiction, can be dismissed once one begins to resurrect the buried facts of Africans and Indians meeting and the profound cultural fusion that took place once they met. . . . The Europeans and the English introduced the plantation, a highly specialized system of capitalist production, to the New World. The division of labour made the plantation and the absolute need to make profits created a situation in which economic imperatives overrode considerations of humanity, race, colour or creed. This was true in particular of the sugar plantation.
>
> The slave was chained to the plantation on which he worked under a system of terror and forced labour. But one of the neglected facts of life in the plantation system was that the slave from Africa, forcibly inducted into a modern system of production, did a wide range of both skilled and unskilled jobs. The white overseer class was not recruited for their skills. They policed the plantation and were symbols of authority, and when necessary, of terror. So that slaves were field hands, domestics, technicians, coopers and everything else that the plantation system demanded. . . . The illusion that the African slave was a dumb beast, performing mindless tasks in the field under the whip bears little relationship to the reality of the plantation system. The African's survival through a grim and more extended phase as a plan-

> tation worker is one of the great epics of human endurance against seemingly impossible odds.
>
> Enough has been written about the plantation system to fill whole libraries, but of the African culture that secreted itself away in the very heart of this system, there is very little indeed. There is much talk about the plantation culture, but all cultures are based on man's creative labour, and creative labour must of necessity be labour with a modicum of freedom attached to the offering of it. Whips, chains, bloodhounds, guns and terror hardly inspire people to work creatively. The plantation, therefore, so long as slavery existed, was a system, not a culture. The workers carried their culture within themselves and found a thousand and one ways of preserving it.

This culture Africans took with them in the nightmare journey across the Middle Passage seas. It was something which could not be broken by the whips and manacles of slavery. It has survived as a legacy on which to build. The education of Francis Williams was superimposed on this cultural inheritance. The same thing can be said of whole generations of descendents of those ancestors whose slave labour was not in vain.

Francis Williams went on teaching in Spanish Town until his death in 1772 at the age of seventy. But he was not the only black scholar who, during the years of African slavery, showed that slaves could master not only English and Latin, but other difficult languages as well. There was Anthony William Amo who was born on the coast of Guinea. He studied at the University of Wittenberg at Halle, Saxony, and wrote and spoke fluently, Greek, Latin, Hebrew, Dutch, French, and German. He obtained his doctor's degree for a philosophical work called *The Want of Feeling.* A second book by Amo was published in 1734. It was also philosophical and dealt with the sensations which involve the mind and the organic workings of the body.

Another slave scholar, Jacobus Eliza Capitein, studied at the University of Leyden, earning a degree in philosophy in 1740. He published two works: one a treatise on the calling of the Gentiles, *De Vocatione Ethnicorum,* which ran into three editions; and the other a book of sermons in Dutch. Juan Latino, a black, was a professor of poetry at the University of Granada in Spain. His remarkable book on Don Juan of Austria at the Battle of Lepanto was published in Granada in 1573 and won him respect as a scholar. It is one of the most prized of rare books in the world today.

Although Amo, Capitein, and Latino did not settle in England, they are included here to show that scholarship, even in those years, was not the sole prerogative of the white man. However, there were two blacks, Job Ben Solomon and Sake Deen Mahomed, who lived in England and were just as learned.

The Fula slave, Job Ben Solomon, became one of the leading Arabic translators of his time. In the early 1730s he worked in London in close collaboration with Sir Hans Sloane, botanist and doctor. One of his scholastic feats was to write three copies of the Koran from memory. After he had finished working on the first copy he did not need to refer to it while writing the other two.

London society went into ecstasies over this tall, brilliant, handsome African who carried himself in the Georgian salons with a natural pride. His patron, the Duke of Montagu, was so taken with Job that he presented him at court. After a few years in London he asked the directors of the Royal African Company to send him home.

Sake Deen Mahommed was of East Indian and African ancestry. He had been barber to George IV and William IV of England, but was gifted in surgery and medicine. Historians of the period list him as one of the foremost experts on cholera and muscular ailments. He was born in 1749 and died, at the ripe old age of 101, in 1851.

Most of the African students who came to England seemed, at first, to have been given an elementary education in reading, writing, and arithmetic. By 1788, it was estimated that there were over fifty such students in London. Some then went on to profesional studies. In 1791 the best known student in England was Prince Naimbanna of Sierra Leone. While in England he was given a classical education by two clergymen—one a Mr. Gambler in Langley, Kent, and the other the Vicar of Rothley in Leicestershire.

Prince Naimbanna was the eldest son of the Temme paramount chief, Naimbanna, of the small kingdom of Robanna. The chief had several sons and being of the opinion that a European education carried with it better advantages, decided to send his sons to Europe. Prince Naimbanna went to England under a trader called Alexander Falconbridge who was the Sierra Leone Company's agent. On arrival in London, Naimbanna was taken to the house of Henry Thornton and there introduced and entertained by other directors of the company, Thomas Clarkson and Granville Sharp. After that he was sent to Leicestershire to begin his education.

The following year young Naimbanna was baptized in the name of Henry Granville, after the first names of his sponsors, Thornton and Sharp.

While studying in England Prince Naimbanna worked hard and was given very good reports by the tutors who supervised his studies and general behavior. The African thirsted after knowledge and would spend eight or ten hours a day in study. In the space of eighteen months he had learned to read and write fluently.

Naimbanna was very popular and his English friends found in him a natural courtesy and even delicacy of manners. He had a kind and affectionate disposition. As his tutors observed, his morals were pure and he seemed to have a genuine loathing for lewd conversation and every kind of vice. Like many blacks, Naimbanna hated anyone who spoke ill of his race. Once, when someone mentioned to him the name of a person who made degrading remarks in public about Africans, Naimbanna got angry and exclaimed, rising from his seat with emotion: "If a man should rob me of my money I can forgive him. If a man should shoot me, or try to stab me I can forgive him. If a man should sell me and all my family to a slave-ship so that we would pass all the rest of our days in the West Indies, I can forgive him. But, if a man takes away the character of the people of my country, I can never forgive him."

Prince Naimbanna's studies in England lasted for one more year. On April 17, 1793, he heard that his father had died. So, on May 18 he left London for Plymouth where he set sail for Sierra Leone on a vessel of the Sierra Leone Company called *Naimbanna.* The journey lasted for several weeks and before the vessel reached Sierra Leone he fell ill of a high fever. In a few days his condition became serious. This prompted him to make a will in which he thanked the Sierra Leone Company for its kindness to him and wrote messages to his family in Temmeland. By the time the ship reached the Sierra Leone river on the morning of July 17, Prince Naimbanna lay dying. He was taken ashore and brought to the governor's residence. His mother, who had come from Robanna to welcome him with his brother, sister, and other relatives was at his side when he died at seven o'clock that evening. His body was taken to Robanna and buried near the grave of his ancestors.

Not so long after the death of Prince Naimbanna the son of another African chief from Sierra Leone came to England for instruction. He was named Anthony Domingo. Like hundreds of other blacks who came to England, Domingo was befriended by Granville Sharp and by the Sierra Leone Company, which paid for his education. On his return to Sierra Leone, Domingo wrote Granville Sharp thanking him for his kindness and help. Judging from his letter, dated Freetown, June 3, 1797, his education in England had achieved the results which the Sierra Leone Company had hoped for. Domingo wrote:

> I have no other way of expressing my gratitude at present, than by my hearty thanks to the Directors of the Sierra Leone Company for giving me education. . . . The distance at which Providence has placed me from you, has neither made me ungrateful nor undutiful. When I left England I felt a violent struggle in my mind between inclination and duty. I could have wished to have spent my advanced years in that place where I first obtained your acquaintance. But I hope I shall be one of the numbers that shall teach my countrymen.

Still more Africans came to be educated in England at the expense of the Sierra Leone Company. This was creating good relations between the people of Britain and "the European colony of freedom"—as Sierra Leone was sometimes called. Students returning home, like Anthony Domingo, played a vital part in introducing the "improvements of science, and the comforts of European civilization into Africa," as well as taking a fair share in the development of Africa. Following after Domingo, a batch of young African students chosen from the schools of the colony sailed from Freetown in 1799. There were twenty-one boys, mainly the sons of local chiefs, and four girls. By 1809 there were over one-hundred West African students in England. Most of them were in schools around Liverpool since they had arrived in vessels which called at that port.

In the latter part of the eighteenth century and during the early years of the nineteenth these students did not experience any serious show of race prejudice. The memories they took back to Africa with them were mainly of pleasant experiences. The idea that they would help in developing their country was not without foundation—Susoo youths, to cite one of many instances, on returning home helped a missionary to draw up a Susoo grammar and vocabulary. But it was from these early student pioneers that the seeds of the ultimate revolt against colonialism took root.

By the turn of the nineteenth century black students arriving in England had already reached secondary school standard. Some came to study theology, others to qualify as schoolmasters at the Royal Free School in Southwark in order to return home and spread education among their people: the education necessary for the long political fight against white domination. In the twentieth century it did indeed become a weapon, but that was almost an eternity away. The other blacks in Britain in the eighteenth century and after had a mountainous struggle ahead of them; first, for freedom, and then for some measure of equality.

BIBLIOGRAPHY TO CHAPTER THREE

Banton, Michael. *The Coloured Quarter.* London: 1955.

Barnes, R. M. *A History of the Regiments and Uniforms of the British Army.* London: 1950.

Estwick, Samuel. *Considerations on the Negro Cause.* London: 1817.

Farmer, Henry George. *Military Music.* London: 1950.

A Genuine "Dicky Sam." *Liverpool and Slavery.* Liverpool: 1884.

Grégoire, H., formerly Bishop of Blois. *An Enquiry Concerning the Intellectual and Moral Faculties, and Literature of Negroes.* Brooklyn, N. Y.: 1810.

Hoare, Prince. *Memoirs of Granville Sharp.* London: 1820.

Little, K. L. *Negroes in Britain.* London: 1948.

Long, Edward. *The History of Jamaica,* Vol. 2. London: 1774.

Mannix, Daniel P. and Cowley, Malcolm. *Black Cargoes.* London: 1963.

Quarles, Benjamin. "Black Exodus," *Negro Digest* (January, 1962), pp. 85–97.

Rydings, H. A. "Prince Naimbanna in England," *Sierra Leone Studies.* New Series. No. 8. (June, 1957).

Smith, John Thomas. *Nollekens and his Times.* London: 1949.

———. *Vagabondiana.* London: 1874.

Stuart, Dorothy Margaret. *The English Abigail.* London: 1946.

CHAPTER IV

ORANG OUTANGS OR NOBLE SAVAGES?

African slaves who came to England received sympathy and help from certain classes of the population. Race prejudice as we know it today and which seems to have sprung up with the abolition of slavery did not exist. As slaves, Africans were looked upon as harmless property. But when freed this same property, plantation owners believed, became not a fellow human but a raping monster. Despite this, in eighteenth-century England many masters showed great consideration, giving their slaves wages, arranging for them to be educated, to be taught crafts and trades and even bequeathing them freedom and money. Several of the leading authors of the day wrote tracts and satirical poems on the slaves' behalf. Some donated money to help them against rapacious slave owners who took them to court in order to claim ownership.

The most bigoted among the population were dealers in the slave trade, owners of slaving ships, planters, ships' captains and others directly connected with the trade. That was to be expected since slaves were viewed as merchandise which enriched the coffers of those who possessed them. This attitude went deeper. Slave barons believed that the termination of the trade would spell economic collapse for Britain and the complete breakup of the British sugar colonies. With over 100,000 slaves being shipped annually to North America and the West Indies at up to £50 per head, it is easy to see how this might have come about.

Although most writers and poets sympathized with the black man, there were some who regarded him as an inferior animal and despised him. One historian, Samuel Estwick, claimed that since the black man was incapable of moral sensations, he was to be classed with the lower animal species. Another, Edward Long, maintained that since apes could be taught how to eat, drink, and dress like men, there might be a chance for blacks! He compared them unfavorably with orang outangs, claiming that the latter possessed more docility of nature than blacks. But underlying this race hatred Edward Long had a weakness . . . for black women. He spoke about black men with repugnance but boasted that there was no sin or shame in white men cohabiting with their "Negresses, free or slaves," and that nineteen out of twenty did so. Long absolved himself of blame by saying that habit and prevailing fashion reconciled such scenes. And how right he was. As soon as a white man arrived in the West Indies he was advised to set up an establishment with a black mistress. If he hesitated he was laughed at by older residents. The result was that in time he fell into the habit, as J. Williamson's observations in the West Indies testify:

> Black and brown mistresses are considered necessary appendages to every establishment; even a young book-keeper coming from Europe, is generally instructed to provide himself; and however repugnant may seem the idea at first, his scruples are overcome and he conforms to general custom.

Granville Sharp denounced Edward Long and others for their hypocrisy. Sharp argued that black men could not be inferior if black women had such strong influence over their white masters.

In the Caribbean a black man caught in a clandestine affair with a white woman, would be killed, but in England there was much more sexual freedom between whites and blacks.

Many black men married English women. The parish register of the St. Marylebone parish church, for instance, which has been kept in the London County Record Office at County Hall, Westminster Bridge, since June 1959, contains several entries of marriages between blacks and white women, and the baptism and burial of children of these unions; also those of adult blacks. Many other parish registers have such entries; this one appeared in the Record of Baptisms for the Parish of Canongate (Edinburgh):

> 30 September, 1686. The same day year was baptized a Blackmore Servant of My Lord Duke of Queensberry, named John; who, being

> about 10 years of age, made public profession of the Christian Faith, and solemnly engaged to live according to it. Witness ye whole session of the Abbey Church.

On the margin is written: "Blackmore John Drumlanrig". (Drumlanrig is the seat of the Queensberry family in Dumfriesshire.)

Certainly one of the most sensational mixed marriages in the early 1800s was that between Lady Jane Ellenborough and Medjuel El Mezrab, a black Arab. Lady Jane was from an aristocratic family, the Digbys. George IV is said to have described her as "the most beautiful woman I have ever seen." Finding her husband, Lord Ellenborough, later a Viceroy of India, incompatible, she took, in the words of historian E. M. O'Donoghue, "three other husbands, all wealthy and of noble birth, but unhappy with them all, she at last found true happiness with El Mezrab."

Love affairs between titled ladies and their black butlers and valets were not uncommon. J. Ashton, a chronicler of the time, mentions a lady who eloped with her husband's black butler. She took her children away with her, saying: "I would live with no other than the black." The Earl of Craven, who caught his black servant and his mistress, Harriette Wilson, locked in an embrace, was reported to have said: "Her dismissal from my cottage was because I caught her on the knee of my black footman, Mungo, and I bundled black and white into the coach together to seek their fortunes." Harriette, perhaps the most talked of female writer of the day, was later to become the mistress of the Duke of Wellington.

Then there was the story told by Mrs. Leigh of Georgia. When she took her black servant to England "the English maidservants preferred him to a white man," and "m'lady's maid preferred to marry him."

In the same way that black men in England were viewed as desirable lovers, black women were adored and sought after by Englishmen who likened them to goddesses. They were so much in vogue in the middle and late eighteenth century that in London a circular was passed around to clients from the nobility advertising black girls who performed for customers "the rites of Venus as they are done in the South Seas." At that time the Caribbean was usually referred to as the South Seas.

One of the most courted women in London in the 1770s was Harriot, a black woman from Guinea. Her master, a planter from Jamaica, found her intelligent, so he educated her, took her to London, and installed her in a grand mansion as his mistress. A writer of the times said of her: "Her person was very alluring; she was tall, well-made and genteel in appearance." When her lover died soon afterwards she found "a Lord S . . . . . who instantly quitted the arms of Miss R . . . . for this black beauty." The same writer goes on to say:

> The novelty so struck him with her unexpected talents that he visited her several successive evenings and never failed giving her at least a twenty pound note. . . . In the course of a few months she could class in the list of her admirers at least a score of Peers and fifty Commoners who never presented her with less than soft paper, commonly called a banknote . . . She grew wealthy, had fine clothes, plate and furniture. Only men of the highest rank and wealth were entertained.

Until the 1820s the picture of black and white mixing could be seen in everyday London life. In Pierce Egan's *Life in London,* sub-titled *Or the Day and Night Scenes of Jerry Hawthorn Esq. and his elegant friend Corinthian Tom in their Rambles and Sprees through the Metropolis,* the heroes Tom and Jerry and their friend Logic go to All-Max in the East End. It is described as a place where everyone regardless of country of origin or color was made welcome. Partners were paired off according to their fancy. Logic was in conversation with Black Sall, who was seated on his right knee. In the print illustrating the scene Black Sall is seen kissing Logic while, to quote the words of Mrs. Mace, wife of the proprietor of All-Max, "That black woman who you sees dancing with nasty Bob, the coal-whipper, is called African Sall, because she comes from foreign parts; and the little Mungo in the corner holding his arms out is her child; yet I doesn't think as how for all that, Sall has got any husband; but la! sir, it's a poor heart that never rejoices, an't it, sir?"

It was not only among the more lowly citizens of London and other English cities that this racial fraternizing went on. Georgian aristocrats and eminent men in the arts rubbed shoulders with blacks who had gained a measure of fame. And it was fashionable among portrait painters, sculptors and other artists like Gainsborough, Nollekens, Hogarth, Reynolds, and Zoffany to use black models because of their exoticism and the element of curiosity. The black man of worth was courted and some even belonged to fashionable clubs. These blacks frequented the more select coffee houses and taverns, went to the opera, drove in Hyde Park, and gambled at the sporting houses.

In music and the other arts the question of color and English attitudes to it were mirrored. The story of the opera *Inkle and Yarico,* with libretto by George Colman the younger and music by Samuel Arnold, is a case in point. It throws light on the problem of mixing between the races in the eighteenth century. From 1788 well into the nineteenth century this opera was tremendously popular. In fact, Yarico and the black charmer, Wowski, were favourite parts of many famous English singers like Mrs. Kemble and Miss George. One of the opera's themes is the love of a white man, Trudge, for the enchantress, Wowski. Trudge, a gay London clerk, turns his back on the English beauties and takes Wowski for his wife. This controversial theme—controversial even for today—helped the opera's success in the latter part of the eighteenth century. And, more important, it showed that the idea of interracial mixing was not as abhorrent as race supremacists believed.

Artists portrayed it on their canvasses. One of Hogarth's pictures is entitled *An Unpleasant Discovery* and shows the friends of an English dandy catching him in a luxurious bed with a black woman. In another Hogarth, *Four Times of the Day (Noon),* a black man is fondling a pretty English wench. Both these prints are omitted from most editions of Hogarth, but a copy of the first one can be found on page 400 in Iwan Bloch's *Sex Life in England.* Hogarth was not the only artist to portray this on canvas. Thomas Rowlandson's *Dairy-Maid's Delight,* which depicts a love passage between a black man and a white girl, is seldom seen.

In fiction, mixed marriages were also approved. In *Slavery* or *The Times* by Anna M. Mackenzie an African prince marries the charming English heiress. Curiously enough, it is the girl who is honored by the match. Also, Juba, the black in Miss Edgeworth's *Belinda* marries the rich farmer's daughter. This theme of mixed marriages, pioneering for the period, recurs in *The Peregrinations of Jeremiah Grant, Esq, Humphrey Clinker, Vanity Fair* and several other novels.

Mixed marriages and other such unions did not cause much surprise in London and the larger seaport towns of England during the riotous years of the Georgian era. Hester Thrale, who was by 1802 Mrs. Piozzi, said of London in one of her letters: "Men of colour in the rank of gentlemen; a black lady covered with finery in the Pit at the opera and tawny children playing in the squares—the garden of the squares, I mean—with their nurses."

Such scenes were commonplace in London where "decent seeming white women" married blacks and where "white women walk the streets with their mulatto children." Professor Silliman of Yale, who visited London in 1820, wrote that on Oxford Street he saw "a well-dressed white girl of ruddy complexion and even handsome walking arm-in-arm and conversing sociably with a Negro man who was well-dressed as she and so black that his skin had a kind of ebony lustre."

The English attitude to blacks in the seventeenth and more especially the eighteenth century is a strange one and poses a paradox, as Dr. Kenneth Little, the anthropologist, noted:

> The Slave Trade and the holding of plantation Negroes abroad, and the treatment of individual Negroes in England are not necessarily the same thing, however strangely economic considerations may have favoured the former.

That does not mean that in England there was no hard core of Negrophobes. Following the lead of Samuel Estwick and Edward Long and spouting the kind of illogical race-hate propaganda which we still hear from fascist elements in Britain and elsewhere, was Gilbert Francklyn. It was his contention that the ideas of liberty, the charms of novelty, and an ignorance of Britain where these slaves had found themselves on terms of equality with the inferior white people had a corrupting effect on the black man's mind. That was why a great number ran away from their masters, plunging into vice and debauchery, claimed Francklyn. He was thoroughly convinced that liberty was not good for blacks and that they were much happier in a state of subjection. It did not occur to him that many preferred to starve as free men roving the city streets than to return to their masters.

Opinion in certain newspapers appeared to be against bringing slave servants into Britain because they would not put up with unequal treatment, or be willing to continue working in more menial jobs than English servants. They were depicted as sullen, spiteful, treacherous and revengeful; the only time they would work was when they were treated with severity. Not surprisingly, the papers forgot to add that trouble started because black servants did not want to work as unpaid slaves. English servants got wages and, quite naturally, blacks expected the same treatment.

In direct contrast to Francklyn, Long, and Estwick and a whole retinue of English planters, owners, and slave merchants were the more celebrated men of letters. They viewed the black man as a "Noble Savage" endowed with exotic charm and great dignity. High priestess of that cult was Mrs. Aphra Behn who, in 1688, published a novel called *Oroonoko* or *the Royal Slave* extolling the lofty ideals and virtues of the African slave.

Just as it is fashionable and enlightened today for writers to occupy themselves with the problems of apartheid, Jim Crow, the Black Revolution, Black Muslims, Freedom Marchers, Black Power, the Panthers and the migration of black people into Britain, so it was in the eighteenth century with the question of slavery. Other writers were quick to follow Mrs. Aphra Behn. Daniel Defoe lashed out at the slave trade. In his *Life of Colonel Jacques* he said that blacks should be treated with kindness; and in his best-known work, *Robinson Crusoe,* he drew a picture of the noble savage—Man Friday. Alexander Pope in his *Essay on Man* and Laurence Sterne in his *Tristram Shandy* were also black sympathisers, but even earlier writers had been airing their views on slavery and the treatment of slaves. A satirical comment appeared in the *Tatler* in 1710 when the essayist, Richard Steele, showed plainly where his sympathies lay:

> As I am a patron of persons who have no other friend to apply to, I cannot suppress the following complaint: Sir,—I am a six-year-old negro boy, and have by my lady's order, been christened by the chaplain. The good man has gone further with me, and told me a great deal of news; as I am as good as my lady herself, as I am a Christian, and many other things; but for all this, the parrot who came over with me from our country is as much esteemed as I am. Besides this, the shock dog has a collar that cost as much as mine. I desire also to know whether, now I am a Christian, I am obliged to dress like a Turke and wear a turban. I am, sir, your most obedient servant, Pompey.

The major poets of the time used their art to plead the black man's cause. Milton, Pope, Richard Savage, Shenstone, Thomson, William Cowper, and Thomas Day, all cried out the anguish of blacks. It was Cowper who wrote lines which were to be used in an English court when the freedom of the thousands of black slaves in England was being argued before Lord Mansfield, Chief Justice of the King's Bench:

We have no slaves at home—then why abroad?
And they themselves once ferried o'er the wave
That part us, are emancipate and loos'd,
Slaves cannot breathe in England; if their lungs
Receive our air, that moment they are free;
They touch our country, and their shackles fall.

But the poem which tugged at the hearts of the English population was *The Dying Negro* by Thomas Day. This was published in 1773 and was based on an incident that had taken place a year or two earlier. A black man had been walking along the streets of London when he was seized and forcibly put aboard a ship bound for the Caribbean. Rather than return to the West Indies and slavery, he killed himself. A frontispiece to Thomas Day's poem showed the black man standing as though making an impassioned plea to Heaven. With the fatal dagger in his hand, he utters his last words:

To you this unpolluted blood, I pour,
To you that spirit, which ye gave, restore.

This poem was one of the strongest written on the subject. So powerful was its impact that Thomas Clarkson, one of the most militant and active of abolitionists in England, observed that it added immensely to the sympathy which the English population had already begun to show for African slaves. Indeed, for weeks it was the talk of London.

Eminent men of letters began taking sides. When the voice of Samuel Johnson was raised against the evils of slavery its tones were fearless. Johnson was a most liberal, progressive-minded man who detested the social evils of the eighteenth century. Once, when in company with some learned men at Oxford his toast was "Here's to the next insurrection of the negroes in the West Indies." His violent antipathy against West Indian and American plantation owners came quickly to the surface. Towards the conclusion of his *Taxation no Tyranny* he shouted "How is it that we hear the loudest yelps for liberty among the drivers of Negroes?" His argument about the case of Joseph Knight, a slave who was seeking his freedom by law in the Court of Sessions in Scotland, was quite simply that men in their original state were equal and by no stretch of the imagination could he see how one man could be beaten into subjection by another; that since no man is by nature the property of another then Joseph Knight should be allowed to go free.

Samuel Johnson certainly practised what he preached. His treatment of his black servant was all protective kindness and fatherly love. This humanitarian attitude to slaves was taking root in the last quarter of the eighteenth century in England and was growing rapidly. From their pulpits Dr. Hayter, Bishop of Norwich, Bishop Warburton, and the celebrated divine John Wesley all preached about the miseries slaves were made to endure. But it was the Quakers who were the earliest and most tireless fighters. By appealing to members, by censuring them and by warning, most of the Quakers in England and the colonies who owned slaves or were in any way involved in the slave trade were encouraged to give the whole thing up. With puritanical determination the Quakers went one step further in 1774. They passed a decree expelling any Friend who had anything to do with the Trade. To show that they meant business, a ruling was passed two years later compelling any Quaker who had slaves to free them.

By then a group of earnest young Englishmen was getting together to fight slavery. These men were to shape the unyielding, fighting spirit of the abolitionists: Granville Sharp who had seen slaves ill-treated in London; William Wilberforce who had observed the slave market at Bristol when he was a boy and had written a letter to a newspaper in York at the age of fourteen declaring that "this odious traffic in human flesh should end"; Thomas Clarkson who had won a prize at Cambridge for a Latin essay on the slave trade and who held strong views on the matter; and the Reverend James Ramsay who had spent nineteen years in the West Indies and had been horrified at the treatment meted out to slaves. With Granville Sharp, Clarkson, and Ramsay, a new society for the Abolition of the Slave Trade was formed. Their spokesman in Parliament was William Wilberforce, Member for Hull. Of these, the man who was to prove the greatest friend of the black man in England was Granville Sharp, a clerk.

Passing judgment on racial attitudes in England during the period of the slave trade and after, Dr. Kenneth Little wrote:

> From a number of historical sources, more particularly the ramifications and implications of the Slave Trade, from various side-references and comments, and from occasional literary material wherein the Negro appears as a character, it is possible to infer a good deal. The main impression so gained is that there was little or no colour prejudice in

> England in the modern sense of the expression until at least the beginning of, and perhaps quite well on in, the nineteenth century.

This statement, though true in a general sense, needs qualification. The English were divided in their attitude to blacks: the haters included English planters, a few minor writers, and others who stood to gain financially from the African Slave Trade; on the other side there were the friends of the black man, far more numerous than the bigots. They included major poets and men of letters, Georgian nobility, artists, enlightened men, the Quakers, ministers of religion, and the poorer classes.

Blacks who lived and worked in London and elsewhere did not depend solely on whites to fight their battles for them. Sometimes they showed their solidarity and gave as good as they got. On February 15, 1764, for example, a club of black servants held a meeting at a public house in Fleet Street. Fifty-seven men and women were present. They wined, dined, and danced to the music of violins, French horns, and other instruments. They refused to allow white people to attend.

BIBLIOGRAPHY TO CHAPTER FOUR

Ashton, J. *Good Old Times*, p. 268. London: 1885.

Ayearst, Morley. *The British West Indies*. London: 1966.

Chancellor, E. Beresford. *The Pleasure Haunts of London During Four Centuries*. London: 1925.

Egan, Pierce. *Life in London*. London: 1821.

Estwick, Samuel. *Considerations on the Negro Cause*. London: 1773.

Faulkner, Thomas. *History of Kensington*, pp. 358–59. London: 1820.

Johnstone, Julia. *Confessions of Julia Johnstone*, p. 28. London: 1825.

Leigh, Mrs. Francis B. *Ten Years on a Georgia Plantation*. London: 1883.

Lindsay, Jack. *1764: The Hurlyburly of Daily Life Exemplified in One Year of the Eighteenth Century*. London: 1959.

Long, Edward. *The History of Jamaica*. London: 1774.

Nocturnal Revels, or History of King's Place. Vol 2, pp. 98—125, 1779. London: 1779.

O'Donoghue, E. M. *Odyssey of a Loving Woman*. London: 1936.

Thrale, Hester (Mrs. Piozzi). *Intimate Letters*. London: 1914.

Records of St. Marylebone Church, Marylebone Road, 1769-1774. London County Record Office, Westminster Bridge, London, S.E.1.

Williamson, J. *Medical and Miscellaneous Observations Relative to the West India Islands*. Vol. 1. London: 1817.

Wilson, Harriette. *Memoirs of Harriette Wilson*. Vol. 1. London: 1909.

CHAPTER V

"THE LAW TAKES NO NOTICE OF NEGROES"

The twenty thousand African slaves who lived in England prior to 1772 had no legal status whatsoever. Their position was a strange one, living precariously outside the protection of the law. They were slaves and were considered the property of their white masters in exactly the same way as they were "property" in the British colonies. To their dismay they learnt that life in England was not quite what they had expected. They came with one expectation—to gain freedom. This caused complications and ill-feeling among some English people who objected to their entry into the country on the grounds that as soon as they arrived they ceased to conduct themselves as slaves. One man who made no bones about the way he felt on this issue was Sir John Fielding, the London magistrate. Like other magistrates and judges who delight in making moral comment from the bench, Fielding said that no sooner had slaves arrived in England than they put themselves on a footing with other servants:

> They became, [he said,] intoxicated with liberty, grew refractory, and either under the influence of others or from their own inclinations, began to expect wages according to their own opinion of their merits. There were already a great number of black men and women who had made themselves troublesome and dangerous to the families who brought them over by getting themselves discharged. They made it their business to corrupt and dissatisfy the mind of every black servant who came to England; first by getting them christened or married, which, they informed them, made them free though it has been decided otherwise by the judges.

Baptism or marriage, as Fielding had stated, did not make slaves free. In the case of marriage there was one way slaves could get round the law:

if a wife showed the court that she was destitute because her husband could not keep her, as in the case of John Caesar's wife (see p. 22).

There was yet another way in which slaves quite often obtained formal manumission: through their masters' wills. Even so, although a master could provide in his will that after his death his black servant was free, this act did not prevent unscrupulous dealers from forcing the servant back into slavery.

The situation before 1772 seems to have been confused and was not helped by statements from various judges. First the Court of Common Pleas made it quite clear that a slave remained a slave while he was in England because he was a heathen. Many of them were therefore converted to Christianity and baptized, thinking that they would automatically be set free. Then, during the reign of Queen Anne, Chief Justice Holt stated that "As soon as a negro comes to England he becomes free." Slave masters paid not the slightest attention to this declaration since it was not a decision given in court and had no real legal weight.

About the same time that Chief Justice Holt aired his opinion, Mr. Justice Powell added to the general chaos making it known that "The law takes no notice of negroes." And in truth he was right. Blacks in England did not know where or how they stood with the law. They were certain of one fact: that they were at the mercy of any white master who apprehended them. In spite of this they were absconding from English homes in increasing numbers, roaming the streets, hanging around the riverside pubs, scraping a bare existence, but living surreptitiously as free men.

The position became uncertain for the slave master as well, since runaway slaves after baptism found "godfathers" who were willing to safeguard them against seizure. For that reason English planters in London appealed to Yorke and Talbot, the Law Officers of the Crown, for a legal decision on African slaves living in England, were they runaways or not. In 1729 the two Law Officers maintained:

> We are of the opinion that a slave by coming from the West Indies into Great Britain or Ireland, either with or without his master, does not become free, and that his master's right and property in him is not thereby determined or varied, and that baptism does not bestow freedom on him, nor make any alteration in his temporal condition in these kingdoms. We are also of opinion, that the master may legally compel him to return again to the plantations.

This decision was welcomed by planters, merchants, and others who gave it much publicity. Nonetheless, more and more slaves ran away, causing masters to advertise for their capture in the newspapers, offering money as reward. In 1749 Yorke, as Lord Chancellor Hardwicke, gave judgment that a runaway slave could legally be recovered. This was accepted unanimously. Slave owners proclaimed it their Bill of Rights. Now slaves were captured in the streets indiscriminately and openly sold by auction or to ships' captains who transported them back to slavery in the colonies. But the conscience of the English public was aroused and something was bound to happen sooner or later.

The change was slow in coming. The man who was to play a tremendously important part in it—helping African slaves to win their freedom in England—appeared on the scene several years after Hardwicke's 1749 judgment. That he came into it quite by accident can be looked upon as an act of providence. He was a little man, neither famous nor wealthy; just an ordinary clerk working for a small salary in the Civil Service. His name was Granville Sharp. He was to become the foremost champion of blacks in England.

Granville Sharp was born on November 10, 1735, son of an archdeacon of Northumberland and grandson of an Archbishop of York. Since a large portion of his father's money was spent on educating the two elder sons, Granville, being the twelfth of fourteen children, had to leave Durham Grammar School at an early age, and in 1750 he was sent to London and apprenticed to a Quaker linen draper named Halsey on Great Tower Hill. He served for seven years under three different masters and then went into the manufacturing business. Before long the venture failed disastrously and Granville Sharp became a junior civil servant in the ordnance office at the Tower—an appointment which a friend of his Tower Hill apprenticeship days had helped him to obtain. By 1764 he was appointed a clerk in ordinary and was removed to the Minuting Branch.

Granville Sharp had a probing, inquisitive, intellectual mind. At that time there was nothing of the reformer in him, although the mid-eighteenth century was certainly in need of reform—child cruelty and slavery being two of its worst evils. Sharp could not, however, help noticing that there was much in the fabric of life in London which was rotten. It was impossible for him not to observe the bawdy, Hogarthian life in the streets during his daily walks between the Tower and his brother William's surgery in Mincing Lane. This rather ascetic-looking son of an archdeacon must have been shocked to notice that Londoners "attached no excessive importance to the virtues of sober living." The effects of gin could be seen among the diseased, debauched, poorer classes. It was not long before his arrival in London that gin taverns were advertising the drink with matter-of-fact bluntness: "Drunk for a Penny, Dead Drunk for Twopence, Clean Straw for Nothing." As he walked through the smaller streets on a rainy afternoon he would see dead dogs, cats, and infants lying in the gutters, which were also cluttered with the sweepings from butchers' stalls.

The incident that triggered his all-consuming interest in the welfare of the underdog occurred on the steps of his brother's surgery and concerned a black man. One morning in 1765, as Granville Sharp was leaving the surgery in Mincing Lane, he bumped into Jonathan Strong, one of William Sharp's poor patients. Strong was on the verge of collapse, and looked to be in such pitiful condition that Granville Sharp went back into the surgery to question his brother about him.

Jonathan Strong had been the property of David Lisle, an irascible lawyer from Barbados. Lisle treated Strong brutally at his lodgings in Wapping, beating him over the head with a pistol. Strong became ill with ague, fever, and was lame in both legs; his eyes were affected to such an extent that he was nearly blind. When Lisle saw that Strong could no longer be of service, he threw him out into the street not caring whether he lived or died. It was at this time that Jonathan Strong came to Dr. William Sharp's surgery and was seen by Granville Sharp. The two brothers decided to help Strong. Dr. Sharp gave him lotion for his eyes and some money, and arranged for him to be admitted to St. Bartholomew's Hospital. He remained there for four and a half months, during which time, to quote Strong's own words, "The gentleman [Granville Sharp] find me clothes, shoes and stockings."

When Strong left hospital, he was cured of his injuries, but his eyesight remained feeble. His helper, once again, was Granville Sharp who paid for his lodgings and gave him money until he got him a job; placing him with a Mr. Brown, an apothecary in Fenchurch Street, as a messenger carrying medicine to patients.

And that might have been the end of the matter. However, two years later Jonathan Strong again came into Granville Sharp's life. The occasion arose when David Lisle, the lawyer who had owned Strong, chanced to see him attending his mistress, Mrs. Brown, behind a hackney coach. He noticed that Strong no longer looked sickly but was in tolerably good condition. The desire to lay claim to what had once been his property and to sell Strong as merchandise took hold of Lisle. So he shadowed the black man to the apothecary's house; and after making certain that he could locate the servant again, he sold Strong to James Kerr, a Jamaican planter, for £30 for shipment to the West Indies. Leaving nothing to chance, Kerr immediately kidnapped the black man after decoying him out of the apothecary's house. To help him carry out his dirty deed, Kerr got two helpers, John Ross, Keeper of the Poultry Counter, and William Miller, an officer under the Lord Mayor. Strong was then dragged to the Poultry Counter Prison, where John Ross agreed to keep him locked up until the vessel was ready to set sail for Jamaica.

The thought of returning in bondage to the Caribbean and the kind of treatment that would be his lot as a slave filled Strong with horror. In desperation he wrote to Granville Sharp, hoping for help. Although Granville Sharp had forgotten the unfortunate black man he had once aided, he immediately went along with his brother to the Poultry Counter. They found Jonathan Strong in a state of panic. Patiently Granville Sharp listened to the tale which the slave told him. By the time he was finished, Sharp had made up his mind that from then on his life's work would be the abolition of slavery in all its ugly forms.

He warned the jailer not to hand over his charge without warrant. Then he called on Sir Robert Kite, the Lord Mayor, and asked that he summon before him any persons who claimed possession of Jonathan Strong. Kerr's attorney, William McBean, and Captain Laird, the master of the ship *Thames*, which was to have taken Strong to Jamaica, appeared before the Lord Mayor with the bill of sale and claimed the slave as Kerr's property. But Sir Robert Kite was of the firm opinion that no person, be he slave or free, could rightfully be imprisoned without an offense being alleged against him.

After much dispute between McBean and Granville Sharp, the Lord Mayor discharged Jonathan Strong, telling him he was at liberty to go where he pleased. On hearing that, the captain, David Laird, grabbed Strong by the arm saying he would hold him as the property of Mr. Kerr.

Granville Sharp immediately told Captain Laird that he would charge him for assault if he continued to hold on to Strong. The captain reluctantly released the black man and everyone was told to go his own way quietly. Strong left—a free man.

Matters did not rest there, however. Lisle and Kerr decided that they must get at this busybody Granville Sharp in some way, put him in his place so that in future he would keep his nose out of affairs which, in their opinion, were no concern of his. They consulted their lawyers and immediately started an action for damages amounting to £200. The prospect looked gloomy for Granville Sharp because his lawyers had advised him that it would be pointless to fight the case. They told him he would most certainly lose and, to back up their views, they pointed out that authorities like Yorke and Talbot had maintained that a slave coming to England from the West Indies (whether he was with his master or not) was not free and that his master still had power over him. To make their point final and unarguable Sharp's lawyers added that no less a person than Chief Justice Mansfield himself, had on more than one occasion confirmed that opinion in King's Bench. Consequently they assured their client that his best course of action would be to settle the dispute out of court on the best terms he could get and leave the black man to his fate.

That attitude angered Granville Sharp. Although his knowledge of law was slight he calmly told his lawyers that he would not believe the law of England had no respect for the natural rights of man. Since they would not take up the fight on his behalf he told them that he proposed to "search through the Indexes of a Law Library" for books in which he could find a defense.

For two years Granville Sharp, with the thoroughness which was inherent in his makeup, studied law books, finally preparing a lengthy memorandum. This memorandum resuscitated Holt's statement that every slave coming to England became free, and supported it with "an exposition of the principles of villeinage and the common law."

Granville Sharp presented this memorandum to Sir William Blackstone, the celebrated judge, who had himself quoted Holt's views in his famous *Commentaries.* But Blackstone, who had a great respect for Lord Mansfield's views, had taken out the controversial passage from the last edition of his work. Although he did not decry Sharp's case, he warned him that "it would be uphill work in the Court of King's Bench." And, in point of fact, although Blackstone himself, the Solicitor-General, and the Recorder of London were retained for Sharp's defense, he agreed with his colleagues that they could not fight the case.

All was not lost, however, for Granville Sharp decided to send twenty manuscript copies of the memorandum which Blackstone had treated so lightly to eminent lawyers. The move was successful and very favorably received in the Inns of Court. The Lisle and Kerr lawyers became so alarmed that they postponed the suit. Finally they had to pay treble costs for not bringing it forward.

In 1769 Granville Sharp published the memorandum as a tract on *The Injustice of Tolerating Slavery in England.* There was a remarkable introduction addressed to Lisle, Kerr, and the others who were involved against Jonathan Strong. In the tract he explained his motives thus: "If I appeared in favour of the Negro, it was because he was in distress."

There were many more blacks who were to find distress in England, especially one James Somersett. Once again Granville Sharp's humanitarian instincts were awakened and he was "to appear in favour" of this black slave.

The case of Jonathan Strong prevented no one from kidnaping blacks found walking the streets, selling them and imprisoning them on ships bound for the Indies where they were once again put in bondage. In fact, in 1768, while Granville Sharp was fighting to gain Strong's freedom another case occurred. It concerned one Hylas and his wife, both slaves, who had met each other in England. They were married with the consent of their respective masters. Hylas's master granted him formal manumission, and he and his wife lived together in London enjoying their freedom. Then, one day the wife was seized on behalf of her former master and transported to the West Indies to be sold once more into slavery. Hylas, with the aid of Sharp took action against the kidnapper, Newton, and won. He was awarded one shilling damages and the defendant ordered to bring back the woman to England either by the first available ship or within six months of the court's decision.

Two years later Granville Sharp was called upon again, to help in a similar case: on a dark, murky night one Robert Stapylton, who resided in Chelsea, aided by two watermen, John Malony and Edward Armstrong, seized Thomas Lewis, an African slave and Staplyton's property, and dragged him to a boat moored on the Thames. They gagged him, tied him with a cord and rowed him down the river to a vessel waiting to raise anchor for Jamaica. This kidnaping happened near the garden of a Mrs. Banks, mother of Sir Joseph Banks, the naturalist and explorer who bequeathed his collection and library to the British Museum. Mrs. Banks' servants heard the screams and struggles of Lewis and ran to help him but found the boat already gone. They reported this to their mistress, who sent for Granville Sharp and told him that she was prepared to stand the costs involved in bringing the kidnapers to justice.

Granville Sharp, realising that speed was essential in order to stop the ship leaving British waters, hurried to the Rotation Office, and had a warrant dispatched to Gravesend for the return of Thomas Lewis. But it was too late. The vessel had been cleared and was putting out to sea. However, there was very slim chance of catching the ship in the Downs so a writ of habeas corpus was obtained and taken post haste to Spithead by Mrs. Banks's servant. Luckily, the winds were blowing against the vessel and this forced it to a standstill in the Downs. So the messenger, to use his own words, "found the unhappy negro chained to the mainmast, bathed in tears, and casting a last mournful look at the land of freedom."

The writ was served on the captain and Thomas Lewis was allowed to go ashore and thence to London. Straightaway Granville Sharp instituted criminal charges in Lewis's name against Stapylton and the two watermen. He was doubtful about the charges being accepted, as they were against white men. But the case was heard "without the least demur or doubt on account of the plaintiff's complexion or idea of private property." It resulted in the jury finding that the plaintiff was not the property of the defendant. Several jury members were moved to cry out "No property, no property."

Still blacks were pounced upon in the streets of London, Liverpool, and other English cities and held for sale. The abolitionist Thomas Clarkson wrote

> One or two other trials came on, in which the oppressor was defeated, and several cases occurred, in which poor slaves were liberated from the holds of vessels, and other places of confinement, by the exertions of Mr. Sharp.

Granville Sharp was not happy about this state of affairs, although, as Kenneth Little observed, "A number of Negroes were rescued by the

Courts on some technical point." The fact of the matter was that lawyers and judges had no desire to challenge Hardwicke's authority: that runaway slaves could be legally recovered. Little wonder that "capturing slaves and putting them safe on board ship became almost a trade in the East End of London." Hardwicke had been a celebrated chancellor and a ruling given by him was not lightly to be set aside. Consequently, wrote historian O. A. Sherrard, "Better to let sleeping dogs lie." Though Sharp was able from time to time to secure the release of individual slaves, in each case the judges burked what seemed to Sharp the main issue; they invariably gave as the grounds of release the lack of proper warrant, or disputed ownership, or some other such technical matter, but never the indubitable rights of the slave given him by law." Granville Sharp was determined to put this issue to the test at the next opportunity. He would go to all constitutional and legal lengths to obtain a ruling on "whether an African slave coming into England became free?"

Such an opportunity occurred in 1772. It was the case of *Knowles* v *Somersett* in the King's Bench Court:

James Somersett, a slave, was brought to England from Virginia in 1769 by his master, Charles Stewart, a plantation owner. Somersett found, to his pleasant surprise, that Londoners were not as hostile to blacks as slave masters were in the colonies. Some even urged him to escape. He did.

For a time Somersett enjoyed a spell of freedom around London, having found shelter among the large black population. Eventually, he was seized by his master and "confined in irons on board a ship called the *Ann and Mary*, John Knowles, commander, lying in the Thames, and bound for Jamaica." There, Somersett was to be sold as a slave for the second time. His London friends informed Granville Sharp and a writ of habeas corpus was issued on December 3, 1771, requiring the captain, Mr. Knowles, "to return the body of Somersett before his lordship, with the cause of the detainer."

From the very beginning there were adjournments and it looked as though the case was going to be a long-drawn-out affair. By the time of the first full hearing on February 7, 1772, Granville Sharp had obtained two adroit barristers to plead on behalf of James Somersett.

The case opened in the King's Bench, presided over by Lord Mansfield, the Chief Justice of the King's Bench, assisted by Justices Ashton, Willes, and Ashurst. The point to be argued was: "Is every man in England entitled to the liberty of his person unless forfeited by the Laws of England?"

Mr. Sergeant Davy, for Somersett, began by declaring: "My Lord, no man at this day is or can be a slave in England. All the people who come into this country immediately become subject to the laws of this country, are governed by the laws, regulated entirely in their whole conduct by the laws, and are entitled to the protection of the laws of this country and become the King's subjects." Davy continued, stressing the distinction between England and its colonies. The laws of Virginia, he argued, had no more influence, power or authority in England than the laws of Japan. He then went on to discuss the arguments of "convenience" and ended by naming his authorities for stating that "No man could be the property of another."

Mr. Sergeant Glynn, also for Somersett, followed by enforcing with great emphasis the arguments set forth by Davy "particularly in the point respecting the importation of laws of other countries into our own." By now, Lord Mansfield began to have doubts about the opinion of Talbot and Yorke, who maintained that a slave who came into Britain or Ireland with or without his master did not become free and "his master's right and property in him is not thereby determined or varied." For, at the conclusion of Mr. Sergeant Glynn's speech, Lord Mansfield added: "This thing seems by the arguments, probable to go to a great length, and it is the end of the term; and so it will be hardly possible to go through it without stopping: therefore, let it stand over to the next term."

This gave Granville Sharp time to strengthen the case in favor of Somersett. He sought public sympathy by interviewing people, haranguing and writing letters and pamphlets. Sharp was so dedicated to this cause it never entered his mind that he was a civil servant who might, by remonstrating so much with the government, risk losing his post. He even wrote to the prime minister, Lord North, saying: "My Lord, presuming that information, concerning every question of a public nature, must be of course agreeable to Your Lordship, I venture to lay before you a little tract, against tolerating slavery in England . . ."

Around that time Lord North had his hands full with the taxation troubles in North America and, according to existing records, does not seem to have replied. Undeterred, Sharp continued his efforts.

The Somersett case was resumed on May 9 with the defense restating the arguments of Davy and Glynn. But another adjournment followed and when hearing recommenced five days later Mr. Hargrave and Mr. Alleyne took up the defense. Hargrave harped on the point that if "the right claimed by Mr. Stewart to the detention of the Negro, is founded on the condition of slavery, in which Somersett was before his master brought him into England" and if that right were to be recognized there, then domestic slavery with the horrid evils associated with it would be lawfully imported into Britain. Mr. Alleyne followed by repeating: "The man is here: he owes submission to the laws of England, and he claims the protection of these laws."

The pleadings for James Somersett were at this stage closed and then Mr. Wallace rose for the plaintiff, whose claim he defended with great ability. He reminded the court that "as to England not permitting slavery, there is no law against it; nor do I find any attempt has been made to prove the existence of one. Villeinage itself has all but the name."

Supporting Wallace in his usual able manner was Mr. Dunning. His appearance on behalf of the plaintiff aggravated Granville Sharp. For it was Dunning himself who defended the black Thomas Lewis in a like case and won. Sharp was heard to observe, acidly: "This is an abominable and insufferable practice in lawyers to undertake causes diametrically opposite to their own declared opinions of law and justice."

For yet another time the case was adjourned. It was claimed that the Chief Justice was reluctant to free over 20,000 slaves worth £50 apiece by means of a judicial decision. There was no doubt that Lord Mansfield still retained some confidence in the Yorke and Talbot pronouncement.

On May 21 Mr. Dunning rose to state that the statutes of the British Legislature confirmed James Somersett's condition: that he was a slave both in law and in fact and "I have not heard, nor, I fancy is there any intention to affirm the relation of master and servant ceases here?" After counsel on both sides had summed up, Lord Mansfield abstained from giving judgment on the same day. All along he showed reluctance to arrive at a decision on the general question. Twice he threw out a suggestion that "the master might put an end to the present litigation by manumitting the slave."

At long last, on Monday, June 22, in Trinity term, 1772, the Chief Justice delivered judgment in the case of Somersett and Knowles upon the return of the habeas corpus. Lord Mansfield first stated the return and spoke as follows:

> The only question before us is whether the cause on the return to a Habeas Corpus is sufficient. If it is, the Negro must be remanded; if it is not, he must be discharged. Accordingly, the return states that the slave departed and refused to serve; whereupon he was kept, to be sold abroad. So high an act of domination must be recognised by the law of the Kingdom where it is used. The power of a master over his slave has been extremely different, in different countries. The state of slavery is of such a nature, that it is incapable of being introduced on any reasons, moral or political, but only by positive law, which preserves its force long after the reasons, occasion, and time itself from which it was created, is erased from memory. It is so odious, that nothing can be suffered to support it, but positive law. Whatever inconveniences may follow from the decision, I cannot say this case is allowed or approved by the law of England; and therefore the black must be discharged.

A packed, hushed court heard this memorable decision. It established the axiom, as proposed by Mr. Sergeant Davy that "As soon as any slave sets his foot on English ground, he becomes free." The same applied to Ireland, but not to Scotland until 1778 when the Scottish courts ruled in the case of the slave Joseph Knight that "The dominion assumed over this Negro, under the law of Jamaica, being unjust, could not be supported in this country to any extent."

As was to be expected the planter and commercial classes viewed the Somersett decision with strong disfavor. A planter wrote. "The planters of course have been left as much puzzled by this Delphic Ambiguity, as the sages themselves appear to have been, in forming their judgments upon the subject. The matter having been confounded in this grand uncertainty." Gilbert Francklyn, the pro-slavery champion, commented with bitterness on the twenty thousand and more, freed slaves: "As most of them were prime, young, seasoned, or Creole slaves, the loss to their owners, the planters, has not been less than from £1,000,000 to £1,200,000 sterling: a large sum to be sacrificed to the mere names of liberty and humanity." But, he admitted, the imagination of the populace of London was heated by the cry of liberty and people were jubilant about Lord Mansfield's ruling. Quakers, men of letters and the abolitionists treated the Somersett decision as the first blow against the African Slave Trade and slavery. Granville Sharp, although preparing for the long battle which lay ahead, made this short entry in his diary.

> June 22nd. This day James Somersett came to tell me that judgment was today given in his favour. . . . Thus ended G. Sharp's long contest with Lord Mansfield, on the 22nd June 1772.

But the ruling on the Somersett case did not prevent some slave masters from ignoring authority and hanging on to their slaves in England. Whenever these cases were taken before the courts, the owners were forced to release their slaves or employ them as paid servants. In fact a large number of blacks remained with their former masters under these conditions. Many thousands, however, wandered off and proceeded to live as free men in London, Liverpool, Bristol, and other English cities. Some, it was said, "regarded freedom as immunity from work" and joined the bands of robbers and footpads who roamed the streets.

Poverty and starvation lay ahead for the unfortunate ones in the cold air of eighteenth-century England, which, in the words of the poet William Cowper, would make slaves free "the moment their lungs received" it. As they were soon to find out, the act of achieving freedom was not enough. They had to seek out a living on their own—masters, for the first time, of their destiny.

BIBLIOGRAPHY TO CHAPTER FIVE

Birkenhead, Earl of. *Fourteen English Judges.* London: 1926.

Campbell, John Lord. *Lives of the Chief Justices of England.* Vol. 3. London: 1874.

Clarkson, Thomas. *Abolition of the African Slave Trade.* London: 1808.

Coupland, R. *The British Anti-Slavery Movement.* London: 1933.

The Gentleman's Magazine. (London: 1764). 492.

George, W. Dorothy. *London Life in the Eighteenth Century.* London: 1930.

Goodhart, A. L. (ed.). *The Law Quarterly Review* 50 (1934).

Greenidge, C. W. W. *Slavery.* London: 1958.

Hoare, Prince. *Memoirs of Granville Sharp.* Vols. 1 and 2. London: 1820, 1828.

Howell, T. B. (compiler). *The Case of James Somersett.* Vol. 20. London: 1814.

Klingberg, Frank J. *The Anti-Slavery Movement in England.* New Haven: 1926.

Lascelles, E. C. P. *Granville Sharp and the Freedom of the Slaves.* London: 1928.

Little, K. L. *Negroes in Britain.* London: 1948.

Mackenzie-Grieve, Averil: *The Last Years of the English Slave Trade.* London: 1941.

Quennell, Peter. *Hogarth's Progress.* London: 1955.

Sherrard, O. A. *Freedom From Fear.* London: 1959.

Stevens, William. The Slave in History. London: 1904.

Warner, Oliver. *William Wilberforce and his Times.* London: 1962.

CHAPTER VI

THE BLACK POOR AND THE SIERRA LEONE SETTLEMENT

The thousands of freed slaves in England soon learned that finding employment was going to prove difficult. To begin with, dispossessed slave owners were still fuming over Lord Mansfield's ruling. They were not prepared to pay wages to blacks whom they continued to regard as their rightful property, and as such not entitled to payment for their labors. Some blacks not wanting to face destitution in the frost-bitten city streets ran back to their former masters begging to be taken back, wages or no wages. Naturally, the more rapacious masters took advantage of these offers and proceeded to treat the "Uncle Toms" with greater severity. The humane ones were prepared to pay their black servants and give them the same consideration they gave their English domestics. Many freed slaves found some form of work. Some joined the navy. Several were accepted in the army as drummers and tambourine players. A few managed to learn trades and work as carpenters and builders' assistants. And there were those who were forced to accept jobs as crossing sweepers. Lastly, quite a lot took to selling tracts and patent medicines at street corners, to begging, and to crime.

And so, for the next eleven years the freed blacks in England seemed to have succeeded in earning some kind of a living, and in integrating themselves into English life. The majority married English women and raised families without experiencing racial animosity. The authorities did not put any restriction on their liberty or movements as long as they lived by the law of the land. Those who did turn to crime, however, were treated more harshly than English criminals. They were sent to Newgate, at which grim jail they were subjected to the worst forms of torture. As is the case with West Indians in Britain today, they faced deportation, and many were sent to work on the plantations of Virginia and Maryland. They were referred to as "apprentices."

For those freed blacks in Britain, the situation was deteriorating steadily. The reason for this was the heavy increase in their numbers—twenty thousand more by the time the war with America ended in 1783. This increase was caused partly on account of the fact that royalists and English families, to quote Gilbert Francklyn, "have been forced from the Southern colonies of the American continent by the late unhappy contest," and they took the slaves who attended them back to England.

Granville Sharp himself accounts for the rise thus:

> Some [blacks] have been brought as servants, but chiefly by officers; others were royalists from America; but most are seamen, who have navigated the King's ships from the East and West Indies, or have served in the war, and are thereby entitled to ample protection, and a generous requital.

Present-day historian Michael Banton gives one more reason for this increase by maintaining that there was also "a steady stream from the West Indies which seems to have included not a few stowaways."

All in all, therefore, the number of blacks living in Britain in the latter part of the eighteenth century was close on forty-five to fifty thousand, if those living in Liverpool, Bristol and other parts of the country are included.

Granville Sharp had claimed that the blacks who had served Britain on ships of war, merchant vessels and as soldiers were "entitled to ample protection and a generous requital." They received neither. Instead, hostile attention began to be focused on the entire black population. For, being unable to find immediate employment hundreds, nay thousands, became penniless, and roamed the streets begging, stealing, and turning more and more to crime in order to fill empty stomachs and keep warm. London streets, as well as the streets of several English towns and cities, became overrun with black paupers. Whereas under the Poor Law of the time paupers would be sent back to the parish of their birth to get relief, blacks born in other lands did not qualify for assistance. Since blacks regarded Granville Sharp as their champion many flocked to him in their turn for support: and he occasionally relieved them, finding himself with over four hundred black pensioners whom he had to keep alive with food and clothing. These became known as the St. Giles Blackbirds since they congregated in the London district of that name when receiving their weekly pittance.

For a few years the more fortunate blacks managed to subsist, as John Thomas Smith who became Keeper of the Prints in the British Museum, observed; and for this reason: "Black people, as well as those destitute of sight, seldom fail to excite compassion." Paradoxically, black beggars "achieved a certain fame amongst the London public."

What really worsened the position of the thousands of blacks in England was the presence of lascars who were as conspicuous as the blacks and, in many ways, more unfortunate. They were brought in on the East India Company's ships, discharged and left in London for several months before being shipped back to India. Estimates showed that about 2,500 lascars came annually to London. The English language and way of life were alien to them. (A parallel can be seen today with the Pakistani, Indian, and West Indian migrants in Britain.) To make matters worse the lascars were exploited by each other and, adds historian M. Dorothy George: "by the worst products of the riverside slums of Wapping and Shadwell and Poplar. Some of them made their way as beggars to the west of London and found shelter in the common lodging-houses of St. Giles."

Trouble, sparked off by jealousy and rivalry, began between black and lascar beggars. In 1784 a pamphlet was issued protesting against the beggars of Westminster and those who gave way to their pleas for alms. Curiously enough, the pamphlet made an exception in favour of the "vagrant blacks." In spite of this favoritism, destitute blacks became a problem, and one which caused a great deal of worry to the authorities a couple of years later.

Something had to be done to relieve the distress of blacks starving on the streets. Rather than amend the statutes so that parishes could take care of them, the Poor Law authorities decided to "send the blacks home" to Africa; or, as the government cleverly phrased their decision, there was "no place so fit and proper [for them] as the grain coast of Africa."

(These sentiments are voiced in Britain even today when discussing black immigrants.)

Granville Sharp fell in with the scheme readily. In the past he had aided the Black Poor with money and comforts and had even got help for them from "a voluntary subscription of charitable people." Prince Hoare who wrote Sharp's memoirs claimed: "He [Granville Sharp] determined upon sending them to some spot in Africa, the general land of their ancestors, where—when they were once landed, under a proper leader, and with proper provisions for a time, and implements of husbandry—they might, with but moderate industry, provide for themselves." Hoare declared further that Sharp's determination to send the settlers to Africa "did not originate merely in his own view of their misery, but was the consequence of applications made to him by the distressed Blacks themselves."

By the time the repatriation scheme was put forward the government and the Poor Law authorities were only too glad to get off their shores "this new class of pauper," whom they "regarded as a nuisance." What happened to them afterwards was not their concern. Although Granville Sharp and Jonas Hanway, chairman of the committee for the Relief of the Black Poor, and other philanthropists did not share that attitude they went into action to get the scheme going.

The first step was to buy the necessary land. With the aid of a Mr. Smeathman, a naturalist who had recently returned from West Africa, Granville Sharp persuaded the British government to acquire twenty square miles of coastline in Sierra Leone from paramount chief King Naimbanna. This 256,000 acres could not have been better placed. It was, noted Granville Sharp, well-watered "on a fruitful peninsula, between two noble navigable rivers, the great river of Sierra Leone and the Sherbo which receives the waters of many others . . ." Regulations ensuring the safety of the colonists had to be drafted. So, in the words of Sharp, "A code of laws, not marked with any refined traits of subtlety, but founded on principles of purest rectitude was drawn up." The settlers, he said, were to be "prohibited from holding any kind of property in the persons of men as slaves, and from selling either man, woman or child."

The government now put up posters all over London, inviting blacks who were "desirous of settling in one of the most fertile and pleasant countries in the known world" to apply for free passage. In its anxiety to rid the country of those down-and-out blacks the British government offered, as an added incentive, £12 per head for subsistence during the voyage and for the early settling down period. The seven hundred black poor who applied were described by the government, with a touch of hypocrisy, as "men of ardent passions, whose only lessons had been stripes, and whom experience had instructed to start with dread from their fellow-creatures."

Arrangements for this important journey were made in detail and with precision, with Granville Sharp at the head of things: "At this critical point Smeathman died of the fever, which he had managed to escape in Sierra Leone, and the burden of the scheme devolved upon Granville Sharp," wrote Prince Hoare. Sharp advised the government to appoint a naval officer, Captain Thompson, to take charge of the expedition and to lay the foundation for the settlement. Ships were chartered, food supplies and equipment bought and the contingent supplied "with necessaries during the first six or eight months of their residence in Africa."

In spite of Granville Sharp's tireless industry the scheme met with setbacks from the start. First, there was dishonesty. Stores were stolen and fraudulent transactions exchanged between friends and associates. The man who exposed all this was a freed African slave who had lived in London and who was to join in the fight for abolition. His name was Olaudah Equiano, but he was given the Christian name of Gustavus Vassa.

The government had appointed him their commissary in charge of stores. He was to travel to Sierra Leone with the contingent. Naturally, there were loud objections from the racists, but at first these were of no avail. However, Equiano was finally dismissed because of his honesty in reporting to the Commissioners of the Navy all the villainy which took place. Through the corridors of power in the City of London pressure was put on the Commissioners. They gave in. Nevertheless, Equiano came out of the affair with his integrity unblemished. The Commissioners were satisfied with his conduct and wrote to Captain Thompson expressing their approval. To salve his disappointment and appease their consciences the Commissioners paid him £50 sterling for four months work because, as Equiano himself, said, "I acted a faithful part in their service."

Putting Equiano's dismissal aside, as obviously brought about by racial foul play, more important was the fact that—to quote Equiano—"These poor people suffered infinitely more; their accommodations were most wretched; many of them wanted beds, and many more clothing and other necessaries." These commodities were not forthcoming because both money and stores had found their way into the pockets and homes of pilfering agents and officials associated with the scheme!

In the spring of 1787, headed by the *Nautilus* sloop of war under Captain Thompson, the little fleet sailed for Sierra Leone. Of the seven hundred "black poor" who applied for passages, only 351 turned up! Included on this voyage were "about sixty Europeans, chiefly women," observed Prince Hoare in his memoirs of Granville Sharp.

White historians have made much of these sixty travellers. Edward Lascelles wrote, "It included sixty unhappy white prostitutes, who had been decoyed to Wapping, made drunk, and shipped off as 'wives' for some of the settlers." Kenneth Little takes up this same tune: "Some sixty white prostitutes were shipped along with them in the same transport." Averil Mackenzie-Grieve goes some steps further: "By some extraordinary and still unexplained negligence, several prostitutes had been permitted to accompany the settlers to Africa, degenerate white women whose presence caused constant quarrels and discontents. One of these wretched women explained that she had been taken, with others of her kind, by prospective customers to Wapping, there plied with drink and taken on board the ship and 'married' to a negro. She herself admitted that she had been too drunk to remember anything that had happened the previous night, and the following morning was obliged to enquire who her husband was." But it was the late O. A. Sherrard who came out with the classic white supremacist cliché: "Negroes, it is well known, possess a fascination for the more unstable and abondoned types of white women, and some sixty prostitutes from the slums were sufficiently attracted to throw in their lot with them." Sherrard has bent the historical facts out of proportion to suit his own bias. The unhappy blacks, who had no hand in this, were given the blame. However, a statement by Olaudah Equiano gets closer to the truth: "A gentleman in the City empowered the same agent [the fraudulent one] to receive on board, at the government expense, a number of persons as passengers, contrary to the orders I received." The truth of the matter, which no historian has seen fit to explain, was that these prostitutes were being shipped out as undesirables (a not uncommon act in those days) to the colony of Sierra Leone.

The scheme met with other vicissitudes which hampered progress. Some of the "black poor" died at sea "from disorders brought on board with them," said Prince Hoare. Others were worn out by the long voyage, declared Equiano, and "wasted by sickness brought on by want of medicine, clothes, bedding, etc., they reached Sierra Leone just at the commencement of the rains."

It was virtually impossible at that time to cultivate the land. Provisions ran out and so did many of the colonists, especially some lascars who were included among the blacks. Several, having spent many months cooped up in the ships, could not withstand the harsh climate. They died. The remainder, approximately 276, were still sufficient to start a small town.

By the following March, only 130 of the hardier types remained. They owed their survival to a stock of provisions which Granville Sharp had sent out at his own expense with a party of new settlers. The difficult task of building began and after a year's hard work the settlers succeeded in hewing out a rough town for their capital—a capital which was to be named Freetown.

Fresh disasters followed: King Jemmy, one of the local chiefs, claimed that an American slave ship captain had unlawfully spirited away two of his men, and was impatiently awaiting a chance for revenge. Since the American captain responsible had escaped, King Jemmy swore that the first American to set foot on his territory would suffer. The opportunity came when an American ship's boat was seen rowing slowly upstream in the direction of the nearby slave factory. King Jemmy and his warriors attacked and plundered it, killing three of the crew of four. The lucky seaman who escaped traveled up the river bank to the factory and told his story to the agent. After lengthy consultation with Captain Savage of *H.M.S. Pomona,* which was anchored in the river, the factor decided to punish the culprits.

First, overtures were made to King Jemmy to pay a social visit to the ship of war. These attempts proved futile with the wily chief. After three days the factor's patience had worn thin. Accompanied by a naval lieutenant and an escort of sailors and marines, he set out for the king's village, taking with him two of the free blacks from the settlement as guides. They were reluctant and afraid and did not want to get involved in an affair which could mean the loss of their freedom and, perhaps, their lives. However, the factor was adamant and with his armed sailors and marines surrounding the two men, they were left with no other choice.

When news reached King Jemmy that the attacking force was after him, he and his subjects retreated from the village into the forest. The sailors then set fire to the deserted village. But King Jemmy's retreat was a planned strategic move, with men hidden at vantage points all along the path. They remained almost motionless in ambush waiting for the party to return. As it grew dark the factor and his men began their journey back to the slave factory feeling satisfied with the easy success of their venture. The free blacks in the party were less happy about it. Their fears were justified when suddenly musket shots began flying all around them from the dense undergrowth. Before the sailors and marines could load their muskets the lieutenant and sergeant of marines were killed and King Jemmy's men surrounded them blocking the narrow path. In the skirmish some of the sailors were wounded while the black force lost several men before it could withdraw.

King Jemmy's anger rose higher and he was determined to avenge his followers. He placed most of the blame on the factor but since that gentleman decided that his wisest course of action was to leave the coast immediately, King Jemmy had to find other scapegoats. For that purpose he summoned a council of neighboring chiefs. They decided that every person, no matter how remotely connected with the chief offender, should be punished. And since two men from the newly set-up colony had been members of the attacking party, King Jemmy ruled that Freetown should be burned to the ground. He made his decision known to the settlers. The two guides pleaded that they had been drawn into the affair very much against their will and by threats. King Jemmy remained firm. He replied that he viewed their participation as deliberate and announced that he would grant the settlers three days' grace in which to leave. True to his word, on the last stroke of the hour of the third day King Jemmy's men burned Freetown to the ground. The settlers scattered. Less than half of them reached the comparative safety of a malarial island in the Sierra Leone River. Nothing remained.

Despite these disasters the Freetown experiment was not dropped. Granville Sharp and his abolitionist colleagues were still set on re-establishing the free blacks on their own soil. In 1790 the St. George's Bay

Association was founded for opening and furthering a trade in Africa's natural produce. In the following year an Act of Parliament was passed granting the association a charter and incorporating it as the Sierra Leone Company. Granville Sharp was president of the company, and Henry Thornton, chairman. Among the directors were William Wilberforce and Charles Grant, who, like Wilberforce, Thornton, and Granville Sharp, was a member of the wealthy and philanthropic group known as The Clapham Sect. In January of that same year Alexander Falconbridge, a former surgeon on a slave ship, was sent out to Sierra Leone in order to bring together what remained of the scattered free blacks and to rebuild a settlement. He found only sixty of the original settlers alive. "But," writes historian Edward Lascelles, "He brought them together from the scattered huts where they were hiding from the attentions of King Jemmy, and persuaded them to build a new capital. This achievement convinced them that the settlement could be saved."

By July, 1791, when the Sierra Leone Company was incorporated by Parliament, it was obvious that for the settlement to survive not only were more settlers required, but also more capital. The company immediately started looking for both. It was at this timely moment that one Thomas Peters, a representative of the Free Blacks, or "Black Pioneers" as they were called in Nova Scotia, appeared in London to lodge complaints about the ill-treatment his black colleagues had received since they fled from their homes in the rebellious thirteen American colonies. He asked that the free blacks of Nova Scotia should be allowed to join the colonists in Sierra Leone. The British government and the Sierra Leone Company agreed to his proposals and Lieutenant John Clarkson, R.N., offered to go to Nova Scotia in order to supervise the removal of the free blacks to Sierra Leone. The feeling of the government was that the Black Pioneers were entitled to some consideration—for a very sound reason.

When the war with America began in 1776 the British authorities promised by proclamation that any slave who ran away from a rebel owner to fight for the government would automatically be freed. Straightaway thousands of black men, women, and children escaped from slave masters to the British lines where they were given a certificate of protection. The majority of the men were formed into companies called "Black Pioneers" or "Guides and Pioneers." At the beginning they were mainly labor battalions, but as the war progressed they were equipped with muskets and played an active part in the fighting. Pay lists and muster rolls show that they were commanded by European officers.

This tendency on the part of slaves to join the British side was widespread. When the governor of Virginia, then Lord Dunmore, was driven away from the colony by patriots, he rallied to his support several blacks to help him regain his power, promising them freedom from their masters. And it was Sir Henry Clinton who proclaimed in 1779 that all slaves in arms should be bought from their captors for the public service, and that every black who deserted the "rebel standard" could come over to the British lines and take up any occupation he wished. These plans were, in fact, carried out. The British made efforts to organize two black regiments in North Carolina. Between the years 1775 and 1783 the state of South Carolina lost 25,000 blacks to the British. One-third of the soldiers garrisoned at Fort Cornwallis at the siege of Augusta were blacks loyal to the English. There was a corps of fugitive slaves who called themselves the King of England's soldiers. For several years they harassed the people living on the Savannah River.

When the war ended in 1783 and America had won her independence, the various black combatants found themselves in a sticky position. By a clause in the Treaty of Paris, the British were obliged to hand back all American property. And since slaves were listed as property, the British authorities in New York—where the defeated army had assembled and was awaiting shipment to Great Britain—found themselves faced with two alternatives. They had either to break their promise to the Black Pioneers and return them to slavery, or ignore the clause in the Treaty of Paris.

The British found a way around this clause in the treaty. They compromised by declaring that any American who came to New York and could prove beyond all doubt that he was the master of a slave, would be allowed to take him away. After that, those slaves who were not claimed would be evacuated with the army. In making this stipulation the British authorities knew only too well that it would be difficult for any master to get to New York since the war had only just ended, leaving everything in chaos and making travel a risky business. To make the position even more awkward the establishment of proof of ownership was by no means easy, since the British authorities put all sorts of red tape obstacles in the way. That is why very few of the Black Pioneers were given up, and thousands taken away.

In a list of three thousand Black Pioneers there appeared the name of Thomas Peters (spelt Petters), a sergeant whose age at that time was forty-five; and who, before running away at the start of the war, had been a slave, the property of William Campbell of Wilmington, North Carolina. When the Black Pioneers were about to embark from New York with the rest of the English loyalists, Peters had with him his thirty-year-old wife Sally who had also been a slave near Charleston, South Carolina. She too had escaped to the British lines, where she met Thomas Peters.

Several of the vessels taking the loyalist contingents away sailed north from New York to Nova Scotia, the nearest remaining British colony. The one on which Peters sailed put in first at Bermuda, but in May, 1784, he landed at Annapolis on the western part of the Nova Scotia peninsular. There Peters hoped to make a living, earning wages like any other free man, as a millwright.

But Thomas Peters and the rest of this contingent of three thousand Black Pioneers were to face disappointment. To begin with, they formed only a very small proportion of the British loyalists who left the United States at the end of the war. Over 28,000 loyalists settled in Nova Scotia, which at the time was a sparsely settled, underdeveloped colony covered with wild forests. These loyalists—the white ones—were given preference over the three thousand Black Pioneers by the British government. The "free Negroes" were shamefully neglected. They had been promised land but few of them got any. What little they were given was thick pine forest which was virtually impossible to clear. Worse than that was the severe winter when all the land was encased in hard, unmelting layers of snow for four months of the year. Nevertheless the black war veterans decided that there was nothing to do but settle down as small peasant farmers. They knew very well that without land they would have no alternative but to work as farm laborers for employers who had once owned slaves and who would not welcome the idea of paying them. Nor were these fears their only misfortune. When the British government stopped sending supplies of food to the loyalists and their slaves, many free blacks died from hunger.

Among those who did not get the land promised by the British government was Thomas Peters. He waited six months for his claim to be examined and his argument that he had no guarantee from the authorities that his case would be heard was a sound one. A statement that it would have been heard in a matter of months came at the time when Peters declared that he would go to England and tell the government about the injustices he and his people were having to suffer.

This was certainly a courageous decision. For one thing he was then in his fiftieth year and had no influential friends to back his proposal. What was worse, the government of Nova Scotia quite naturally objected to a complaint of this nature and was against Peters' trip to England. Thomas Peters faced still graver risks. As a former slave traveling alone, he would be at the mercy of any rapacious ship's captain who might take him to an American port where the British certificate of freedom would be worthless, and then sell him. Thomas Peters braved all these perils and arrived in London in 1791.

His voyage was not in vain. At the very beginning he met the right person—Granville Sharp, who had fought tirelessly and successfully on behalf of slaves in England. Straightaway Sharp and Thornton, chairman of the Sierra Leone Company founded in 1791, championed Peters' cause. It was included in a Memorial to the Secretary of State who accepted it wholeheartedly, at the same time sending a despatch to the governor of Nova Scotia—Governor Parr—ordering him to investigate the grievances of the Black Pioneers and put them right. When the scheme to take the blacks of Nova Scotia to Sierra Leone was proposed the secretary of state approved of it—not only because he wanted to help the poverty-ridden blacks of Nova Scotia: the slaves, seamen, soldiers, and servants who had left after the war with America had already doubled London's black population. (A mere 351 had left on that first voyage of the Sierra Leone Settlement Scheme, and an even smaller number on the second one.) Since many of those who remained found themselves literally in the London gutters and forced to beg on the streets, the secretary of state did not welcome the prospect of another three thousand to further aggravate the problem of the "black poor."

With his task accomplished, Thomas Peters, after being royally treated in London, returned to Nova Scotia as the representative of the wealthy and influential directors of the Sierra Leone Company who were also helping to finance the project. He had the power to offer his people a new home in Sierra Leone. From then on Peters was their leader.

In Nova Scotia thousands of Black Pioneers applied when the company's notice appeared, promising to accept those who could produce satisfactory testimonials of character. Peters' job was to go across to St. John, New Brunswick, and then to Annapolis, and bring to Halifax those who wanted to go to Sierra Leone. From Halifax they would sail to Africa. The major task of collecting the emigrants scattered all over Nova Scotia, of chartering ships at Halifax and organizing the expedition, was put in the hands of John Clarkson, the young naval lieutenant.

By November, 1791, Thomas Peters had gathered eighty-four emigrants and, with his wife and children, sailed to Halifax to wait for ships to take them across to Africa. Eventually on January 15, 1792, Lieutenant Clarkson, with 1,198 Black Pioneers including Peters and his contingent, sailed from Halifax to Sierra Leone. On March 8, the emigrants arrived. Sixty-five had died at sea. On arrival Clarkson thanked the "Nova Scotia Blacks for their regular and orderly behavior during the voyage."

Thomas Peters did not live to enjoy life in Sierra Leone. On June 16, 1792, less than four months after he landed, the man whose determination had taken him to London to plead the cause of his comrades in Nova Scotia, died. His memory did not die, for his exploits were not trivial. It was because of his faith and courage that the Nova Scotia settlers, without whom the colony could not have survived its earlier misfortunes, went to Sierra Leone. Thomas Peters has always been looked upon and honored as one of the Founding Fathers of Sierra Leone.

With the help of the original settlers the 1,133 Nova Scotians wasted no time in building a new capital, "gratefully and hopefully christened Freetown." Governor William Dawes had been sent out with his second-in-command, Zachary Macaulay, who, two years later succeeded him as governor. The territory was vested in the Crown so that it became a British possession.

At every turn troubles descended on the settlement and its settlers, almost shattering their hopes, as O. A. Sherrard wrote:

> In 1793 war broke out between England and France, and the next year an embittered American slave-trader, whose victims had occasionally escaped to the new settlement and there found refuge,— avenged himself by guiding a French revolutionary squadron to the

> spot, where the exponents of liberty manifested the fruits of their faith by burning Freetown and making themselves drunk on looted spirits and ridiculous in stolen feminine finery. Macaulay was left with nothing but a heap of ruins, but like Sharp he was not discouraged. He was determined to succeed and he did.

More and more back-breaking work had to be put in. Finally, the settlement was rebuilt. When it was taken over by the government as a Crown Colony in 1808, Sherrard observed, "it was already a shining light in the Dark Continent. . . ."

However, even then the going was not smooth. The fortunes of the settlement still remained chequered. In the end perseverence in the face of nearly insurmountable obstacles was rewarded. The colony became prosperous and peaceful. It was this which caused abolitionist Fowell Buxton fifty years later to announce:

> With all its defects, if anything has anywhere been done for the benefit of Western Africa, it has been there. The only glimmers of civilisation; the only attempt at legitimate commerce; the only prosecution however faint, of agriculture, are to be found at Sierre Leone. . . . And there alone the Slave Trade has been in any degree arrested.

In honoring Thomas Peters as a Founding Father, history will not forget the role played by Granville Sharp in the Sierra Leone project. For without his tenacity and dogged courage the scheme would have been still-born in the streets of London, already full of the dead and dying "Black Poor."

BIBLIOGRAPHY TO CHAPTER SIX

Banton, Michael. *The Coloured Quarter.* London: 1955.

Buxton, Sir Thomas Fowell. *The African Slave Trade and its Remedy.* London: 1840.

Equiano, Olaudah *The Interesting Narrative of the Life of Olaudah Equiano.* (new edition) Written by Himself. 2 vols. London: 1809.

Francklyn, Gilbert. *Observations on the Slave Trade.* London: 1789.

George, M. Dorothy. *London Life in the Eighteenth Century.* London: 1930.

Hoare, Prince. *Memoirs of Granville Sharp.* London: 1828.

Lascelles, Edward. *Granville Sharp.* London: 1928.

Little, K. L. *Negroes in Britain.* London: 1948.

Mackenzie-Grieve, Averil. *The Last Years of the English Slave Trade.* London: 1941.

Marshall, Dorothy. *The English Poor Law in the Eighteenth Century.* London: 1926.

Mayhew, Henry. *London Labour and the London Poor,* Edited by Peter Quennell. London: 1952.

Richmond, Anthony H. *The Colour Problem.* London: 1955.

Sherrard, O. A. *Freedom From Fear.* London: 1959.

Smith, John Thomas, *Vagabondiana.* London: 1874.

Stevens, William. *The Slave in History.* London: 1904.

West, Richard. *Back to Africa. A History of Sierra Leone and Liberia.* London: 1970.

CHAPTER VII

AFRICAN ABOLITIONISTS

The Sierra Leone Settlement was not the only project in which abolitionist Granville Sharp was engaged. For him, the fight would continue until the African Slave Trade and slavery in the colonies were totally abolished. Already, in 1772, through his efforts, slaves were pronounced free once they lived in England. That was the first step. Other abolitionists like William Wilberforce and Thomas Clarkson had dedicated their lives to crushing slavery.

It was not only English abolitionists, however, who were doing all the campaigning against the slave trade and slavery. A few African slaves and free black men in London joined in the crusade. Most prominent among the Africans was Olaudah Equiano, who played a useful role in the Sierra Leone project. He took part in all matters affecting blacks and the slave trade, and was a tireless abolitionist worker around London, often in collaboration with Granville Sharp. A man of great talent and strength of character, Equiano became well known and respected among his illustrious contemporaries.

Olaudah Equiano was born circa 1745 at Essaka in Benin, Northern Nigeria. As a young boy of ten he was captured with his sister and taken from their home in Iboland. He was thrown into the hold of a slave ship anchored off the coast of Guinea and never saw his sister again. After a long and miserable journey across the Middle Passage the frightened young boy reached Barbados, where he was sold. He was then shipped off to Virginia where he was again purchased on the slave market. Later he was re-sold to Henry Pascal, captain of a vessel of war, the *Namur*, bound for England.

Equiano accompanied his master to Guernsey. He remained with Captain Pascal and travelled with him on his voyages, witnessing many naval battles between the English and French, notably the siege of Louisbourg in Canada in 1758. He was also an observer at the siege of Belle-Isle in 1761. However, on setting foot in North America he was once more put in irons as a slave. In 1766, through hard work and thrift, he managed to purchase his freedom and continued to sail in merchant ships until 1777. Up to that time his life had been full of excitement. He travelled as far afield as Spain, Portugal, Italy, Turkey, and Greenland. Having escaped the dangers of the sea, being several times shipwrecked and having also avoided the cruelties of many slave masters—one of whom, in Savannah, proposed to assassinate him—Olaudah Equiano decided to make London his home.

No sooner had Equiano (Gustavus Vassa) settled in London than he busied himself in the campaign to get justice for his people. In 1783, Granville Sharp noted in his diary:

> March 19.—Gustavus Vassa, a Negro, called on me, with an account of one hundred and thirty Negroes being thrown alive into the sea, from on board an English slave ship (the *Zong*).
>
> 20th—Called on Dr. Bever this evening to consult about prosecuting the murderers of the Negroes.

The ship's Captain, Luke Collingwood, and crew were not even taken before the courts. The solicitor-general asserted:

> To bring a charge of murder against those who had acted in this part of uncontrolled power, into an English court of law, would argue nothing less than madness in him who brought it thither.

And what was the reason for throwing these slaves alive into the sea on the pretext that there was a severe shortage of water on board?

To begin with the slaves were sick. Some had already died. If all of them died a natural death the loss would fall on the owners of the vessel. However, if they were thrown alive into the sea, on any sufficient pretext of necessity for the safety of the ship, it would be the loss of the underwriters. The law of the land at that time was prepared to protect the slave traders rather than the slaves.

The *Zong* affair caused deep distress to Equiano, Sharp, and the anti-slavery elements in the country, but it did not diminish their abolitionist zeal.

Olaudah Equiano was next involved in the Sierra Leone Settlement Scheme—the part he played in it having been described in the previous chapter. That, too, turned out unhappily for the African. But, undaunted, he refused to give up, and applied to the Bishop of London to be sent as a missionary to Africa. As in the Sierra Leone Settlement project his request was turned down. Then in 1788 he petitioned Queen Charlotte, on behalf of his fellow Africans, to help relieve them "of the grossly cruel act of slavery."

Equiano was not content to remain out of the fight while the English abolitionists were pitting their might and resources against the slave trade. So he did what he considered best. In 1789 he wrote his autobiography—*The Interesting Narrative of the Life of Olaudah Equiano or Gustavus Vassa, the African.* It was published in two volumes and dedicated to "The Lords Spiritual and Temporal, and the Commons of the Parliament of Great Britain." It was written with the express purpose of being used in Parliament when the motion against the slave trade was being debated. It was the first and only time that a book was dedicated to members of Parliament in England. This vivid personal account of the sufferings of a captured African was widely quoted whenever the motion for abolition was being debated in the House. Equiano's account of how he felt when he was first taken on the slave ship at Guinea is most moving:

> When I looked around the ship, too, and saw a large furnace of copper boiling and a multitude of black people of every description chained together, everyone of their countenances expressing dejection and sorrow, I no longer doubted of my fate; and quite overpowered with horror and anguish, I fell motionless on the deck and fainted. I was soon put down under the decks, and there I received such a salutation to my nostrils as I never experienced in my life. Two of the white men offered me eatables and, on my refusing to eat, one of them held me fast by the hands, and laid me across, I think the windlass, and tied my feet, while the other flogged me severely.

The book was exceedingly successful. Within five years it ran into eight editions. The subscription list of the first edition numbered three hundred and nine and included George III's sons, the Duke of York and the Duke of Cumberland, eminent personalities like Hannah More, Samuel Whitbread, Henry Thornton, John Wesley, Sydney Smith and Granville Sharp. In fact, in a preface to a later edition the printer, James Nicholas, wrote: "The subscription list of the first edition could boast that it was graced by the names of more wealthy characters than had before adorned the pages of any book published in this country."

Equiano's autobiography became a minor classic. The narrative, everyone who read it agreed, had a continuous flow, an unaffected style, and a pictorial quality that not only carried conviction, but enthralled the reader. The reviewers of the period sang its praises. The magazine *Monthly Reviewers* wrote:

> We entertain no doubt of the general authenticity of this very intelligent African's story. The narrative wears an honest face. His publication appears very seasonable, at a time when negro-slavery is the subject of public investigation; and it seems calculated to increase the odium that has been excited against the West Indian planters, on account of the cruelties that some are said to have exercised on their slaves, many instances of which are here detailed.

Another critic of the time wrote:

> The heart of the work is his own. Its very ingenuousness gave power to its human appeal.

In the year 1792 at Soham in Cambridgeshire Olaudah Equiano married a Miss Susan or Susanna Cullen, daughter of James and Ann Cullen, an English couple of Ely in the county of Cambridgeshire. It was claimed that Equiano had a son who later became librarian to Sir Joseph Banks, the celebrated scholar and man of letters who was Secretary to the Vaccination Committee. But this son was probably that of Ignatius Sancho who did in fact work for Banks, and whose name was William.

Right up to his death in 1801 Olaudah Equiano remained in London helping, as he himself wrote, to stop "the miseries which the slave-trade has entailed on my unfortunate countrymen." He led a deeply religious life, having been baptized in 1759 in St. Margaret's Church, Westminster. In assessing his work and his life, emphasis has always been placed on his book, but the reason for writing it is of greater significance. A historian has described Equiano or Gustavus Vassa, as "one of the greatest anti-slavery agitators" of his time. After completing his book Equiano traveled throughout Britain selling copies and making speeches against the slave trade in several towns and cities. Letters of recommendation from his friends show that he visited Birmingham in 1789, and Manchester, Sheffield, and Nottingham in the following year. Further notes prove that he was in Belfast on Christmas Day 1791, Dublin and Hull in 1792, and in the West of England at Bath and Devizes, in 1793. During those campaigning years he made many enemies among those who stood to profit from the slave trade. Those enemies made charges against him in *The Oracle* of April 25, 1793, stating that he was not a native of Africa, but was born on the Danish island of Santa Cruz in the West Indies. This story was reprinted in *The Star* two days later. However, Equiano was able to furnish proof positive that he was born in Essaka, in Benin, Africa; and the editor of *The Star* apologized, admitting that the story must have been a total fabrication of the enemies of abolition, who were prepared to do anything to weaken the force of arguments against the slave trade. After his 1798 visit to Birmingham, where he was well received, he wrote:

> These acts of kindness and hospitality have filled me with a longing desire to see these worthy friends on my own estate in Africa, where the richest produce of it should be devoted to their entertainment. They should there partake of luxuriant pineapples, and the well flavoured virgin palm-wine, and to heighten the bliss I would burn a certain tree, that would afford us light as clear and brilliant as the virtue of my guests.

Olaudah Equiano always longed to return to Africa but that desire, unfortunately, was never fulfilled.

While Olaudah Equiano was agitating in London and other English towns and cities, two other Africans were using their pens to bring the horrors of slavery before the public. One was Ottobah Cugoano (sometimes spelt Cuango and also known as James Stuart), a freed slave—the other, James Albert Ukawfaw Gronniofaw. Cugoano's book, more than Gronniofaw's, dealt strongly with the evils of slavery with a devastating denunciation of the slave trade. One historian described it as "abolitionist rhetoric, demanding a heightened style."

Books by slaves were always popular in England and were sure to raise passions. They gave the abolitionists more fuel for their fire and angered the pro-slavery factions. Cugoano's book, titled *Thoughts and Sentiments on the Evil and Wicked Traffic of Slavery and Commerce of the Human Species* and published in 1787, was the first and one of the most impressive of the books written by slaves. But it is Equiano's work which has remained a classic.

Ottobah Cugoano, a Fantee, was kidnapped as a boy and taken to Grenada. He was subsequently liberated and brought to England. There he worked for Cosway the miniaturist and having acquired an education became a leading abolitionist. In his book Cugoano gives a poignant description of his departure from the coastal fort, Cape Coast Castle, where he was kept prior to being taken aboard the slave ship:

> There was nothing to be heard but the rattling of chains, smacking of whips, and the groans and cries of our fellow-men. Some would not stir from the ground, when they were lashed and beat in the most horrible manner. I have forgot the name of this infernal fort; but we were taken in the ship that came for us to another that was ready to sail from Cape Coast.

In the fight against slavery, these works, together with those of major English writers, clergymen, and abolitionists, played a great part in changing the attitude of the English people and causing them to realize the enormity of the crimes their slave barons were committing against Africans. They helped greatly in bringing about the abolition of the slave trade in 1808.

Although not an African by birth, there was a man, Richard Hill, who would carry on Olaudah Equiano's good work several years later. He was a devoted fighter in the emancipation struggle. Hill was the son of a well-to-do English father and a mother who was part African and part East Indian.

Born in Spanish Town, Jamaica, in 1795, Richard Hill was sent at the age of five to England to be educated. His father hated slavery intensely. On his death bed he said to his son: "Richard, before I die you must promise me one thing; you must swear that—even as I have done—you will use all your strength in the struggle for freedom for the coloured race to which you belong; that you will not rest until they achieve equal rights with all other races—until the whole rotten system of slavery is ended. Promise to do this. Swear now."

Richard Hill, proud of his African descent, kept this promise to his dying father. When he had completed his studies in England he returned to Jamaica. Soon afterwards he made journeys to Cuba and America and studied in those countries. Then after a short stay in Canada he sailed to

England to join the Anti-Slavery Society. He met William Wilberforce, Thomas Clarkson, Thomas Fowell Buxton, and other abolitionists, and presented a petition to the House of Commons for the removal of the civil restrictions on the free black people of Jamaica and the freeing of the slaves. He was received with great respect in the House, and Canning, foreign secretary and later prime minister during the reign of George IV, made his last speech in favour of the petition.

Richard Hill stayed in London for the next few years and continued the struggle. Although short of money he managed to make ends meet by contributing literary and scientific articles to the leading newspapers and periodicals. He worked tirelessly with both pen and voice to make the English public aware of conditions in Jamaica, and to arouse their passions against slavery. The abolitionists recognised the good work he was doing and the Anti-Slavery Society sent him to Haiti to report on the natural resources of the island then under the rule of President Boyer. He remained there for two years studying the soil, animals, plants, fish, insects, as well as the effect of freedom on the Haitians. On his return to England he took with him several notebooks filled with valuable information and sketches.

Back in London Richard Hill resumed his work against slavery until emancipation in 1834. Then he returned to Jamaica to help in the period of adjustment. The post given him was that of head of the special magistrates appointed to settle disputes between freed slaves and their former masters. He held this appointment ably for thirty-eight years.

To honor him for the work he had done for the people of Jamaica and the rest of the British Caribbean territories, the British government offered him the appointment as governor of St. Lucia. He politely declined the offer. Richard Hill felt that he could do more for his people if he remained free of imperialist plumes and trappings of governorship. When he died in 1872, aged seventy-seven, he was honored and respected not only for his untiring struggle against slavery but for his high principles in putting the welfare of his race before personal glory.

On the night of July 31, 1834, thousands of blacks sat in the churches in Jamaica, the Leeward and Windward Islands, Barbados, Trinidad and Tobago, and British Guiana. They were offering prayers for their deliverance from bondage. At midnight the bells began to peel out the joyful news. For eight hundred thousand slaves under the flag of Britain it meant they had reached the end of the freedom road. But the journey along that road had been long and thorny and littered with the dead: the slave dead who had been ravaged by ill-treatment and disease; the slave dead who had stirred up rebellion against their white oppressors and paid the supreme penalty for it. Fellow travellers along the freedom road had been the abolitionists who doggedly and passionately campaigned through legal and humanitarian channels for over fifty years until, as one black poet so lyrically put it: "My dungeon shook, and my chains fell off."

The toil of the slave writers and abolitionists in London, like Olaudah Equiano, James Albert Ukawfaw Gronniofaw, Ottobah Cugoano and Richard Hill, not forgetting Granville Sharp, William Wilberforce, Thomas Clarkson, Thomas Fowell Buxton, Zachary Macaulay, John Smith, David Livingstone, and other English abolitionists, had not been in vain. For, in the words of historian Eric Williams "the humanitarians were the spearhead of the onslaught which destroyed the West Indian system and freed the Negro." To disregard this fact, would, again to quote Dr. Williams, be "to commit a grave historical error." However, Williams adds, and quite rightly: "The establishment and development of the Caribbean slave system were basically the result of the importance of that system to the economy of the metropolitan governments. Conversely, the abolition of the slave system was basically the result of the fact that the system had lost its former importance, in the nineteenth century, to the metropolitan economy. The first aspect of this economic revolution was that, on the eve of emancipation in the several Caribbean territories, Cuba excepted, production was either static or declining. Thus, by that time, substantial economic interests in Britain were actively in support of abolition which, to a large number of abolitionists and others, had been, and still was, a moral issue."

BIBLIOGRAPHY TO CHAPTER SEVEN

Brawley, Benjamin. *Early Negro American Writers.* Chapel Hill, N.C.: 1935.

Cugoano, Ottabah. *Thoughts and Sentiments on the Evil and Wicked Traffic of Slavery and Commerce of the Human Species.* London: 1787.

Equiano, Olaudah. *The Interesting Narrative of the Life of Olaudah Equiano.* (new edition) Written by Himself. 2 vols. London: 1809.

Grégoire, H., formerly Bishop of Blois. *An Enquiry Concerning the Intellectual and Moral Faculties and Literature of Negroes.* Brooklyn, N. Y.: 1810.

Hoare, Prince. *Memoirs of Granville Sharp.* Vol. 1. London: 1828.

Hodgkin, Thomas. *Nigerian Perspectives.* London: 1960.

Rogers, J. A. *Nature Knows No Color Line.* New York: 1952.

Sherlock, Philip M. *West Indian Story.* London: 1960.

Scobie, Edward. "Jamaican Abolitionist." *Flamingo Magazine* (August, 1964).

Williams, Eric. *From Columbus to Castro: The History of the Caribbean 1492–1969.* London: 1970.

Woodson, Carter G. *The Negro In Our History.* Washington: 1922.

CHAPTER VIII

DARLING BLACKS

Out of the throng of courtesans, blackamoors, butlers, beggars, black abigails, jingling johnnies and slave writers came some who gained positions of eminence and even immortality for their contributions to Georgian society. In the arts as elsewhere they had something to offer. They moved in an atmosphere of tolerance and admiration for their accomplishments and benefited from their uniqueness and exoticism.

Those blacks who managed to develop their talents and personalities and receive adulation were usually "blackamoors," black children adopted by Georgian aristocrats. They became M'Lord's and M'Lady's "darling blacks": the favored few, the lucky ones. Others, usually those who had gained prominence in other lands and who visited Britain were also idolized. Such a one, the Chevalier de St. Georges, was a darling of society. Titled persons fawned on him. They called him "the most seductive of coloured gentlemen." Society hostesses sought his company and invited him to their homes and their exclusive parties. His handsome presence—for he was over six feet and well-built—his talents, his learning, his refinement were of the quality found in gentlemen of breeding. He fascinated everyone who came into contact with him, his color being an attraction rather than a cause for prejudice.

Historian Kenneth Little wrote:

> There is plenty of evidence that individual Negroes in England won respect and a position for themselves on their own merits. Coloured men who acquired wealth and patronage were received without reser-

> vation in the very highest circles. A French mulatto, the Chevalier Georges de St. Georges, son of the Marquis de Langley and a Negro slave, was a personal friend of the Prince of Wales, afterwards George IV, and as the champion swordsman of his day, and an accomplished rider, skater and violinist, once set the fashion in the English courts.

The Chevalier de St. Georges, a contemporary of Mozart, was also a composer of note. Among his most performed works is a *Symphonie Concertante in G* for two violins and string orchestra.

Dr. Little went on to write that it seemed evident that "Until at least well on in the eighteenth century Englishmen saw nothing extraordinary in a Negro possessing talents equal to their own." That may have been the view of most Englishmen of intellect and learning and birth but it was certainly not a widely accepted one among the proslavery elements of the English population.

This English love of the "Noble Savage," the black man of talent and accomplishment, has never failed to excite wonder and bewilderment; for, while the English will put up all sorts of social and constitutional barriers in order to prevent black people from entering and living in Britain, they will, at the same time, sing the praises of black writers, poets, singers, musicians, cricketers, athletes, or boxers. This has been true throughout a long association with blacks, especially in the eighteenth century. Although this attitude appeared to be changing in the nineteenth century, it is very much in evidence in the twentieth.

Another black visitor to receive the adulation of the English was the American slave poet Phillis Wheatley. Brought to America on a slave ship in 1761 when she was about six or seven and described by the Boston auctioneer as "naked as a little savage and fine as a suckling pig" Phillis was bought by a tailor, John Wheatley, and his wife Susannah. They treated her with the same affection that they gave their own twins, Mary and Nathaniel. When she was thirteen Phillis began to display a talent for writing poetry in the style of Alexander Pope.

It was in the summer of 1773, and on the advice of the family doctor, that Phillis was sent on a sea voyage to England with Nathaniel Wheatley. The sea air, Mrs. Wheatley felt, would do her good. Not wanting her servant to travel as a slave, Mrs. Wheatley gave her formal manumission.

On her arrival in London Phillis Wheatley was introduced to the Countess of Huntingdon, who acted as her patroness and gave receptions for her. At one such gathering Phillis met the Duke and Duchess of Gloucester, Lord Dartmouth, and the Honourable Brook Watson, Lord Mayor of London, who presented her with a copy of the 1770 Glasgow folio edition of *Paradise Lost*. (This book is now at Harvard University; at the National Gallery in London there is a portrait of Phillis receiving it from the lord mayor.)

While in London, Phillis Wheatley's first book of thirty-eight poems called *Poems on Various Subjects, Religious and Moral* was published under the patronage of the Countess of Huntingdon. It represented the bulk of her poetic output for the past six years. The majority were written for occasions—especially deaths, twelve of the poems being on this theme. In a preface to the volume Phillis Wheatley stated that the poems were written during her leisure hours for her amusement and that it was due to the kindness of her many friends that they were published. Her portrait appears in the book and shows her to be pretty.

Black critics claim, with some justice, that Phillis, in her poetry, was merely parroting the language of gentility, or poetic expressions, mostly from Pope, which were foreign to her; or, as the late Langston Hughes once said, that being a slave she would have used her talents better in writing more about the inhumanities of slavery.

By 1777, after having achieved some eminence in London, Phillis Wheatley returned to Boston.

In general, blacks who were protégés fared better than those who had to fend for themselves. For instance, when Staten Island was taken over by the British during the War of the American Revolution, one black boy named Bill Richmond came to the notice of General Earl Percy, who immediately took him under his protection as his servant. In 1777, after traveling abroad with the Earl for some time, Richmond arrived in England at the age of fourteen. The Earl, having discovered that Richmond was an intelligent youth, put him in a school in Yorkshire, where he received a tolerably good education. But it was as a boxer that Richmond became known and is remembered. It was said of him that he was "a complete Harlequin in the ring."

Bill Richmond fought fourteen times in all, losing only three of his fights. One was to Tom Cribb who became the Prize Ring champion of

England four years later. Pierce Egan, a writer and journalist who saw him fight was, like many of his contemporaries, much impressed: "I saw Richmond when he was fifty-five years old, enter the lists with a tall, strong, and young fighter; and win the battle in twenty minutes."

He married an Englishwoman by whom he had many children. Although at times subjected to taunts because of his color, Richmond, whom associates described as "intellectual, witty, and well-informed," moved in circles which shielded him from the insults of the vulgar. After he retired from the prize ring, he ran an inn and boxing academy in Martin's Street, near Leicester Square, London, called the Horse and Dolphin. The inn was much frequented by Lord Byron and other bluebloods. On December 28, 1829, during the reign of George IV, Bill Richmond died at Tichbourne Street, London, at the age of sixty-six.

It would be no exaggeration to state that of all the "darling blacks" in England during the eighteenth century none was more petted, more loved, more spoilt than that of Kitty—Catherine, Duchess of Queensberry—the wealthiest, prettiest, wittiest blue-stocking in the reign of the first three Hanoverian kings. His name—Julius Soubise. He was brought to England from St. Kitts in 1764 when he was ten. The duchess, a friend of celebrated men of letters like John Gay, Dean Swift, and the poet Alexander Pope, was so "struck with his manner and address" that she begged him of her cousin, Captain Stair-Douglas, R.N., to whom the boy belonged. She noted:

> I at once felt an interest for the orphan, promised to provide for him, and faithfully kept my word. I named him Julius Soubise, sent him to school, supported him genteely and provided him a good education.

Most of the duchess's friends who came into contact with Soubise felt that her favors were not ill-bestowed for Soubise was grateful and affectionate. He soon ingratiated himself with the duke as well as the duchess, becoming the pet of each and a favorite with the whole household. He grew fast, was engaging in his manners and soon manifested a disposition for gallantry. One of his friends at that time was Henry Angelo, son of the celebrated Italian riding and fencing master, Domenico Angelo, whose academy, Carlisle House, was in Soho Square, London. The duchess who admitted that "he was very attractive to women and my maids called him the young Othello," sent Soubise to learn fencing and riding with Angelo.

Very soon Julius Soubise became one of the most accomplished riders at Angelo's manège. The Duchess of Queensberry and other ladies used to sit in a gallery for spectators watching "her protégé perform his equestrian exercises." He was an equally proficient fencer, and acquiring grace of manner and blessed with a handsome presence "it was said he was to be sent to one of the universities to finish his education." There is no record that he did attend a university, but what he lacked as a scholar he made up in his expert riding and fencing. He became one of the chief riding and fencing masters at Domenico Angelo's school. His popularity soared and he made friends with the young bloods he taught. At the same time the duchess's attachment to Soubise, in the words of Henry Angelo, Domenico Angelo's son, "increased every day and she was accustomed to drive him around in her carriage." She never hid from her friends her fondness for the teenage black, allowing him privileges which were denied others of her household; something which one of her close friends, Lady Mary Coke, thought was very uncommon: "I made a visit to the Duchess of Queensberry and found her at home half dressed and half undressed. She was talking to Soubise who indeed seems to have a very extraordinary capacity."

Soubise became the talk of the town and was even satirized in the newspapers.

William Austin, the caricaturist, published a print in 1773, with the tall duchess and Soubise engaged, like D'Eon and St. George, in a public fencing match. Soubise is shown with his sword aimed at the duchess's heart and saying "Mungo here, Mungo there, and Mungo everywhere. Above and below. Hah! What your Grace think of me, now?"

There was more than a measure of truth in Austin's caricature, as Henry Angelo observed: "There are ladies who fence, but the most striking example is the Duchess of Queensberry who does, in fact, practise fencing with her Negro protégé." The handsome Soubise with his "well-formed legs and well-proportioned body" was a source of interest to everyone who came into contact with him. One evening during dinner at Carlisle House some friends of the elder Angelo—Thomas Sheridan, a professional lecturer, a physician named Dr. Kennedy, and Samuel Foote, the actor-dramatist—were discussing Soubise. Sheridan remarked: "Considering all circumstances, Soubise is the best behaved, unassuming minion of the great that I have ever known. What say you, Kennedy?"

"Yes, yes . . . and so modest withal," Kennedy replied.

To which Foote added: "Sheridan is right; but damn me, for all Soubise's modesty, I never saw him blush."

This repartee offended the elder Sheridan, and as Angelo observed: "I might add, Soubise had other admirers who were always ready to defend him. He was a great favourite of Garrick's too."

At that time, Soubise, because of his physical attractiveness, was being sketched, painted, and sculpted by famous artists and dilettantes. Thomas Gainsborough made a sketch of his head, the size of life, Johann Zoffany, a small whole-length of his person, and Henry Angelo himself painted him for pleasure. When all this attention was being paid him Julius Soubise was nineteen, a truly gifted and unusual young man by any standards. Henry Angelo said of Soubise's talents:

> Soubise played upon the violin with considerable taste. The elder Sheridan gave him some lessons in elocution. He studied the speeches of Othello and declaimed in the grand manner of the tragedian at the sporting clubs, with mighty applause: one of his favourites being Othello's speech in the bed-chamber of the castle while Desdemona is asleep.
>
> As an orator, another of his favourite exhibitions was Romeo in the garden scene. When he came to the part, "O that I were a glove upon that hand, that I might touch that cheek," Soubise would hold his black hands up in front of him and with one of them, the right, go through the motions of putting on a glove. Then he would give a sigh of longing. General applause always ensued; which was not discouraging to his vanity.

But there were more parts to this talented slave. He not only "played upon the violin with considerable taste," but had a good voice and was a minor composer meriting attention, as Henry Angelo admitted: "Soubise composed several musical pieces and sang them at sporting clubs, too, in a manner that would have fitted him for a role at the Opera-house." One of the songs, it is claimed, was "Kate of Aberdeen." A favorite performer at London's Vauxhall pleasure gardens, Soubise always won mighty applause and an encore for his comic opera rendering of a popular ditty of the period called "As now my bloom comes on apace the girls begin to tease me."

During that period, Julius Soubise gained promotion at Domenico Angelo's manège. Other instructors included Domenico's fourth brother, Leonardo Maria, his nephew, Anthony, and the famous French master, Chevalier Charles D'Eon. Henry Angelo—himself an expert at both riding and fencing, and also an instructor at his father's manège—had gone to live in Paris. One of the duties of Soubise in his new post as assistant master in fencing and riding was to attend as the usher of Domenico Angelo when he gave lessons to the pupils at Eton. As the elder Angelo himself observed, "Soubise was no less a favourite with all the pupils."

Loved by his patroness, trusted by his employer, mothered by his employer's wife, lionized by eminent actors, writers, and painters, the pet of Georgian aristocrats, the attractive Soubise could do no wrong. Up to the age of twenty-one he had led a reasonably well-ordered life, but it was too much to expect all this adulation not to have some effect. By 1775, Henry Angelo, who had returned from Paris and had rejoined his father's manège as an instructor, began to notice a change in Soubise. Supplied with pocket money by the duchess, for the first two years he worked with the Angelos he passed his time happily and without incident, until "he suddenly changed his manners and became one of the most conspicuous fops in town." He began to dress in the fashion of members of the Macaroni Club—a band of young men of rank who had visited Italy and affected a Latin elegance of manner and dress. Henry Angelo described this change in Julius Soubise:

> "Bourgeois Macaronis" was the term given to the queer characters of the day—the dandies—like Lord Littleton, Sherwin, Watts and Major Topham. I called Soubise the Mungo Macaroni. Others addressed him as the Black Prince—a term which he loved.

Dressed in powdered wig, white silk breeches, very tight coat and vest, with enormous white neck-cloth, white silk stockings, diamond-buckled red-heeled shoes, and at all seasons of the year with a bouquet of the choicest flowers in his bosom, the black dandy presented a most striking appearance. Soubise was the gayest of all the "macaronis." He frequented the opera and the theatre; sported a fine horse and white groom in Hyde Park, and became a member of many fashionable clubs (among them The Thatched House Club in St. James's street, a rendezvous for wits, politicians, and men of fashion). His insinuating manners, his accomplishments, his drollery, and that amusement from his endeavors to do the "agréable" made him a general favorite at the club. When singing and late hours were the order of the night, Soubise went to the Brush Club in Long Acre. The Black Prince most certainly cut a figure. But it was his attraction for the ladies which caused eyebrows to be raised and then frowns to gather on the foreheads of Georgian society. Henry Angelo claimed that although "Soubise always boasts to me of his amours, he had a way with women," and, "in truth, he is as general a lover as Don Juan and writes as many sonnets to his lady loves as Charlotte Smith." Angelo illustrated his extrovert behavior with the following story:

> I remember seeing him, when presenting a chair to a lady—if [at] some distance—make three pauses, pushing it along some feet each time, skipping with an "entrechat en avant" then a pirouette when placed. That never failed to coax a fond gaze and sweet smile from his lady admirers.

As an instance of his dashing spirit, while teaching riding and fencing at Eton, he frequently entered Windsor with his *chère amie* in a post-chaise and four. In the words of Henry Angelo:

> There, Madame awaiting his return from the college, he would meet her, dine in style at the Castle Inn, take his champagne and claret, entertain half a dozen hangers on, and return to town by the same expensive conveyance.

Soubise, even whilst at Domenico Angelo's, had private apartments, unknown to the family, where he conducted himself in the manner of an extravagant man of fashion. He had a succession of lady visitors, and his rooms were supplied with roses, geraniums, and other expensive greenhouse plants in the spring. His perfume was equally expensive. In fact, when fops and frail fair would see Soubise coming they would whisper to each other "I scent Soubise," so lavish was his use of it. These extravagances were finally discovered by the elder Angelo, who, to his great surprise, found that Soubise's bills at the inn and elsewhere were paid regularly, as his noble patroness supplied her darling protégé liberally without asking him any questions about his mounting extravagance. Even if anyone were indiscreet enough to tell the duchess she would not listen and would dotingly lavish more and more money on Soubise.

Eventually, after repeated entreaties from Domenico Angelo, the Duchess of Queensberry discussed her protégé with Ignatius Sancho, an older black man and friend of Soubise, asking him to give the latter some wise counsel. But Sancho's advice fell on deaf ears. For nearly two years Soubise lived a life of excess. So, when Domenico found that admonition was fruitless, he was obliged to dispense with his services, recommending that the black fop be sent to India at the expense of his patroness so that he might mend his wild ways away from the high life of the rakes and fops of London.

On July 15, 1777, Julius Soubise, fop, man about town, riding and fencing master, singer and actor, was put on the *Bessborough* at Portsmouth, bound for Madras. Seven months later he set foot on the soil of India to start a new life, hoping in time to win his way back into the heart of his devoted Duchess of Queensberry. But Sancho wrote to tell him that two days after he left Portsmouth his "noble, friendly benefactress, the good Duchess of Queensberry entered into bliss."

Julius Soubise, though he was an out and out rake, was charming and made friends easily. People were always ready to help him. When he reached Calcutta later in the year 1777, Memory Middleton, a gentleman who held a high station in the east, became Soubise's friend. Through Middleton and other distinguished patrons he obtained numerous pupils and accepted an appointment, with a large salary, to break in horses for the government. Soubise also taught fencing.

Julius Soubise never returned to England but attained respectability during his twenty-one years in India. He died as he would have wished: taking risks. His death at the age of forty-four was reported in the *Calcutta Monthly Journal:*

> As Mr. Soubise was exercising a spirited young Arab horse near the riding school, he tripped and fell off, by which unfortunate accident he received a violent contusion on the head and was otherwise much bruised. He was immediately carried to the General Hospital where he lingered through the day, and notwithstanding every possible assistance was afforded him, died the same evening, Friday, the 25th of August, 1798.

His friend and colleague in London, Henry Angelo, made this note in his *Reminiscences:*

> When lucklessly engaged to subdue a fine Arabian, the terror of everyone, mounting the unconquerable beast—for he was the boldest of horsemen—he was thrown, and, pitching on his head, was killed. Thus

> ended the Black Prince, as he was self-dubbed and so designated in a portrait, a small whole-length, published by Darling in Great Newport-Street.

It would be unfair to say that Catherine, Duchess of Queensberry wasted her love, her affection, her money, in making a gentleman out of her darling black, Julius Soubise. He did nothing worse than gamble, spend money recklessly, and have many lady loves; pursuits many an English blueblood enjoyed and got away with. But for Soubise's color he, too, would have been allowed to lead his merry life, giving pleasure to those of his acquaintance, and would not have been "sent to the colonies" (India) as punishment. In any case, he made amends. He is remembered in eighteenth-century memoirs and reminiscences as one of the most fascinating characters in a fascinating age. That he had been a slave and was black makes the life of Julius Soubise all the more remarkable.

There were other blacks of different inclinations. Three stand out above the rest—Ignatius Sancho, Francis Barber, and George Augustus Polgreen Bridgtower.

Of them all, Ignatius Sancho is the one who has the strongest claim to being a man of culture and learning. Yet he started life with more obstacles piled against him than many. In 1729 he was born of slave parents on board a ship sailing from Guinea to the Spanish West Indies. At Cartagena in South America, a Portugese bishop baptized him Ignatius. Soon after, his mother contracted a fever and died; and, not wanting to face the tortures of slavery, his father committed suicide.

At the age of two he was taken by a ship's captain from the West Indies to England where he was handed over to three sisters who lived in Greenwich. From the time he went to live with the spinsters, Ignatius was treated with sternness and cruelty. They kept him in ignorance, maintaining that to teach a slave how to read and write would prove dangerous for his mistresses. When he tried to run away they threatened to send him back to serfdom on a West Indian plantation where menials were treated with much greater severity.

The sisters named him "Sancho," claiming that he resembled the squire in Cervantes' *Don Quixote.* It was a lucky thing for Sancho that John, the second Duke of Montagu, lived nearby at Blackheath; after a visit to the sisters, he grew fond of the boy, admiring his frankness and quickness of mind. The duke took him to his house regularly, and taught him to read and write. His wife Mary, youngest daughter of the Duke of Marlborough, used to give Ignatius books which he read avidly, unknown to his mistresses.

On many occasions the duchess begged the three narrow-minded spinsters to educate Sancho but they refused. When he was twenty, feeling that he could not stay with them any longer, to be beaten, starved, and forced to sleep on the floor in a cold backroom, Ignatius Sancho ran away. He was certainly no "darling black" to the three old maids. However, he was to find kindness with the Montagues, where he was taken in to the duchess's household as a butler. (Just at that time, 1749, John the second duke of Montagu died.)

When the second duke's widow died in 1751, she left Sancho £70 and an annuity of £30. He gave up his job and went to London, but fell on hard times. He felt an urge to live in luxury like a man about town, gambling and going to the theatre. As soon as his money ran out and he lost his clothes in games of cribbage, this urge disappeared, and, swallowing his pride he returned to the Montagues. George Brudenell, who was created the Duke of Montagu in 1766, took a lenient view of his behavior and made him his personal attendant. Sancho became deeply religious and settled down, with his wife Anne, described as "a deserving young woman of West India origin." They had six children.

This period of Sancho's life was a very significant one. While at Montagu House he struck up a friendship with novelist Laurence Sterne who had just written his greatest work of fiction, *The Life and Opinions of Tristram Shandy, Gentleman.* It was Sterne's sympathetic reference in his novel to the horrors of slavery which caused Sancho to write to him in 1766:

> Reverend Sir, It would be an insult on your humanity (or perhaps look like it) to apologize for the liberty I am taking. I am one of those whom the vulgar and illiberal call negroes. The first part of my life was rather unlucky, as I was placed in a family who judged ignorance the best and only security for obedience. A little reading and writing I got by unwearied application. My chief pleasure has been books. I think you will forgive me; I am sure you will applaud me for beseeching you to give one half-hour's attention to slavery, as it is this day practised in our West Indies. The subject handled in your striking manner would ease the yoke (perhaps) of many.

Laurence Sterne's reply paved the way to a life-long friendship with Ignatius Sancho and stirred up in him the desire to be a "man of letters." Sterne wrote:

> There is a strange coincidence, Sancho, in the little events (as well as in the great ones) of this world: for I had been writing a tender tale of the sorrows of a friendless poor negro-girl, and my eyes had scarce done smarting with it, when your letter of recommendation in behalf of so many of her brethren and sisters, came to me. It casts a sad shade upon the world, that so great a part of it are and have been so long bound in chains of darkness and misery.

In the spring of 1767 Ignatius Sancho solicited subscriptions for the ninth volume of Sterne's *Tristram Shandy, Gentleman* from the Duke and Duchess of Montagu and their son, Viscount Mandeville. The friendship grew and by that summer Sterne's letters to Sancho were addressed to "his good friend Sancho." The connection, said one of the black man's contemporaries, extended his reputation, "and on 29th November, 1768, Gainsborough, while at Bath, painted his portrait, at one rapid sitting." This portrait (now hanging at the National Gallery in Ottawa, Canada) is twenty-nine inches by twenty-four and took exactly one hour and forty minutes to complete. It was engraved in stipple by Bartolozzi in 1781, and shows Sancho to be of a pleasant and intelligent countenance.

Ignatius Sancho said in his first letter to Laurence Sterne that his pleasure was books. The black slave also read books to educate himself. He was in the literal sense of the phrase "a self-taught man," learning and mastering the intricacies of music. Proof of this came when Sancho composed and published a collection of minuets and country dances, some of them scored for strings and two horns, and some just on two staves, and described as suitable for violins, mandolins, German flute or harpsichord. This collection was "Humbly Inscribed to the Right Hon'ble John, Lord Montagu." John, Lord Montagu, was the son of George, Lord Brudenell, for whom Sancho worked as personal assistant; and Sancho was devoted to all his master's children, especially John. In 1767 when Lady Betty Montagu, his master's twenty-three-year-old daughter, married Henry, third Duke of Buccleuch, Ignatius Sancho once again composed minuets, cotillions and country dances, again scored for strings, German flute, two horns and harpsichord to mark the occasion, and dedicated to the bridegroom.

These two works cannot be dismissed as amateurish. Musicologists are agreed that they are far superior to much of the musical trivia which minor composers foisted on the long-suffering eighteenth-century public. In form and style they are typical of the late baroque music of the third quarter of the eighteenth century. They resemble and are equal in merit to some of the work of Johann Christian Bach, Bach's youngest son who lived in London, and his contemporaries. (These compositions can be seen at the British Museum.)

In 1773 Ignatius Sancho, who was suffering from repeated attacks of gout, left the Montagues to open a grocer's shop at No. 20 Charles Street, Westminster, a house which stood on the southwest corner of Crown Court. With his wife and children he began to enjoy a life of domesticity, finding time to satisfy his thirst for literary matters. As John Thomas Smith observed, "In his leisure hours he indulged his taste for music, painting, literature; which procured for him the acquaintance of several persons of distinction." The shop of "this extraordinary literary character" soon became a meeting place for Joseph Nollekens the sculptor, the violinist Giardini, Laurence Sterne, John Hamilton Mortimer, painter, Julius Soubise, Sancho's good friend, John Thomas Smith, the Duchess of Queensberry and actor David Garrick—to mention only a few. Sancho also had a penchant for acting, having tried his hand at the parts of Oroonoko and Othello on the London stage; but a lisp prevented him from continuing with a stage career.

Not only did Ignatius Sancho run his shop, write innumerable letters—158 of them being published after his death—converse with the many friends who dropped in on him, but he was also busy as a critic and writer. He wrote several pieces of poetry, two plays for the stage and a work entitled "*The Theory of Music*" dedicated to the Princess Royal. His art reviews appeared in the magazines of the day and were read by artists and art lovers with interest and respect. Joseph Jekyll, a member of Parliament, said of him: "Painting was so much within the circle of Ignatius Sancho's judgement and criticism that Mortimer came often to consult him. Several artists paid great deference to his opinion."

Ignatius Sancho fell ill with internal disorders in December, 1780. On the morning of the 14th, his wife, children, and a few close friends were at his bedside when he passed away. He was buried at Westminster Broadway in London.

Some men of letters gain greater recognition after death. So it was with Sancho. One of his correspondents, a Miss Crewe, collected and edited his letters, publishing them in 1782 in two volumes. This devoted correspondent had a sound reason for publishing the letters of the former slave:

> My motives for laying them before the public were, the desire of showing that an untutored African may possess abilities equal to an European; and the still superior motive, of wishing to serve his worthy family. And I am happy in thus publicly acknowledging I have not found the world inattentive to the voice of obscure merit.

One of Miss Crewe's motives was the same as that which prompted the Duke of Montagu to educate the Jamaican Francis Williams in England, a habit quite common in the eighteenth century among enlightened men in England, to show that "darling blacks" were equal in intellect and learning to whites.

The reception which the work enjoyed was tremendous. In fact, the subscription list was even lengthier than that of Joseph Addison's *Spectator,* which, up to then, had been unbeaten. Among the names of the numerous (1,216) subscribers to Sancho's book were the Duke and Duchess of Buccleugh and George Brudenell. Mrs. Sancho received part of the royalties. The publication, called *Letters of The Late Ignatius Sancho,* was so popular that a fifth edition was printed in 1803. Gainsborough's portrait of Sancho engraved by Bartolozzi was prefixed to the book. The publisher of the fifth edition was Sancho's son William, who had taken over his father's shop in 20 Charles Street, turned it into a bookshop, and was fast becoming one of the most successful booksellers in London. (The portrait of Sancho by Gainsborough was presented by Sancho's daughter Elizabeth to her father's friend, William Stevenson of Norwich; and it was subsequently sold at Norwich by auction in March 1889, with the property of Stevenson's son, Henry Stevenson F.S.A.)

Ignatius Sancho's letters were brimming over with advice and philosophy gained from a hard experience of life. It was his insatiable curiosity about life which prompted this letter to a "worthy friend":

> You will of course make Men and Things your study—their different geniuses, aims, and passions. Continue in right thinking, you will of course act well; in well-doing, you will insure the favour of God, and the love of your friends.

A contemporary critic claimed that the black man's letters showed traces of Laurence Sterne's literary style. Others disagreed, maintaining that Sancho's manner of writing was his own. To quote one reviewer, Sancho's writing "exhibited epistolary talent, rapid and just conception, wild patriotism, and universal philanthropy."

The letters show Sancho to be a man of principle, free from any form of hypocrisy. He was deeply conscious of the miseries of his people and would write to newspapers such as the *General Advertiser* under his favorite pen name "Africanus," protesting about the treatment of slaves and the evils of slavery. His letters were also full of his love for England. He took a great interest in the affairs of the country. He even wrote to the *General Advertiser* suggesting a plan for "greatly diminishing the national debt, or, in case a war with the House of Bourbon should be inevitable, for raising three or four years supplies, without oppressing the merchant, mechanic, or labouring husbandman . . ."

If one is to find fault it is not with Sancho's letters, for they are honest, humble, with no pretensions, respectful and an interesting indication of his personality. At times, he tended to preach to the numerous friends who sought his advice, but above all, he was always sincere. In an age when eccentricity and dandyism were cultivated, Ignatius Sancho was a rarity—a man of utter integrity and strength of character.

Ignatius Sancho's frugality during his lifetime, except for one early lapse, proved a blessing to his family whom he left well provided for. In the fascinating canvas of eighteenth-century notables, Ignatius Sancho more than deserves his share of praise. Maybe that is one of the reasons why the former slave retains a place of honor in the *Dictionary of National Biography* under the heading: "Ignatius Sancho, Negro writer."

A black man perhaps less honoured than Ignatius Sancho but equally deserving was Francis Barber, household favorite of that literary giant of eighteenth-century England, Dr. Samuel Johnson.

From the very beginning Johnson showed great paternal love for the ten-year-old Frank who had been brought to England by Colonel Richard Bathurst. Bathurst had owned a plantation called Orange River Estate in the parish of St. Mary, Jamaica. The Colonel was the father of Johnson's very intimate friend Dr. Richard Bathurst of Guy's Hospital in London. Since Barber was born of slave parentage on Orange River Estate he automatically became the property of the colonel. The exact date of his birth has never been established as it was not usual during the years of slavery to register the births or deaths of slaves. However, he told James Boswell that when he was brought to England in 1750 he was eight years old.

Colonel Bathurst's treatment of Francis Barber was enlightened and certainly did not follow the pattern of most slave masters, who maintained that to educate a slave would give him aspirations above his station. By the time the colonel took Frank to England his business seemed to be in total ruin. This apparently did not concern him since he felt that if he had no estate in Jamaica, he would not be tempted to own slaves. And he certainly did not treat Francis Barber in the manner of master to slave. Instead, he had the black boy baptized and named Francis Barber and sent him to school at Barton-upon-Tees in Yorkshire under the tuition of the Reverend Jackson. The colonel, by his will, left him his freedom, and Dr. Bathurst was willing that Francis Barber should enter Johnson's service, which he did.

Francis Barber was to play a very important part in Dr. Johnson's life, yet, unlike the other Johnsonians, he remains a shadowy character in the historical literature of the period. Several of Dr. Samuel Johnson's associates are as familiar to us as our own circle of friends: Mrs. Thrale, at whose residence in Streatham Johnson spent many tea-drinking hours; Sir John Hawkins and Sir Joshua Reynolds who were both executors of the Doctor's will. But the one whom we recognize most easily is James Boswell, the Scottish lawyer and biographer from Auchinleck. It is he who jogs side by side with his hero through the highlands of posterity. However, one person who remained in close association with Johnson for over thirty-two years, and who should have been well-known to us, finds himself hidden in the pages of Mrs. Thrale's *Anecdotes of Dr. Johnson* and Sir John Hawkins' *Life of Samuel Johnson* and dismissed as "Dr. Johnson's negro servant Francis Barber." From the diary of Reynolds we learn only that in April, 1767, Francis was one of his sitters. Lastly there is Boswell. When the occasion arises he speaks favorably of Barber, faithfully recording the various chores, like buying coffee for breakfast, booking rooms for Johnson and himself, and the other incidents in Dr. Johnson's life with which the black servant was directly associated.

It is unfortunate that Barber should have been allowed to remain largely unknown, because he turned out to have been more than a faithful servant. His first-hand knowledge of events during his long service with Dr. Johnson proved very helpful to Boswell. In fact, the shrewd Scotsman, when compiling the life of Johnson in 1786 used Barber, to quote biographer Aleyn Lyell Reade, as "the humble instrument of his biographical zeal."

That Dr. Johnson should have a manservant in his employ seems somewhat odd. The figure which the Doctor presented to his friends was certainly not one of sartorial elegance but rather, because of his portly form, ungainly amble, unorthodox mannerisms, and facial twitches, that of an untidily dressed, gruff bear. Once when Hogarth saw Johnson dining at Samuel Richardson's he seriously believed that the novelist was entertaining an idiot dressed up in ill-fitting clothes and wig. And, in the words of Hawkins himself: "The uses for which Francis Barber was intended to serve his master were not very apparent, for Diogenes himself never wanted a servant less than he [Johnson] seemed to do."

It is probable that Dr. Johnson's demands on his manservant for fresh linen went no further than a clean shirt, but the question of whether he needed a manservant or not is unimportant. Johnson developed a lasting devotion for Frank—the pet name he used when addressing the West Indian—and he left him all his personal belongings and £1,500, nearly every penny of his meagre savings.

Francis Barber first went to Dr. Johnson's at Gough Square about two weeks after the death of Mrs. Johnson on March 17, 1752. Anna Williams, a blind woman, was part of Johnson's household and did not take kindly to the idea of Frank's intrusion on her influence over the Doctor, who usually gave way to her moods. She found fault with everything Frank did and never let any mistake of Frank's escape his master's notice. Adopting an I-told-you-so attitude she would throw up at Johnson: "This is your scholar! Your philosopher! On whose education you have spent so many hundreds of pounds." Except for a few short intervals, Anna Williams and Frank both remained with Dr. Johnson for over thirty years.

Some years after Frank joined Dr. Johnson's household, Robert Levett, an unlicensed medical practitioner described as "an obscure practiser in physic amongst the lower people" and a friend of Johnson's since 1746, moved into Gough Square, where he waited on Johnson every morning through the whole course of the latter's late and tedious breakfast. Levett had a strange, grotesque appearance, was stiff and formal in his manner and seldom spoke while company was present. Until his death on January 17, 1782, he lived with Johnson together with Barber, the latter's English wife Elizabeth, and Anna Williams. (In 1776 Barber had married a pretty English woman from Blackfriars whom Johnson always called "Betsy.")

Except for three brief excursions, Barber was always a member of the Doctor's household. He first went to work as an apothecary in Cheapside; then, tired of "washing bottles and wrapping up pills," he joined the navy. Finally, Johnson sent him to a grammar school at Bishop's Stortford. When Johnson went to live in chambers in the Temple, he found Miss Williams lodgings elsewhere, paying the rent and other living necessities out of his own pocket. On his return from a European tour, he once again moved to Johnson's Court in Fleet Street where his three companions joined him. Anna Williams had an apartment on the ground floor while Frank and Levett were installed in the garret. And when Johnson, Frank, Levett, and Anna Williams moved to Bolt Court, Mrs. Demoulins with her daughter and the eccentric Poll Carmichael joined the household. Mrs. Demoulins added to domestic dissensions by her persistent quarrels with the others. This odd assortment of people was privileged to serve the great man of letters and to listen to the conversation of eminent and lesser personalities of the eighteenth century who clustered round Dr. Johnson.

Hester Thrale and Sir John Hawkins were the only people in Johnson's circle known to have shown a positive dislike for Barber. Their reasons were personal. Hester Thrale's dislike for the black man can be attributed to the fact that Frank was "no small favourite" with Johnson. The tiresome and overbearing Mrs. Thrale of whom Dr. Johnson once said that she would be the first woman in the land were it not for her naughty tongue, resented anyone who competed for Johnson's affection. Her resentment became more marked when she discovered that the old desk, carpet, silver tea kettle and lamp—which had belonged to her mother and which she had given to Dr. Johnson—had become Frank's property.

Hawkins' attitude to Barber was no less intolerant. After Johnson's death he seized the doctor's gold watch although he knew that it had been given to Barber. When the other two executors of Dr. Johnson's will, Sir Joshua Reynolds and Sir William Scott, forced him to return the watch to Frank, Hawkins felt disgraced. It is not surprising that he sought to violate Barber's character in his *Life of Samuel Johnson.* Dr. Johnson himself, however, who was entitled to criticize Barber discovered not an iota of evil in "dear Frank" after three decades.

After Samuel Johnson's death in December, 1784, his close friend, James Boswell, set about collecting material for his biography. One person who could furnish him with the kind of personal detail that he needed to make the literary giant human was certainly the forty-two-year-old Francis Barber who accompanied Johnson on several journeys and had observed him in all his moods. Johnson himself had once observed that:

> Biographers so little regard the manners or behaviour of their heroes, that more knowledge may be gained of a man's real character, by a short conversation with one of his servants, than from a formal and studied narrative begun with his pedigree and ended with his funeral.

Boswell's choice was in fact the only one left open to him. Blind Anna Williams and Robert Levett, who had also been given shelter under Dr. Johnson's roof, were both already dead when Boswell began gathering his material.

Even before Johnson's death, James Boswell—with the biography in mind—had enlisted Barber's aid. He wrote from Edinburgh on January 30, 1784:

> Mr. Francis, I will be obliged if you will once a week at least let me know with minute exactness how Dr Johnson is, who are with him and in what manner his time is employed. I shall in the meantime depend upon full intelligence from you. I am, Sir, Your sincere friend, James Boswell.

The following year, James Boswell was busy gathering data. Barber, as beneficiary under the will, had been left all Johnson's papers and other personal belongings together with an annuity of seventy pounds from the bequest of fifteen hundred pounds. Boswell noted in his Journal:

> Thursday, December 22nd: Met Dr Johnson's Frank in the street, and he promised to search for every scrap of his master's handwriting and give all to me.

This Barber did. On January 7, 1786, Frank, who was still living in London, wrote Boswell enclosing three letters Dr. Johnson had written to him during the four years he was attending Bishop's Stortford grammar school. They were letters of encouragement that a father might have written to a son he loved.

In the words of Boswell, himself:

> Johnson's sincere regard for Francis Barber, his faithful Negro servant, made him so desirous of his further improvement that he placed him at a school at Bishop's Stortford in Hertfordshire. This humane attention does Johnson's heart much honour.

Boswell included those letters in full in his *Life of Johnson*. Much correspondence passed between him and Barber while work on the *Life* was in progress. In a letter which he wrote to the West Indian in 1786, James Boswell said:

> Good Mr Francis, I beg you may oblige me with answers to the following questions for the Life of your late excellent master, which you will be pleased to write under each question. I am, Sir, Your sincere friend, James Boswell.

There were eight questions in all and Barber answered six of them. The replies form the basis for the part of the *Life of Johnson* relating to Barber's entry into Johnson's service and the state of the household at that time. Barber also gave the names of Johnson's friends, his tailors—a Mr. Thomson of Ludgate Hill and later Mr. Cooke of Bloomsbury—and that of his barber, Mr. Collet who lived in Plumbtree Court.

Sir John Hawkins, not content with casting the vilest aspersions on the good name of Johnson and Frank, carried off some of the papers and personal belongings which were the rightful possessions of the Jamaican under his master's will. James Boswell wrote this letter to Barber on June 29th, 1787:

> Dear Sir, Sir John Hawkins having done gross injustice to the character of the great and good Dr. Johnson, and having written so injuriously of you and Mrs. Barber, as to deserve severe animadversion, and perhaps to be brought before the spiritual court, I cannot doubt of your inclination to afford me all the helps you can to state the truth fairly, in the work which I am now preparing for the Press.
>
> I therefore beg that you will without delay write three copies of the Letter No. 1 which I enclose, directing one to Sir Joshua Reynolds, one to Dr. Scott, and one to Sir John Hawkins putting to each the date of which you write, and enclose them to me, together with a letter to me in the words of No. 2. I have mentioned the business to Sir Joshua and Dr. Scott. When I have received the said letters distinctly written out by you, I shall proceed in an effectual manner.
>
> Please to enclose your packet to me under cover of The Honourable William Ward M.P., London. You may at the same time let me have a private letter informing me how you are, and mentioning anything

that occurs to yourself. Be assured that I am ever sincerely concerned about your welfare. I send my compliments to Mrs. Barber and am with much regard Dear Sir, Your steady friend, James Boswell.

Frank's private letter, which had been written on July 9 of that same year from Lichfield, where he was then living, was included with the three to the executors, Dr. Scott, Sir Joshua Reynolds, and Sir John Hawkins. In it, he said to Boswell:

Sir, I take pen in hand to inform you, that, I am happy to find there is still remaining a friend, who has the memory of my late good master at heart. If necessity should require it, if God spares my life (for I am at present poorly) I would willingly attest what I have related personally—with which, I beg leave to subscribe myself, Your most obedient, humble servant, Francis Barber.

The West Indian was a willing helper and Boswell sought more information from him. On March 3, 1788, he sent a letter to Barber, asking:

Dear Sir, you have been so obliging, that I trouble you with a further application, which is to copy, date, and subscribe the enclosed, and transmit it to me under cover of J. B. Garforth, Esq., M.P., London. You will be so good as at the same time to authorise me to receive from my brother what Sir John Hawkins delivers to him. I flatter myself that my book will do justice to the character of your excellent master. It will not be published before September or October.

Barber replied on March 12th:

If you can inform me of any other papers which he has in his possession belonging to me as residuary legatee please to give me a line or two and shall upon the receipt of which impower you to demand them from Sir John Hawkins.

Back to Barber came this answer that same month:

Dear Sir, I thank you for your attention. As I cannot specify exactly what papers Sir John Hawkins may yet have, you will please to write me thus—

"Sir, I hereby authorize you to demand from Sir John Hawkins all books or papers of any sort which belonged to the late Dr. Samuel Johnson, that may be in his possession, and your receipt to him shall be sufficient on my account as residuary legatee."

Let this be copied over in your own hand, dated and signed and addressed to me. I give you a great deal of trouble; but I am very desirous to collect all I can concerning your excellent master.

James Boswell got all that he wanted from Hawkins, for he made the following entry in his Journal on the 19th of April:

> Having received from Francis Barber a letter authorising me to demand from Sir John Hawkins all books or papers that belonged to Dr. Johnson which remained in his possession, of which I had acquainted Sir John and begged to know when I might wait on him to receive them, I received from the Knight a very civil answer. I found him with a crimson velvet night cap on and his eldest son with him, who stood by all the time while Sir John and I settled the business, which we did in perfect humour. He complimented me on my coming exactly to my time. I said, "I am as regular as you, Sir John; at least, I wish to be so." There were but three pamphlets, the three diplomas of degrees from Dublin and Oxford, and a few papers, for which I gave a receipt "as witness my hand at Westminster." We parted quite placidly.

Still the Scottish biographer continued to elicit material on Johnson from Barber, who said to him: "I shall ever be happy to obey any command wherein I am capable by any means to give you satisfaction."

In yet another letter to Boswell on December 20, 1789, Francis Barber answered more questions about Johnson, and enclosed a copy of the inscription on the inside of the box containing Mrs. Johnson's wedding ring. In that letter Barber wrote:

> Soon after the death of my master, I made a journey to Lichfield in order to take a house, at which time I took the ring with an intent to present to Mrs. Porter, being her mother's wedding ring, but she refused accepting the same, and upon my return to town I had it enamelled and converted into a mourning ring for my wife to wear in remembrance of my master, which she now has in her possession.

Apart from aiding Boswell, Francis Barber was responsible for saving two valuable works for posterity—*An account of the Life of Dr. Samuel Johnson, from his Birth to his Eleventh Year,* written by himself, and *A Journey Into North Wales in the Year 1774.* Strangely enough, Boswell did not know of their existence. About the first, Dr. Richard Wright, the Lichfield apothecary, said:

> This volume was among that mass of papers which were ordered to be committed to the flames a few days before Johnson's death, thirty-two pages of which were torn out by himself, and destroyed; the contents of those which remain are here given with fidelity and exactness. Francis Barber, his Jamaican servant, unwilling that all the manuscripts of his illustrious master should be utterly lost, preserved these relics from the flames.

It was not only to James Boswell that the West Indian gave information about Dr. Johnson. In 1793 while living at Lichfield he was interviewed by a reporter from *The Gentleman's Magazine*, who said:

> Francis is low of stature, clean and neat. He spends his time fishing, cultivating a few potatoes, and a little reading. I asked him: You never heard your master swear? No, Francis replied. The worst word he ever uttered when in passion was, "you dunghill dog."
>
> Mr Barber appears modest and humble, but to have associated with company superior to his rank in life.

James Boswell had great confidence in the accuracy of the material he received from Francis Barber. Commenting on Dr. Johnson's state at the time of his wife's death, Boswell remarked:

> That Johnson's sufferings upon the death of his wife were severe, beyond what are commonly endured, I have no doubt, from the information of many who were then about him, to none of whom I give more credit than to Mr. Francis Barber, his faithful Negro servant, who came into his family about a fortnight after the dismal event.

The Scottish biographer goes further than that. In his *Life of Johnson* he quotes Barber's reply to one of his questions about Johnson, in the letter of July 15, 1786, word for word.

> From Mr. Francis Barber I had had the following authentic and artless account of the situation in which he found him [Dr. Johnson] recently after his wife's death:
>
> "He was in great affliction. Mrs. Williams was then living in his house, which was in Gough Square. He was busy with the dictionary. Mr. Shiels, and some other of the gentlemen who had formerly written for him, used to come about him. He had then little for himself, but frequently sent money to Mr. Shiels when in distress. The friends who visited him at that time were chiefly Dr. Bathurst and Mr. Diamond, an apothecary in Cork Street, Burlington Gardens, with whom he and Mrs. Williams generally dined every Sunday. There was a talk of his going to Iceland with him, which would probably have happened, had he lived."

There is no doubt that it was largely through the painstaking efforts of James Boswell and with the aid of the Jamaican, Francis Barber, that the name of Dr. Johnson has been immortalized.

During Dr. Johnson's lifetime Francis Barber and his wife Betsy lived under the same roof with him, and he was as fond of her as he was of Frank. Naturally, this mixed marriage aroused curiosity and incurred the displeasure of some of Dr. Johnson's friends, notably Hester Thrale and Sir John Hawkins, who cast the vilest aspersions on Mrs. Barber's fidelity. Of Betsy Barber's four children, three—Elizabeth born 1783, Samuel, 1785, and Ann 1786—survived their infancy. Soon after Dr. Johnson's death in December 1784, Frank Barber journeyed to Lichfield as he said to Boswell, "in order to take a house." Then, around 1797 Francis Barber and his wife and family went to live at Burntwood, a village about four miles west of Lichfield. He was fifty-five at the time. With his wife Betsy he kept a small school there, and he was described in the parish register as a "yeoman." However, he was, as a friend noted, "suffering from a troublesome disorder" which was diagnosed as kidney trouble. Dr. Richard Wright of Lichfield had been treating him but when his ailment became worse in 1801 he was removed to Stafford Infirmary. He died there, and was buried at St. Mary's Churchyard, Stafford, on the 28th of the month, leaving his wife and three children to survive him.

Mrs. Barber came upon hard times after her husband's death because his income from the annuity Dr. Johnson left him died with him. For a while she continued to live and to teach school in Burntwood. Her daughter Elizabeth died there on March 9, 1802, just over a year after her father's death. Some time later Mrs. Barber returned to Stowe Street at Lichfield where she had lived with her husband. She kept a day school for children and was helped by her daughter Ann up till the year 1810. Mrs. Barber died in 1816 and of her children only Samuel survived her. He was first put at a boarding school in Lichfield and given a very liberal education. Later he became a personal aide to Dr. Gregory Hickman, of Burslem, grandson of the Gregory Hickman to whom Johnson's first known letter was addressed. He afterwards became a disciple of William Clowes and a well-known local preacher in the Potteries, having joined the Methodist church. When he died on July 6, 1829, he had been living in Tunstull where he had been prominent as an eloquent and zealous preacher. He left an English wife and six near-white children. His son, also a Methodist, emigrated with his mother to North Carolina.

Mrs. Rowell, a custodian of Dr. Johnson's house in Gough Square, Fleet Street, London, tells the following story which supports anthropologists like Dr. Kenneth Little in their claim that there is evidence that many Englishmen today have ancestors who came from Africa or the West Indies:

During World War II a thirty-year-old American soldier visited Dr. Johnson's House in Gough Square. He said that he came from New York and that his name was Samuel Barber. He was blonde, blue-eyed and Caucasian—in every respect a "white" American. He told Mrs. Rowell that when he was a child he learned from his grandmother that he was named after his grandfather, the grandson of Dr. Johnson's Francis Barber. His grandfather was the Samuel Barber who migrated to North Carolina. He was quite proud of his African ancestry, even though the United States Army authorities were unaware of it.

Of all the "darling blacks" George Augustus Polgreen Bridgtower, a child prodigy, was by far the most talented. Born in 1779 in Biala, Poland, the son of an African adventurer who named himself John Frederick Bridgtower and a Polish woman named Maria, the young Bridgtower and his father first made their appearance in England in 1789, finding themselves in the aristocratic company of Mrs. Papendiek, Assistant Keeper of the Wardrobe and Reader to Queen Charlotte, wife of George III. Young Bridgtower was then described as "a most prepossessing lad of ten years old, and a fine violin player." His first concert in England was a very important one. He was commissioned by their majesties to perform at Windsor Royal Lodge, where he created a sensation when he executed a concerto by Viotti and a quartet of Haydn's with all the mastery of a mature and accomplished player. Society wasted no time in accepting both father and son with open arms. Mrs. Papendiek went into ecstasies over them and noted in her diary:

> Both father and son pleased greatly. The son for his talent and modest bearing, the father for his fascinating manner, elegance, expertness in all languages, beauty of person, and taste in dress. He seemed to win the good opinion of everyone, and was courted by all and entreated to join in society.

From very early on, the child prodigy received instruction from the ablest tutors in Europe—Barthelemon, Thomas Attwood and Haydn—and he had already made a name for himself in France. When he appeared with his father at the fashionable English watering place of Bath in the winter of 1789, the *Morning Post* reported the event thus: "Amongst those added to the Sunday promenade along the South Parade were the

African Prince and his son who has been celebrated as a very accomplished musician."

All Bath was excited over the prospect of hearing the young violinist. His first concert there was held at the New Assembly Rooms on Saturday December 5, 1789. The *Bath Journal* summarized the general opinion of young Bridgtower's talent:

> The amateurs of music in this city received on Saturday last at the New Rooms the highest treat imaginable from the exquisite performance of Master Bridgtower, whose taste and execution on the violin is equal, perhaps superior, to the best professor of the present or any former day. The concert room, recesses and gallery were thronged with the very best of company, who were enraptured with the astonishing abilities of this wonderful child.

Having created a sensation at Bath, the boy violinist was taken to London by his father. His London debut was at the Lenten Oratorio performances at Drury Lane Theatre on February 19, 1790. The London papers were no less enthusiastic about young Bridgtower's virtuosity. The *London Advertiser* said: "Master Bridgtower is a complete master of the violin," and the *London Chronicle* admitted that "Master Bridgtower performed with great taste and execution."

London society buzzed with praise about the good-looking boy violinist and his charming father, whose claim to royal African blood even though completely unfounded was accepted by everyone. However, this sudden success affected the relationship between father and son. Young Bridgtower told Mrs. Papendiek that his mother was left in distress in Poland and that the money he earned by his music was wasted. He added that the brutal severity of his father would surely lead him to do something desperate. And, in fact, matters came to a head one evening when his father returned home with a female companion and told the boy to get under the sofa and go to sleep. He obeyed, but watching his opportunity, made his escape. He ran to Carlton House, where, from having often been there to perform, he was well known to the Prince of Wales, later George IV. (Another of the prince's personal friends was Prince Saunders, the Afro-American writer from Boston who became very popular in antislavery circles in England.)

The prince took an immediate interest in young Bridgtower. He at once sent for his father and ordered him to leave the country forthwith, saying: "I will furnish you with a proper sum of money for your journey. When I hear of your return to your wife I will remit a trifle for present emergencies that you might have the opportunity of looking out for employment." With his father gone, George Bridgtower found a new parent—the Prince of Wales. The young lad was first stripped of the fancy Polish dress which he usually wore, and clad in the English fashion of that day. A proper person was appointed to instruct him, and as he was not then to depend upon the public for support, he had time to develop his great musical gifts. The atmsophere at Carlton House was ideal for the talented, serious-minded youngster. He practiced steadily, and listened to the first-class performers who were constantly at Carlton House. Daily, he associated with such masters as Giardini, Cramer, Salomon, and especially Viotti, from whom he learned much and whose style appeared to suit him, "for Bridgtower had always been remarkable for his elegant and bold manner of drawing the bow."

The Prince of Wales allowed his black protégé to appear at many London concerts. By 1794, when Bridgtower was fifteen, he became the first violinist of the prince's private orchestra, playing at Carlton House and the Royal Pavilion in Brighton. In 1802 Bridgtower was granted leave of absence by the Prince of Wales to visit his mother, who was living in Dresden. The following year, having been allowed an extension of leave, he went to Vienna. There, he met Ludwig van Beethoven, who introduced Bridgtower to Viennese society. In a letter of introduction to Baron Wetzlar, dated May 18, 1803, Beethoven wrote:

> Dear Baron Wetzler, I do not hesitate to recommend Mr. Bridgtower. He is very clever and a thorough master of his instrument. I do hope that you will be able to increase his circle of acquaintances. I know that you yourself will thank me for this introduction. Yours obediently, Beethoven.

Beethoven and Bridgwater saw a lot of each other, as this note from the former shows:

> My dear B, come today at twelve o'clock to Count Deym's where we were together the day before yesterday. They perhaps wish to hear you play something or other, but that you'll find out. I rejoice at the mere thought of seeing you today, Your friend, Beethoven.

The friendship blossomed and on May 24, 1803, the two gave a concert together at the Augarten-Halle. The black violinist had induced Beethoven to compose a piece—*Sonata No. 9 in A Major Opus 47*. From what Bridgtower said, this sonata was finished barely in time for the concert which was due to begin at eight o'clock that morning:

> Beethoven called upon me at half-past four on the morning preceding the concert and asked me to copy out with all speed the violin part of the first Allegro—his regular copyist being otherwise engaged. The slow movement variations were literally finished at the last moment, and I had to sight read my violin part as best I could from Beethoven's more or less illegible manuscript. . . . When I accompanied Beethoven in the Sonata-concertante at the repetition of the first part of the Presto, I imitated the flight at the eighteenth bar of the pianoforte part of this movement. He jumped up and embraced me: "Noch einmal, mein lieber bursch—Once more, my dear fellow." Beethoven's expression in the andante variations was so chaste, which always characterised the performance of all his slow movements that it was unanimously hailed to be repeated twice.

This Beethoven sonata, inspired by his friend George Bridgtower, came to be called later the Kreutzer Sonata. Bridgtower told a contemporary violinist named Thirwall how this happened:

> When the sonata was written Beethoven and I were constant companions, and on the first copy was this dedication: "To my friend Bridgtower." But, ere it was published, we had some silly quarrel about a girl, and in consequence Beethoven scratched out my name and inserted that of Kreutzer—a man whom he had never seen.

George Bridgtower returned to London in July 1803 where he rejoined the prince's orchestra and gave several concerts under royal patronage. Then he became a student of music at Cambridge University, where he received a bachelor's degree in June, 1811. His name is entered at Trinity Hall. Bridgtower composed an anthem as one of the exercises for his degree. It was played on June 30, 1811, at Great St. Mary's Church in Cambridge for the installation of the Duke of Gloucester as Chancellor of the University. *The Times* reported: "The composition was elaborate and rich; and highly accredited to the talents of the Graduate. The trio struck us, particularly, by its beauty."

Back in London, Bridgtower continued to give concerts, to compose and to teach music. He married an Englishwoman whose maiden name was "Drake" but no record has so far been traced of this marriage. One item of information appears in April, 1819, concerning his wife who had been invited to attend a concert given by the Philharmonic Society of which Bridgtower was a member.

In 1812 he published a manual of study called *Diatonica Armonica for the Pianoforte.* Of this work Bridgtower said:

> In presenting the following work, I am influenced by a desire of offering to students in Music, that which may unite instruction and amusement: the former as necessary for their improvement; the latter, as an inducement to frequent practice on the pianoforte. This I shall call the Diatonic Style.

In London musical circles George Bridgtower was held in high esteem, and was on very intimate terms with leading musicians like Viotti, Cramer, Thomas Attwood, and Samuel Wesley. He wrote many violin concertos and other instrumental pieces but one of the only pieces that has so far been unearthed—apart from the *Diatonica Armonica* and the *Anthem*—is a ballad called "Henry." It was one of the most charming songs in Regency England, and, in the words of Bridgtower, himself, it was "composed and humbly dedicated with permission to Her Royal Highness the Princess of Wales." The Princess of Wales to whom "Henry" was dedicated was Caroline, wife of the Prince Regent—Bridgtower's royal guardian, who lavished so much care and attention on this very talented, very cultivated, "darling Black."

George Bridgtower seems to have fallen on hard times in later years. He died on February 29th, 1860, in Peckham, London, at the considerable age of eighty-one.

BIBLIOGRAPHY TO CHAPTER EIGHT

Angelo, Henry. *Angelo's Pic Nic* or *Table Talk*. London: 1834.

———. *Reminiscences of Henry Angelo*. Vol. 2. London: 1828.

Aylward, J. D. *The House of Angelo*. London: 1953.

Balderston, Katherine C. (ed.), *Thraliana. The Diary of Mrs. Hester Lynch Thrale* (later Mrs. Piozzi). Vol. 1 (1776–1809). London: 1962.

Baring, Mrs. Henry (ed.). *The Diary of Rt. Hon. William Windham* (1784–1810). London: 1866.

Batchelor, Denzil. *Big Fight*. London: The Sportsmans Book Club, 1955.

Bengal Past and Present. Vol. 14 (1917), pt. 1.

Biddulph, Violet. *Kitty, Duchess of Queensberry*. London: 1935.

Boswell, James. *The Life of Dr. Johnson*, Edited by G. E. Fletcher. With marginal notes by Hester Lynch Thrale. London: 1938.

Boswell-Barber Letters (unpublished) 1786–1789. Yale University collection.

Bridgetower, George. *Diatonica Armonica for the Pianoforte*. London: 1812.

———. "Henry" (ballad). London: 1812.

Broughton, Mrs. Vernon Delice (ed.). *Mrs. Papendiek's Journals*. Vols. 1 and 2. *Court and Private Life of Queen Charlotte*. London: 1887.

Calcutta Chronicle, 1787–90.

Carey, W. H. *The Good Old Days of Honourable John Company*. Vol. 1. Calcutta: 1906.

Coke, Lady Mary. *Journal of Lady Mary Coke*. London: 1889.

Colles, H. C. (ed.) *Grove's Dictionary of Music and Musicians*. 3rd. edn. London: 1927.

D' Arblay, Madame. *Memoirs of Dr. Burney*. By his daughter. London: 1832.

Dictionary of National Biography. Vols. 6 and 50. London: 1886, 1897.

Durant, John. *The Heavyweight Champions*. London: 1960.

Egan, Pierce. *Boxiana*. 3 vols. London: 1820.

———. *Sporting Anecodotes*. London: 1820.

Falk, Bernard. *The Way of the Montagues*. London: 1948.

Gentleman's Magazine. London (July–December, 1811).
"George Bridgtower and the Kreutzer Sonata." *Musical Times.* 49 (May 1, 1908).
George, Dorothy M. *Catalogue of Political and Personal Satires.* London: 1935.
Griswold, R. W. *The Female Poets of America.* Philadelphia: 1849.
Hawkins, Sir John. The Life of Dr. Samuel Johnson. London: 1787.
Heartman, C. F. *Phillis Wheatley: A Critical Attempt and Bibliography of her Writings.* New York: 1915.
Hughes, Langston. *Famous American Negroes.* New York: 1954.
Jekyll, Joseph. *Letters of the Late Ignatius Sancho.* 5th edn. London: 1803.
Johnson, Samuel. *Diary of a Journey into North Wales.* (1774). Edited by Birkbeck Hill, revised by L. F. Powell. London: 1934.
Kalischer, A. C. *Beethoven's Letters.* Selected and edited by A. Eaglefield-Hull. London: 1926.
"Letters of a Bachist—Samuel Wesley." *Musical Times.* 49 (April 1, 1908).
Little, K. L. *Negroes in Britain.* London: Kegan Paul, 1948.
Melville, Lewis. *Life and Letters of Laurence Sterne.* Vol. 2. London: 1912.
"Memoir of Samuel Barber" by a local preacher. *Primitive Methodist Magazine.* 10. London: 1829.
"A Meteorologist's Tour from Walton to London." (An interview with Frank Barber) *Gentleman's Magazine* (London: 1793).
Nocturnal Revels. 2. London: 1779.
Ottley, Roi. *Black Odyssey.* New York: 1948.
Reade, Aleyn Lyell. *Johnsonian Gleanings. Pt. 2. Francis Barber—The Doctor's Negro Servant.* London: 1912.
Rogers, J. A. *World's Great Men of Color.* Vol. 2. New York: 1947.
Scott, Geoffrey and Pottle, Frederick A. (eds.). *Private Papers of James Boswell from Malahide Castle.* Vols. 6, 11, 16, 17. New York: 1928–34.
Seton-Karr, W. P. *Selections from Calcutta Gazettes,* Vols. 1 to 5. Calcutta: 1864–65.
Shepherd, T. B. *The Noble Art.* London: 1950.
Smith, J. T. *Nollekens and his Times.* London: 1949.
Smith-Dampier, J. L. *Who's Who in Boswell.* London: 1955.

Thrale, Hester. *Anecdotes of the Late Samuel Johnson during the Last Twenty Years of his Life. By Mrs. Piozzi.* London: 1786.

———. *Letters To and From the Late Samuel Johnson. By Mrs. Piozzi.* London: 1788.

Wake, Joan. *The Brudenelles of Deene.* London: 1953.

Wignall, Trevor C. *The Story of Boxing.* London: 1923.

CHAPTER IX

BLACK JACKS, BOXERS, ARTISTS

After the Sierra Leone Settlement Scheme, when less than four hundred Africans left England, thousands of blacks continued to live there. Although other blacks left to work as laborers in the West Indies, "blacks continued to be conspicuous among London beggars." Their position became so desperate that in 1814 a parliamentary report stated that there were very many blacks in London whose condition merited the attention of the House of Commons. The Sierra Leone Settlement Scheme had not done so much to alleviate the condition of "the black poor" as had been hoped. Black beggars in English city streets were as much in evidence in the early years of the nineteenth century as they were in the latter years of the previous one.

By the time the early years of the nineteenth century had disappeared the age of the "darling black" had also come to an end, having faded with the elegance and eccentricity of the eighteenth century. The general attitude in Britain to blacks was by then undergoing change. It has been said of eighteenth century England, "the spirit of humanitarianism was the age's most precious gift," but there was precious little of that spirit left for the following century. This was especially true of the English on the question of race. Dr. Kenneth Little wrote:

> By the end of the nineteenth century, however, attitudes towards the Negro, as well as notions concerning him, seem to have undergone a considerable change. No doubt the emotions of sympathy aroused on his behalf had a great deal to do with this. An object of pity becomes very often an object for condescension. The difficulty was that

> by emancipation (1834) he had theoretically ceased to be either. It was no longer possible to regard him merely as a faithful black, a typification of servile devotion and fidelity. It was as if in becoming a "man and a brother" as one anonymous commentator put it, "he forthwith ceased to be a friend." Members of the public who had known the Negro in his servile days looked back to them and to him with sentiment and affection, but it is doubtful if they could bring themselves to recognise and to relish him on terms of equality.

It is not only that the English refused to treat blacks with any semblance of equality in the years before the turn of the twentieth century. To them blacks were also objects of fun. That elegant, Edwardian man-of-letters Max Beerbohm in writing of the 1880's, said that on the evidence of the music hall and comic papers the English populace thought blacks "mirth-provoking." The reason he gave for this was that the English always showed "contempt for the unfamiliar." He did not state the whole truth for he knew, as did most enlightened men and women of that period, that this contempt for blacks went deeper. Unfamiliarity was only a minor factor. Underneath this "not being used to" blacks, was the feeling that blacks were inferior morally, socially, and intellectually, in spite of the fact that preceding generations of the English in the eighteenth century had seen differently. In fact, way back in the sixteenth century Britons should have grown accustomed to the blacks continually settling in their midst. The hostile racial attitude which was taking root from emancipation right through to the turn of the century and after must have grown and developed for other reasons more serious than the fact that blacks were "mirth-provoking" because they were "unfamiliar." Who were the blacks living in Britain in the racial climate of the nineteenth century?

During the earlier decades of that century, blacks in Britain were employed as regular footmen and coachmen in the houses of the wealthy. The black footman was often a portly person with his hair well powdered and dressed in brilliant livery. One of the best-known footmen of this time was Andrew Bogle, a Jamaican, who was a key figure in the case of the Tichborne claimant, one of the most celebrated lawsuits in the annals of imposture. Although the claimant lost his case and Andrew Bogle had given evidence on his behalf, Sir Alexander Cockburn, the Lord Chief Justice, praised him in his summing up, saying: "The truth is that Bogle made a very good impression as an honest man." Cockburn called Bogle "a very fine specimen of the Negro race" and suggested that he might have been mistaken in his recognition of the claimant, but that it was an honest mistake. In 1880 Andrew Bogle died in peaceful respectability in North London.

Some blacks were accepted in the army as bandsmen. In the main, however, the less fortunate blacks sold songs, were street singers, swept crossings, knitted night-caps and socks and manufactured garden nets. Some begged for alms or turned to stealing. But it was as "black jacks"—seafarers—that blacks were known during the nineteenth century. They played a vital part as able seamen and as stewards on sailing ships. Dr. Little writes:

> Sometimes, before the abolition of slavery in America they were impounded by the local authorities when their ships put into such ports as Charleston in the American south. Generally, the exchanges which ensued between the British Consul and the local government touching the rights of a British subject, appear to have been settled in favour of the Negroes concerned.

But as contemporary writer Pierce Egan noted in 1821, the population of the East End of London in the early years was quite a cosmopolitan one with "lascars, blacks, jack tars, women of colour, old and young and a sprinkling of the remnants of once fine girls." To which must be added Scots, Irish, Welsh, Americans, Chinese, Africans, West Indians, and others. By the end of the Napoleonic wars the number of white and black beggars increased greatly in London, and the sale of crossing sweepers' pitches had become a scandal. The officers of the Society for the Suppression of Mendicity were quite active in discharging their duties, with the result that after a few years very little was seen or heard of the black beggars. As has been written already, the initial effect of emancipation was to increase destitution among the black population. Slowly, however, they were encroaching on the English working class, moving into the East End parishes of London. This caused friction. It is no wonder that the early years of the nineteenth century were notorious for the hostility between the different ethnic groups in East London. In 1808 and 1809, for instance, the weavers of Bethnal Green rioted against the Irish. Whole areas barricaded their doors and windows and the rioters tore stones from the pavements to use as weapons. Down on Ratcliffe Highway the lascars held a pitched battle with the Chinese in which several hundred men were involved. In the 1840s and 1850s, with London's death rate mounting, lascars and blacks were occasionally found dead from exhaustion, cold and hunger in the Stepney Streets. It was this sad condition which brought about the opening in 1857 of "The Stranger's Home for Asiatics, Africans and South Sea Islanders" in the West India Dock Road. Africans do not seem to have made much use of this home, but from there many Asiatics were repatriated. In a period of sixteen years more than £16,000 sterling and property were deposited there by men who wanted to take their savings back to their families.

Living conditions for blacks and other immigrants in the dockland areas of English cities were very bad. An idea of how terrible these conditions were can be gleaned from an account in *The Times Police Reports* of 1855 which recorded the prosecution of an Irishman who kept a common lodging house. The floors and stairs "were in a filthy and dilapidated condition, covered with slime, dirt, excrement, and all kinds of odious substances." In that house the police found five lascars, nine Chinese, two prostitutes, one poor Irish widow, and two dead bodies. Had the house been properly registered as a lodging house only twelve tenants would have been permitted to live there.

By the 1850s black beggars had disappeared from the London streets. Those who attracted most attention came mainly from America as seamen, but sometimes as stowaways. Seamen who settled in Britain during that period naturally chose dockland districts. As far South as Loudoun Square in the Tiger Bay area of Cardiff in South Wales black communities began to grow in number until by the nineties they were quite sizeable. This happened in all the major ports—London, Liverpool, Bristol and South Shields, as well as in Cardiff. The black man was assumed to be a seaman; a man who would return to a home in Africa or the West Indies one day. Usually, however, he did not return and therein lay the beginnings of racial animosity. Many of the blacks who settled in London, and in the other British ports married white women and so began "a measure of amalgamation." From records of these years, in the latter half of the century, it can be concluded that in the latter half of the century there were many blacks living in these seaport towns, not as separate groups, but "mixed in with the other immigrants and the locals of the area." More and more black settlements grew up as the years passed, especially in London. One of the most prominent was near the docks in Canning Town, London. (Some of the very oldest blacks now living in

Stepney, Canning Town and other dockland areas were born there during the nineties.) The men who made their homes there were mostly West Indians and other black seamen. This caused a contemporary writer to observe:

> Black Jack, very woolly-headed, and ivory grindered, cooking, fiddling, and singing, as it seems the nature of Black Jack to cook, fiddle, and sing. Where the union-jack flies Nigger Jack is well treated. English sailors do not disdain to drink with him, work with him, and sing with him. . . .

This writer went on to draw comparisons between white American and British attitudes to Black Jacks. Naturally, his conclusion was that blacks fared better on British ships than on American ones. They claim that white and black people in those districts lived on very amicable terms with little awareness of race or color, but that relations deteriorated later on. In many respects the English writer of the time viewed the black man in the same way as succeeding generations of English writers were to look at him: as a flamboyant creature who generated a certain amount of amusement and who was tolerated within well-defined limits. Arthur Morrison, an English writer with great knowledge of the East End of London wrote of that time:

> The best dressed, and the worst, were the Negroes; for the black cook that was flush went in for ornaments that no other sailor man would have dreamed of: a white shirt, a flaming tie, a black coat with satin facings—even a white waistcoat and a top hat. While the cleaned out and shipless nigger was a sad spectacle indeed.

During the early years of the nineteenth century, although blacks were thought of either as beggars, sellers, crossing sweepers, or seamen, individuals achieved fame in the boxing ring and on the London stage, while others became prominent in the labor movement. By the turn of the century, there were frequent visits from colonial potentates of African origin, and the beginning of the great influx of colonial students into Britain.

The writers of the nineteenth as of any other century reflected the attitude of the English to blacks and can be used as guides to the racial feeling of the period. This is particularly true of the novels of Douglas Jerrold and William Makepeace Thackeray, from which it appeared that the lower rather than the better-off classes of society were more race conscious at that time. For instance, in Jerrold's *St. Giles and St. James,* a character called Kitty is a servant in a noble house where her sweetheart, Mr. Caesar, is a footman. Kitty's friend, the muffin-maker's wife, hears about the association, and exclaims:

"Why bless me, she's never going to marry a nigger. She'll never do such a thing."

To this statement comes the reply:

"Miss Kitty is a long way the other side of a chicken. And when women of her time of life don't snow white, they snow black."

Jerrold's treatment of Caesar also bears out the accusation that the English regarded the black man as a buffoon—which was characteristic of racial attitudes in America and other countries until recently. It was a view held by most English writers, particularly in Victorian and Edwardian times.

Anthropologist Kenneth Little claims that "outside the city, however, it is possible that the reaction and attitudes of the rural people towards the Negro were quite different. Thackeray's Gumbo, though looked upon as somewhat of a curiosity, was admired and respected by the domestic circle at Castlewood. He was a universal favorite at the village inn, where he enjoyed considerable prestige as a fisherman, blacksmith and huntsman. No objection was raised, apparently, to his marrying one of the housemaids."

It was perhaps in *Vanity Fair* that Thackeray showed the clearest insight into the attitudes of the middle and upper classes in the early years of the nineteenth century. It is the younger generation rather than the older in *Vanity Fair* which is conscious of race and color as marks of social inferiority. When George Osborne is urged to marry Miss Swartz, a wealthy black woman from the West Indies, he says:

"Marry that mulatto woman? I don't like the colour, Sir. Ask the black that sweeps opposite Fleet Street, Sir. I'm not going to marry a Hottentot Venus."

There were other reasons why the black man in England towards the end of the nineteenth century was viewed with disfavor and growing prejudice. Dr. Little explains it this way:

> Since the cause coincided with a period of acute social distress in Britain, it is not surprising that it came in for a great deal of reproach. Mill-owners were accused of succouring the black slaves out of the

> profits ground out of their white ones, and Michael Sadler in a propagandist ballad told the true story of a factory child who had collapsed and died from overwork and ill-treatment while she was trying to go home through the snow after her day at the loom.

This ballad aroused great pity for poor white children who were forced to work in factories while at the same time it placed the black man in an adverse light:

> *That night a chariot passed her while on the ground she lay,*
> *The daughters of her master an evening visit pay,*
> *Their tender hearts were sighing as Negro wrongs were told,*
> *But the white slave lay there dying who earned their father's gold.*

However, animosity against the black man did not reach the alarming heights which could spark off race riots. This was to come in the twentieth century.

A more deep-seated reason for racial prejudice, one which is still in evidence today, was the age-old question of sex. And sex is no respector of race or color. People will cohabit if and when they want to, and the fact of color becomes irrelevant. So it was in nineteenth century Britain. In fact, blackness seemed an added attraction to English women, signifying greater potency and virility. In 1889, when white women were going wild over Africans brought over to the Earl's Court Exhibition, the London press let out a howl of disgust:

> To anyone who has spent some years in Africa, the familiarity which exists between certain white women visiting the Kaffir Kraal at Earl's Court Exhibition and the blacks on show there, is a peculiarly revolting spectacle; From the hour this "savage" sideshow is opened until late at night, the Kraal is besieged by crowds of females who hustle each other in their rivalry to obtain personal association with the Matabele and other coloured men on view. Some of these women use all their arts of fascination to please these sons of the African wilderness. But lately we saw a European girl detach flowers from her bosom to adorn the person of these niggers and we have seen grown women not only shake hands with them but stroke their limbs admiringly. Nothing is left undone by certain misled English females to gratify the vanity of these miscellaneous African natives in whose delightful manners and customs this show is presumed to instruct us. The Kaffir Exhibition at Earl's Court has in fact degenerated into an exhibition of white women visitors, and a very disgusting exhibition it is. These raw, hulking and untamed men-animals are being unwillingly and utterly corrupted by unseemly attention from English girls.

It is significant here to observe two points: that when it came to sex, white men looked upon blacks as "men-animals"; and that it was not the black man who made sexual advances, but the white woman.

Although there was growing race prejudice in Britain in the years of the nineteenth century, some blacks managed to win a measure of fame. Such blacks—boxer Tom Molineaux, actor Ira Aldridge and composer Samuel Coleridge-Taylor—stand out. There were others, too, mainly visiting black artists, like Thomas Bethune, "Blind Tom", of Columbus, Georgia, an untaught classical pianist who earned over $100,000 in one London season in 1866; slave singer Elizabeth Taylor Greenfeld from Natchez, Mississippi, who thrilled English audiences in 1853 and gave a command performance at Buckingham Palace the following year before Queen Victoria; and the Fisk Jubilee Singers towards the latter part of the nineteenth century.

Tom Molineaux, who was born a slave in Virginia came to London in 1809. He was to create a bigger stir than his predecessor, Bill Richmond. He arrived in the English capital with a record of successes and the claim to be called Champion of America. When he reached England "he roamed the streets, unable to read and without a shilling in his pocket, hoping to stumble across the household of the American Ambassador where he might be taken in and given employment. . . . It was then that chance threw him in the path of Bill Richmond." A racial affinity seems to have drawn the two black men together in an alien land. Richmond's background had been similar to that of Molineaux. He, too, had been a slave and was raised on Staten Island. He lost no time in giving young Molineaux lodgings at his London Inn, becoming his coach.

No sooner had Molineaux settled in London under Richmond's wing than he announced that he had come to England specially to have a crack at Tom Cribb, who was boxing champion of England. This grandiose claim by Molineaux was looked upon as rank impertinence by the British boxing fraternity. Cribb exclaimed that it was unthinkable "that an unknown man from America where the sport was of low order and without standing, would have a chance against the great Cribb. All England was aflame with indignation."

Indignation or no indignation, after proving himself decisively with two tough oponents—one of whom had given Cribb a rough time—and in spite of the fact that Cribb called him "an ebony impostor," Molineaux got his chance on December 10, 1810, at Coptoll Common near East Grinstead in Sussex. At stake in this prize fight was the championship belt, 200 guineas, and "the honour of Old England."

The battle was fought outdoors on the turf in a cold biting wind, driving rain, and before 5,000 wet spectators, almost all of whom were Cribb supporters. It deserves a detailed account because it illustrates the prejudice which tarnished the good name of "Old England."

There were four former champions near the ringside: Dan Mendoza, "Gentleman" Jackson, Jim Belcher, and John Gully; all anxious to see how the man who had defeated them would fare against this fearsome-looking black fighter with extra long arms, weighing over 200 pounds and standing 5 ft. 8 ins. Sir Thomas Apreece "kept the ring." Cribb had Gully and Jim Ward in his corner while Bill Richmond and Paddington Jones were in attendance on Tom Molineaux. Dead silence greeted the arrogant Molineaux when he arrived in Lord Barrymore's chaise and defiantly flung his cap into the ring. With the English champion, Cribb, it was very different. While he was climbing into the ring a burst of cheering resounded though the crowd making him pose and flex the muscles of his massive torso. He stood 5 ft. 10½ ins. and scaled 199 pounds.

The two fighters shook hands. Gusts of rain swept the ring as the fight began. Then Molineaux lashed out viciously, catching Cribb a stinging right on the throat, causing him to retreat. Back he moved, feinting with his straight left as he went, then stopping quickly with rapid punches to the black man's body. These caused Molineaux to wince in pain, but he edged in closer, carrying his long, sinewy arms to the front in order to grapple Cribb around the waist. But the English champion remained as firm as a rock. Then, quick as lightning, he shifted his feet, gave Molineaux the crook, and flung him with a heavy crash to the ground.

The next round was a sensation. Molineaux had a style of his own. He would advance quickly with both arms raised in front of him and then would strike downwards. There was both force and fury behind those blows. Like sledgehammers they fell on Cribb's head and face and one of them cut his lips through like a razor. But he kept very calm and cool and met Molineaux's rush with "good English straight lefts" to the face. Nevertheless, it was "first blood" to Molineaux. Almost before the cheers of the few Molineaux supporters could die down, Cribb drove a smashing right, plumb to the black boxer's nose. Down he went for a second time. A roar of voices shouted "Its all over—Cribb wins."

But it was not. At the call for the next round, Molineaux rushed out of his corner and unleashed a hail of blows at Cribb's head. Bang went the English champion's left into the Virginian's face and for the third time he hit the turf.

During that half-minute interval Bill Richmond took his man severely to task. He was too reckless, he should show more cunning, more caution. Molineaux listened to the advice of his second but still he pressed Cribb hard. The Englishman had to summon all the footwork he knew to keep out of harm's way. Round and round the ring they went, with Molineaux always pressing, always attacking; Cribb "milling on the retreat" and getting that left past Molineaux's guard time and again. The pace was terrific. To the crowd's horror they saw Molineaux brush aside Cribb's attack and batter him to the wet turf in round after round.

At the call of "Time!" to start the twenty-ninth round, Cribb was lying in his corner like a log, unable to get up and start the round. On more than two occasions the referee shouted "Time!" while Molineaux stood alone at the mark awaiting his man. He had won decisively and should have been awarded the fight at that very moment, but Cribb's handlers rushed across the ring and began to wrangle, falsely accusing Molineaux of carrying lead weights in his fists. There were no weights. This was an old trick to gain time, and it worked. The dispute lasted several minutes and when "Time!" was again called, Cribb was able to come to scratch. During that undeserved rest, the black man who was not used to the cold and damp English weather, suffered a chill and when the battle resumed he shook violently and his pace was noticeably slower. Cribb jagged ahead and knocked out Molineaux in the fortieth round. Even the most rabid supporters of Tom Cribb, however, had to admit that Molineaux had been cheated of the championship. England's honor had been saved, but the price left a bad taste in the mouth.

In a return bout staged nine months later, the two men fought on a platform in the open air before twenty thousand people. This time Tom Cribb beat a run-down and overweight Molineaux convincingly. But the memory of the first battle remained.

Tom Molineaux seems to have allowed himself to go to the dogs swiftly after that. He began to drink heavily, and was no longer a potential challenger in the English prize ring. He travelled to Ireland with a troupe of boxers, and there, wretched and penniless, he died at the age of thirty-eight in the Galway barracks of the 77th Foot regiment.

Other black boxers of that era who trained under Richmond were Jim Johnson and Massa Kendrick, but they did not achieve great success. In 1830, the number one black pugilist was Jem Wharton, the Morocco Prince—while Henry Sutton and Sam Robinson also fought with a fair degree of success. In spite of the success of black prize fighters, feeling against black people in Britain ran very high. Sutton married a white woman of considerable beauty. Sutton himself was fairly popular, but when he died the patrons of the prize ring were so disgusted with his pretty wife for marrying a black man that when a benefit was announced for her, they refused to buy a single ticket. Sutton had won four battles out of five, and Robinson five out of eight.

The first really great black fighter in England during the last years of the nineteenth century was Peter Jackson. He was born in Puerto Rico, on July 3, 1861, but learned his fighting skill in Australia. Jackson's greatest fight was against Frank Slavin at the National Sporting Club, London, on May 30, 1892. Leading sportsmen were present, among them the Prince of Wales, afterwards Edward VII. As Slavin stepped into the ring, he shouted: "To be beaten by a nigger is a pill I will never swallow."

He had to swallow that bitter pill. In the tenth of ten gruelling rounds he was plainly beaten, but refused to give in. However, Jackson was proclaimed the winner and the referee's announcement was received with great applause. It was said of Peter Jackson by his contemporaries that his main assets were his excellent behavior and his sportsmanlike qualities—the fact that he did not marry a white woman or consort openly with white women was also a point in his favor in nineteenth-century England where the forces of racial prejudice were gaining ground.

From the first, blacks also showed talent as actors and musicians, and in the nineteenth century the most notable were Ira Frederick Aldridge, the Shakespearean tragedian, and classical composer Samuel Coleridge-Taylor.

Ira Frederick Aldridge can really be termed, with justification, the first black actor to make an impact on the English stage. . . . On April 10, 1833, the twenty-six-year-old black actor, styled on the posters as "The African Roscius," after Quintus Roscius Gallus, the great Roman actor, was billed to play Othello at the Theatre Royal, Covent Garden. His Desdemona was to be Ellen Tree, later the wife of Charles Kean, who himself was cast as Iago. It was the first time that a black man had appeared in tragedy in a first rate theatre and, as was to be expected, voices were raised. Several publications printed articles tending to condemn or rather "to annihilate the Negro actor unheard, and to question the propriety of his being allowed a trial upon the boards of a principal London theatre," as one paper wrote. Another went even further and shouted: "Aldridge shall be jammed to atoms by the relentless power of our critical 'BATTERING RAM' if his name is not immediately withdrawn from the Bills!!!"

But the black tragedian had many actor friends from the Garrick Club and they distributed printed notices about the town on behalf of Ira Aldridge pleading, "To condemn unheard is contrary to the character and known liberality of Englishmen. We beg of a London audience 'fair play' on his behalf when he makes his debut on Wednesday next."

The outcry from certain biased sections of the press did not frighten the Covent Garden management. Ira Aldridge did appear in *Othello* for four nights. Despite this performance, some critics, with eyes blinded by prejudice, did subject the black actor to their critical "battering ram." Two such papers were *The Athenaeum* and *The Times*. That racial prejudice was the basis of their criticism is especially evident in *The Times'* review:

> In the name of common propriety and decency, we protest against an interesting actress and lady-like girl, like Miss Ellen Tree, being subjected to the indignity of being pawed by Mr. Henry Wallack's black servant.

But the Covent Garden audience thought otherwise, as *The Times* critic grudgingly observed: "It is, however, our duty to state that Mr. Aldridge was extremely well received." In truth, not all the newspapers allowed racial prejudice to mar their judgment; *The Globe*, for instance wrote: "Nature has been bountiful to Mr. Aldridge in more than the identity of complexion which she has given him for the Moor. He possesses a good figure and a speaking, intelligent countenance."

Ira Aldridge was born in Chapel Street, New York, in 1807, and like many blacks who settled in Britain in the nineteenth century he had been to sea, having shipped as a steward in a vessel bound for Liverpool. It happened that James Wallack, the English actor, was a passenger in the same vessel. Wallack engaged Ira Aldridge as his personal attendant during the voyage. Aldridge left the ship in Liverpool in 1825, with a view to becoming an actor. He had already gained some acting experience in New York at Brown's Theatre in 1820, the year it opened, and in 1821. His first engagement in an English theatre was on October 10, 1825, at the Royal Coburg Theatre which advertised "First night of the celebrated American Tragedian of a new and most effective melodramatic romance called "The Revolt of Surinam."

The critics sallied to the Coburg en masse to witness the novelty of a black man on the London stage. *The Times,* after lengthy discourse, mainly adverse because of Aldridge's color, had to admit: "The African Roscius played the part of Oroonoko probably as well as was necessary." The other papers paid more attention to Aldridge's histrionic talents, and the consensus of opinion was: "We would say, on the whole, that Aldridge's conception of the character was very judicious and that he rarely overstepped the modesty of nature."

The fact of the matter was that Ira Aldridge had scored a triumph. The black actor was kept on for another week and presented in another West Indian musical melodrama called *The Ethiopian, or the Quadroon of the Mango Grove.* It must have pleased Ira Aldridge when he read this announcement on the playbills:

> The very powerful sensation excited by the brilliant success and astonishing talent of the tragedian of colour, the rapturous applause which has attended each of his performances, and the increasing anxious demand for places to witness his Royal and interesting display of histrionic art, have determined them to gratify the public curiosity, by introducing this unexpected acquisition to the theatrical talent of the establishment, in a new character eminently calculated for the display of his peculiar powers.

Ira Aldridge's appearance at the Coburg Theatre was important, too, for a very personal reason, one which was to have a profound effect on the future of his acting career in England. For it was while he was performing at the Coburg that he met an English woman from Northallerton in Yorkshire, Margaret Gill, whom he married that same year. She was twenty-eight, ten years older than Ira Aldridge.

This marriage angered the pro-slavery forces in London with the result that the black actor was shunned for one whole year. Many pro-slavery newspapers and journals which were mouth-pieces for the very powerful sugar, coffee, tobacco and cotton barons, the estate and plantation owners and slave-traders of the West Indies, organized vile smear campaigns against him. In 1827 he was forced to try his luck in the English provinces. He had great success at the Theatres Royal in Liverpool, Manchester, and Bristol. But it was at the Theatre Royal, Dublin, on December 7, 1831, that he reached the high point of his tour. When Edmund Kean, the celebrated actor, saw Aldridge play Othello he sent for him and not only complimented him highly, but also gave him a letter of recommendation to the manager of the Theatre Royal, Bath, one of the fashionable theatrical centres of the period. In this letter Kean wrote:

> January 3rd, 1832,
> Dear Bellamy, I beg to introduce to your notice Mr. Aldridge, the African Roscius, whose performances I have witnessed with great pleasure. He possesses wondrous versatility, and I am sure, under your judicious generalship, will prove a card in Bath.
> I remain, dear Bellamy, truly yours, Edmund Kean.

Ira Aldridge returned to London in a blaze of triumph to star at the Theatre Royal, Covent Garden. But the same prejudice he had met with from pro-slavery bigots earlier on dogged him to Covent Garden, where his engagement was terminated after four nights. The managers of the two first-ranking London theatres—Covent Garden and Drury Lane—bypassed him completely. Aldridge was forced to accept bookings at London's minor theatres and to undertake quick dashes to make short appearances in the provinces. He noted in his diary:

> Bigotry and fanaticism have excited themselves in all possible shapes to annoy the profession of dramatic art, but I have been very successful, indeed, thank God.

In spite of his successes Aldridge spent the next nineteen years wandering from minor London theatres to provincial ones, with engagements dwindling as the years went by. The pressure of prejudice was great on the black actor. One newspaper admitted:

> Not unconscious of his own natural disadvantage—that of his colour—Mr Aldridge awaited, with characteristic modesty, the invitation to

> appear again. Managers lacked, to say the least of it, the moral courage to engage him when opportunity occurred.

Ira Aldridge was quite definitely aware that his color and his marriage to a white woman were viewed with disfavor among powerful elements in the theatre. And, by May, 1847, another serious factor arose which damned Aldridge even more in the eyes of prudish Victorian England: an Irish lady gave birth to his child, a boy whom he named Ira Daniel Aldridge. On learning about the affair, his wife, Margaret, forgave her husband and took the child to live with her, adopting the role of stepmother. A few more years banging his head against the doors of theatre managers' offices proved a waste of time. So on July 14, 1852, Aldridge left England. Still the English papers were cruel to him, one of them writing: "Mr. Aldridge took his farewell of English audiences previous to rejoining his tribe in some distant part of the world."

Actually, he left for Brussels, in which city he made his first continental appearance at the Theatre Royal St. Hubert as Othello. He afterwards travelled to Aix-la-Chapelle, Elberfeld, Cologne, Bonn, Baden, and Basle. Accompanying Aldridge were his wife, Margaret, and his son, Ira Daniel. The success which had eluded him in England came to him on the European continent. He was showered with honors by the crowned heads of Europe. He received so many decorations in Europe that *The Illustrated London News* commented: "Mr. Aldridge is the only actor, native or foreign, so decorated."

In 1857, Ira Aldridge returned to London with his wife and son. His great success on the continent opened the doors of the London theatre. He was immediately given an engagement at the Lyceum to play Othello. It must have pleased the black tragedian after the performance to see *The Athenaeum* eating the words it had uttered nearly a quarter of a century earlier:

> Mr. Ira Aldridge appeared on these boards in the character of Othello. Not only does the sable artist pronounce our own language distinctly and correctly, but with elocutional emphasis and propriety and his general action is marked with elegance and ease. So far as our own acquaintance with Mr. Aldridge extends we have formed a favourable opinion of his talents.

Aldridge's greatest success was in Russia where he appeared several times in his favorite part, Othello, as well as in other Shakespearean roles.

He became "the lion of St. Petersburg," to quote Théophile Gautier, one of the greatest French critics of the time. He was made an honorary member of the Imperial Academy of Beaux Arts, St. Petersburg, and holder of the Imperial Jubilee de Tolstoy Medal.

Ira Aldridge's wife Margaret died in March, 1864, at the age of 66. In April of the following year he was married again; this time to a thirty-one year-old Swedish opera singer, Amanda Paulina Brandt. They had three children, Luranah, Frederick, and Amanda. But, for fifty-eight-year-old Aldridge the end was not far off. Two years later, in 1867, he went with his wife to Lodz in Poland to play Othello. During rehearsals the actor suddenly fell ill and died at 5 P.M. on August 7, the day before the opening of *Othello,* despite the best medical care. He was given a military funeral with great dignitaries attending, and was buried in the cemetery at Lodz.

Ira Aldridge dreamed of a world where all men lived in harmony. In fact, his life was dedicated to a vision of a world where there were no masters, no slaves, a world in which everyone moved about in freedom, lived as brothers and were equal. He expressed these beliefs with passionate ardor in several of his major roles. The most striking was in the death scene in the melodrama *Dred,* from the antislavery work by Harriet Beecher Stowe in which he played the title role:

> I can see far into the future . . . can behold the time when white and black shall be of equal worth.
>
> Grieve not for me; I go where all are free; I go where my colour is no crime, there—to the abode of bliss—and liberty—liberty!

This was something that was not thought of in Aldridge's time, when nineteenth-century England showed little "humanity" to blacks. The motivating force in Ira Aldridge's work was, as he himself said, over and over again, "the honour of the stage and the dignity of human nature." That was why he gave much of his talent to black causes. It can truthfully be said that he devoted his life to this noble purpose. In writing about this aspect of Ira Aldridge's life historian Owen Mortimer declared:

> This was the man the unhonoured and uncelebrated and unknown people, held in slavery, gave to the world. It was from the epic struggle of his people to overthrow their masters that the great Negro tra-

> gedian derived his inspiration, his strength, his genius, all his magnificent art.

Even the race supremacists of the period did not question the fact that "the greatness of Mr. Aldridge enriches the theatre's long and honourable history. Those who cherish all that is good and beautiful in the theatre will always rank Mr. Aldridge among its most noble leaders."

Nineteenth-century racial attitudes in England might be assumed to have experienced some change for the better, but this was far from the case. Another outstanding black man born in London in 1875, who grew up there in the last quarter of the century was to face the same prejudices. He was Samuel Coleridge-Taylor, musician, conductor, composer. His great talent did not save him from racial insults. His deep awareness of the indignities that blacks were made to suffer had an indelible effect on him and his compositions. He became so race conscious that he came to be known as "the apostle of colour," as well as being one of the most important composers of his time, and one who was to achieve immortality after his early death at thirty-seven in 1912.

Samuel Coleridge-Taylor was born in Holborn, London, the only child of Daniel Taylor, a doctor from Sierra Leone and a member of the Royal College of Surgeons, and Alice Hare, a pretty English girl. From an early age he showed musical talent and as a young man Samuel Coleridge-Taylor entered the Royal College of Music. Quickly, he gained success as a composer. When his *Hiawatha's Wedding Feast* was first performed at the college he was praised by critics, musicians, and composers.

But the advocates of race supremacy sought to dismiss the success. They claimed it was a fluke. Coleridge-Taylor's biographer and friend, W. C. Berwick Sayers, wrote that critics remarked to him: "People of negro blood do not develop beyond a certain point. He's a damned nigger. He'll never do anything more."

This did not deter Samuel Coleridge-Taylor from following his career as a composer. He went on to write works of lasting value: *Hiawatha, A Tale of Old Japan, African Suite, Toussaint l'Ouverture, Othello,* suites for strings, quartets, symphonic poems, keyboard works, sonatas, part-songs, orchestral works, and light romantic songs. He also gained fame as a conductor at Trinity College of Music. When his compositions were ignored by prominent musicians and critics, he became discouraged, and at one period the quality of his work began to suffer. Instead of extending words of encouragement to Coleridge-Taylor, the English press of Victorian times was only too glad to write that his attitude showed "one more outcome of that lack of assurance which is probably racial in origin."

This angered the black composer. In a letter to the Croydon *Guardian* he wrote: "I consider myself the equal of any white man who ever lived, and no one could ever change me in that respect."

As Samuel Coleridge-Taylor walked in the streets of London and Croydon he was pestered by white roughnecks shouting "Blackie," "Nigger." One day, he became so annoyed that he seized one of the hecklers by the neck and gave him a thorough thrashing with his walking stick. All the animosity directed at him gave him a deep preoccupation with his race. He turned away from the classics and sought inspiration in spirituals. The works of black men like Pushkin, Dumas, and Du Bois filled him with racial pride.

Even when Samuel Coleridge-Taylor fell in love and married Jessie Fleetwood Walmisley, an English girl who bore him two children, the question of race marred some of his happiness. Her parents objected to the marriage, because, as they said, "The Negro belongs to the lower stages of human development."

It is little wonder that the black composer became more and more determined to fight this evil which was threatening to drive reason, logic, and understanding from the minds of the English. He was a regular contributor to *The African Times and Orient Review*, a black-oriented magazine founded in 1912 "to advocate the cause of the coloured races in this country [Britain]." Coleridge-Taylor maintained: "It is imperative that this venture be heartily supported by coloured peoples everywhere, so that it shall be absolutely independent of whites."

Samuel Coleridge-Taylor's immense musical talents and his fight against prejudice did not stem the slowly mounting wave of race prejudice which was showing itself in England as the new century was approaching with high hopes for mankind, as everyone thought. These high hopes were not to materialize for blacks, as they were to find out later. They had "to contend with considerable hostility from the white population," wrote Dr. Michael Banton of the Social Research Centre of Edinburgh University some years ago. This deterioration in English attitudes to black people living in Britain appears to have coincided with an increase in the frequency of contacts with blacks in the West Indies and other colonies as a result of imperialistic expansion. As the twentieth century moved past the years of World War I conditions were to become much worse, especially for those who sought employment at a time when the germs of depression were already eating into the economic core of the country.

BIBLIOGRAPHY TO CHAPTER NINE

Aldridge, Ira. Diaries, newspaper clippings, letters, documents, and recorded conversations with Amanda Aldridge about her father and family (in the author's possession).

Anti-Slavery Reports. London: 1913.

Austen, Jane. *Sanditon.* London: 1817.

Banton, Michael. *The Coloured Quarter.* London: 1955.

Egan, Pierce. *Life in London.* London: 1821.

Francklyn, G. *Observations on the Slave Trade.* London: 1789.

George, M. Dorothy. *London Life in the Eighteenth Century.* London: 1930.

Gilbert, Michael. *The Claimant.* London: 1957.

Golding, Louis. *The Bare-Knuckle Breed.* London: 1952.

Hoare, Prince. *Memoirs of Granville Sharp. Pt. 3. Sierra Leone.* London: 1828.

Jerrold, Douglas. *St. Giles and St. James.* London: 1851.

Little, K. L. *Negroes in Britain.* London: 1948.

Mackenzie-Grieve, Averil. *The Last Years of the English Slave Trade.* Liverpool 1750–1807. London: 1941.

Marshall, Herbert, and Stock, Mildred. *Ira Aldridge, The Negro Tragedian.* London: 1958.

Mayhew, Henry. *London Labour and the London Poor.* Edited by Peter Quennel, London: 1950.

Mortimer, Owen. Mr. Aldridge of the Theatre (unpublished mss.), 1954.

Sayers, W. C. Berwick. *Samuel Coleridge-Taylor—Musician. His Life and Letters.* London: 1927.

Thackeray, William M. *Vanity Fair.* London: 1848.

Wignall, Trevor C. *The Story of Boxing.* London: 1923.

Woodruff, Douglas. *The Tichborne Claimant.* London: 1957.

Smith, John Thomas. *Vagabondiana.* London: 1874.

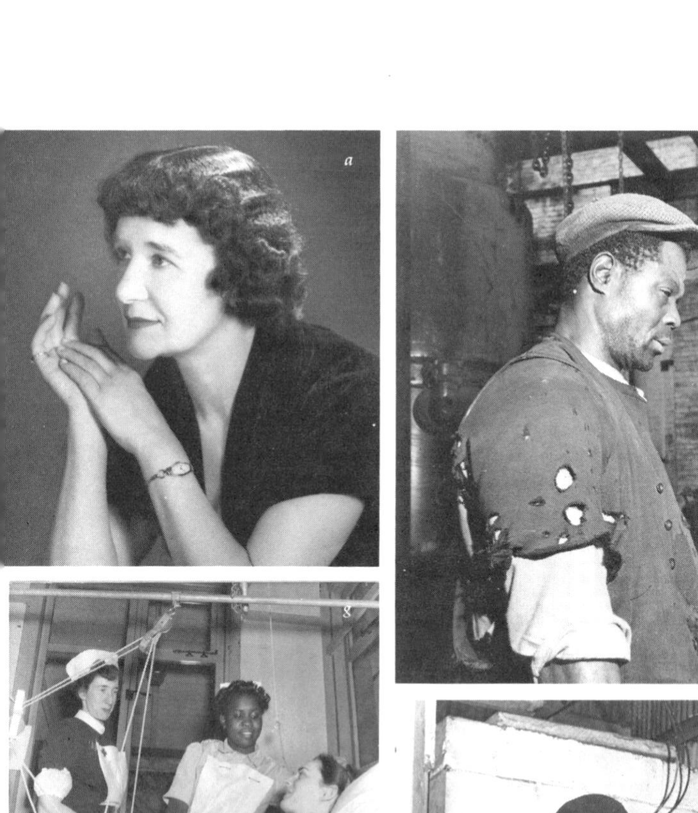

a

b

g

h

l

PART TWO

d

e

f

i

j

k

n

o

Key to Illustrations

a) Averil Coleridge-Taylor, daughter of the composer. (Jane Plotz Art Studios, Johannesburg, S.A.).

b) (Black Star, N.Y.).

c) Edgar Mittelholzer (Ebony files).

d) (Black Star, N.Y.).

e) West Indian immigrants at London terminus (Paul Popper Ltd., London).

f) (Bert Hardy photograph, Picture Post-Pix, N.Y.).

g) Student nurses at Queen Mary Hospital, Sidcup, Kent (Photo from European, N.Y.).

h) (Black Star, N.Y.).

i) (Bert Hardy photo, Picture Post-Pix, N.Y.).

j) Reporters questioning Notting Hill resident after riots. (UPI, N.Y.).

k) (Bert Hardy photo, Picture Post-Pix, N.Y.).

l) Notting Hill race riot (UPI, N.Y.).

m) (Bert Hardy photo, Picture Post-Pix, N.Y.).

n) West Indian batsman (Black Star, N.Y.).

o) Kelso Benjamin Cochrane (Mirrorpic, Daily Mirror, London).

CHAPTER X

STUDENTS AND THE LEAGUE OF COLOURED PEOPLES

By the turn of the century more and more black people of a different kind were coming to England. They were students. Britain had acquired by conquest and colonization nearly a quarter of the earth's countries, especially vast areas in Africa, and had started the business of colonization, John Bull style. Africans, prompted by the zeal of the missionaries had been smitten with the desire for an English education. Towards the end of the eighteenth century, African chiefs and others who could afford it were already sending their sons to England to study. Now, this search for learning was becoming widespread in West Africa. It was the custom, too, for white estate owners in the West Indies to send their mulatto children to school in England. White fathers were particularly fond of enrolling their mulatto daughters at "finishing schools" in order to acquire the social graces. The fashion had been set early in the nineteenth century. Jane Austen, the English novelist, wrote about one of these mulatto heiresses at a boarding-school in her book *Sanditon*, published in 1817.

From those early years Durham University has had a long association with the West Indies and West Africa. Codrington College in Barbados was affiliated to the university in the Easter Term of 1875, and Fourah Bay University, Sierra Leone, in the following year. In 1902, it was felt that more black missionaries were required, so an African Training Institute was founded in Colwyn Bay, North Wales. Each student received an ordinary course of English school training, special attention being paid to the Scriptures. He was also taught a trade, such as printing, tailoring, or carpentry, which would be of some value in earning a livelihood and in teaching other Africans.

As the twentieth century began, the numbers of African students in Britain rose. Before World War I most of them appear to have registered at London University. A few went to Oxford or to Cambridge, and to Liverpool University in the north of England. At Liverpool, wrote the *Anti-Slavery Reporter* of 1913, "The earliest entry of students from the British West Indies, or from West Africa, dates from the year 1909." The great number at that time studied medicine and law rather than theology. However, when those students returned to Africa they found that the administration did not treat them on an equal footing with Europeans, especially in the case of African doctors. European patients, it was argued, had no confidence in them; an attitude which was to change with the times.

In England, African and West Indian students did not experience the harsher forms of race prejudice, which were aimed at seamen and other permanent settlers. These students "were left to live their lives somewhat apart, even from the student class, and some it seems sought companionship in less desirable directions," claimed Dr. Little. At Oxford and Cambridge universities, students encountered prejudice. In London they met tolerance, but also an indifference to their welfare, and it was with a view to putting this condition right that a meeting of persons interested in the welfare of Africans was summoned in London in July, 1913. The question of hospitality was discussed. The gathering was quite well attended. Sir Harry Johnson, one-time governor of Sierra Leone, was a prominent speaker and he spoke quite strongly about the imperial implications of treating Africans in London in a more sympathetic way:

> But if in London we are not actively disagreeable to the negro who comes here, we do not—proportionately with the imperial importance of London—go out of our way to attract hither the negro for his education; to provide him, even, with the means of quickly and cheaply getting that education he wants, and to make the conditions of his stay as profitable to him mentally and as agreeable to him socially as I am sure we should if we were really an imperial people. Of course, if we prefer to be Little Englanders and imagine ourselves the only race worth considering in the world, then it is different. But if we are

> going to maintain this Empire on such lines that all our intelligent fellow-subjects will belong to it of their own free will; then we must minister to their advanced education and make the great educational centres of Great Britain attractive to the coloured peoples who wish to come here to perfect their knowledge. If we do not accomplish this, it will mean that . . . they will go to France and Germany. Germany—quite rightly from her point of view—is doing all she can at the present time to attract the backward races to her centres of education, and I think it scarcely ever arises that a coloured man in Germany receives anything but kind, sympathetic and courteous treatment. I wish I could say the same about my own experience of Great Britain, but it is not so.

Britain's attitude even to students who came to study for professions and then return to their native land was not a friendly one. Though not subjected to outright hostility they still experienced discrimination in one way or another. Several student welfare organizations were formed which catered only to black students. Among the best known from early times were the East and West Friendship Council, the League of Coloured Peoples, of which more will be heard later on, and the West African Students' Union.

From its very beginnings in the 1920s the West African Students' Union (WASU) in London has been one of the most influential bodies devoted primarily to the well-being of West African students. West Indians and other Africans from central and eastern areas, however, were included in several of WASU's activities.

Like all subsequent colonial students, those who arrived in England in the 1920s came with high hopes that they would be treated like brothers of Empire by the English. Anthropologist A. T. Carey described this state of mind:

> In those days, West African students still came from a land of the trader's frontier, administered under different systems of indirect rule: and all were the products of missionary schools. These students looked upon Britain as a land where missionaries came from, a religious country, where all the Christian virtues were practised. The political ideas they brought with them were largely the result of years of colonial rule, although the proclamation of war aims during the First World War had been a stirring influence.

It did not take long for these high hopes to be shattered. Colonial students found that this "land where missionaries came from" was also a land where color prejudice was very much in evidence. One who discovered this was Nigerian law student Ladigo Solanke. He arrived in London in 1922 and was called to the Bar in 1926. Dr. Carey wrote that

> Solanke reacted strongly to the kind of race relations that existed in Britain at that time, and felt personally touched at every form of discrimination. Perhaps as a result of this strong identification, he claimed to have had a dream in which God showed him that only through unity, self-help and cooperation could Africans hope to defeat the colour bar.

Ladigo Solanke devoted his life to making this dream a reality. With this in mind he began by promoting cooperation among students. There were already three organizations working for the welfare of African students in Britain: the African Progress Union, the Gold Coast Students' Union, and the Association of Students of African Descent. Solanke founded a fourth, the Nigerian Progress Union, in 1924, but that did not satisfy him. What he wanted was a union which would be representative of all the peoples of West Africa, so that one day in the future they would be united.

His efforts to start such a union did not meet with much success. Undaunted, Solanke arranged a meeting in 1925 to which representatives of all four West African colonies were invited. Twelve students attended. Many years later all became prominent judges, magistrates, barristers, or politicians in Sierra Leone, Nigeria, Gambia, and the Gold Coast (later to become Ghana). It was this meeting which resulted in the birth of the West African Students Union. A constitution was formulated and a program for the revindication of African political rights was put forward.

From its inception WASU's aim was political: that native African rulers "should regain sovereignty by lawful and constitutional means." In the years that followed WASU made an impact not only on African students in Britain but on the home governments in West Africa, similar student organizations and the Colonial Office in London, receiving funds from the latter as well as from the governments of the West African countries. Although the aspirations of WASU remained, in general, the same with the passing of time, political changes did come about, especially after World War II, when Africa experienced a radical political transformation. Various study groups were formed, the most popular of them dealing with the political and economic problems of the colonies. Just after World War II the membership of the union increased greatly.

The West African Students' Union had been described by many as "a mere training-ground for agitators." Those critics claimed that one had only to look back at the political scene to see that every politician during the fight against colonialism in West Africa had been a very prominent member of WASU. But, Dr. Carey maintained, and with some justification:

> . . . it would be misleading to regard it primarily as a political organisation. Throughout its history, opposition to colonialism and to all forms of racial discrimination have been the leading values of the Union, although the form in which this was expressed had naturally varied with the changing conditions of world affairs.

From the beginning of World War I more West Indian than West African students came to Britain, particularly in the decade 1930–40. For instance, there were 50 West African students in British Universities while there were 128 West Indian—more than twice as many. This ratio remained constant. Even so, it was estimated, according to Dr. Banton, that "before the War [1939–45] there were about five or six hundred colonial students in Britain." After the war the numbers increased by leaps and bounds.

The principal organization devoted to the interests of West Indian students in the 30s was The League of Coloured Peoples, founded at the Central YMCA, Tottenham Court Road, London, on March 13, 1931. The first president was Harold Arundel Moody, M.D., B.S., a Jamaican doctor practising in London. He was regarded as "the recognised leader of his people in the Mother Country," to quote David A. Vaughan, his life-long friend and biographer, who wrote of Dr. Moody's association with the league:

> To its service he was to give himself with devotion, sacrifice, passion and zeal for the rest of his life and he held the office of President continuously till his death in 1947. In many senses the League was his life and it would not be untrue to say that he was the life of the League.

Many meetings were held after that first one in order to crystallize definite aims, objects, and methods for The League of Coloured Peoples. Finally, its purpose was made public:

> To promote and protect the social, educational, economic and political interests of its members.

> To interest members in the welfare of coloured peoples in all parts of the world.
> To improve relations between the races.
> To cooperate and affiliate with organisations sympathetic to coloured people.

Its aims were high but in its first two years of existence The League of Coloured Peoples met with scant success. It catered mainly to the needs of students in London "and arranged many social functions, meetings, and conferences on their behalf." It had a long and uphill road to travel before it could achieve its objects. Apart from an occasional newspaper paragraph, and some letters to editors, the league received precious little publicity. It was difficult to maintain the interest of members and attract the attention of others, so the league decided to start its own journal. Raising the necessary funds for such a venture was difficult but nevertheless in July, 1933, it launched an official organ titled *The Keys.* In describing the new quarterly, David Vaughan wrote:

> It derived its title from the inspiration of that distinguished African, Dr. Aggrey, who asserted that the fullest musical harmony could be expressed only by the use of the black and white keys on the piano. The first issue explained that the name was symbolic of what the League was striving for—the opening of doors now closed to coloured peoples and the harmonious co-operation of the races.

Dr. Moody himself, in the first editorial, set the mood of *The Keys:*

> We are knocking at the door and will not be denied. *The Keys* will, we trust, be an open sesame to better racial understanding and goodwill.

For the thousands (the figure in the years from 1914 to 1945 has always been given as 20,000) of blacks in Britain at that time, this publication was the main vehicle for airing their racial grievances.

The officers and executives of the magazine consisted of Africans, West Indians, and Afro-Americans. The launching was notable, and a copy of the first issue was accepted by the Prince of Wales (who became Edward VIII, later the Duke of Windsor). This copy was especially bound in blue leather and on the front cover was the following inscription in gold letters:

> This, The First Copy of THE KEYS
> The Official Organ of the League of Coloured Peoples
> Is most humbly presented to His Royal Highness
> THE PRINCE OF WALES, K.G.,

By the President and executive of the League
Beseeching His Royal Highness
To honour the League and the Coloured Peoples
Of this Empire by his most gracious acceptance."

All this pomp and patriotism aside, this first issue set to work in accordance with the aims listed by the league. In an article called "The Second Mile-Stone" the achievements of the league were discussed. The article noted:

> The difficulties presenting themselves to men and women of colour who were anxious to undertake their training in London as medical men and nurses soon commanded our attention: One young lady applied to twenty-five hospitals and was refused by everyone on the grounds of "colour." The Overseas Nursing Association to whose notice this case was brought said that they had "applied to eighteen hospitals in London and the provinces and they all said they could not take coloured probationers at present." One young man applied to several hospitals in London and was kept waiting three months without result. We have been able to fix up both these cases, in common with others, quite satisfactorily, but we certainly feel that the best possible training should be made available, without all this bother, for all those who are fitted to undergo such training, regardless of the colour of their skin. As British citizens we claim this as our due.

The League of Coloured Peoples' help was extended to every black man, woman and child; to colonial peoples who experienced difficulties, and to the less fortunate black population of London. The league was constantly in need of funds to continue its work and to finance its journal. In 1934, to raise money, a play, *At What a Price,* by Jamaican Una Marson was put on at London's Scala Theatre for three nights. The cast was made up entirely of league members with three of Dr. Moody's own children, Christine, Harold and Joan taking part. The project unfortunately turned out to be a disaster, but this did not dampen Dr. Moody's fighting spirit. His only comment was: "We have not made money, but we have made history, as it is the first time that a play written and performed by coloured colonials has been staged in London."

Harold Moody always maintained that while the League of Coloured Peoples would campaign for the rights of black people living in Britain, it wanted to work in collaboration and in harmony with English officials, organizations, and people sympathetic to the cause of the black man. His English friend, David Vaughan, explained it in this way: "Moody loved the British though he often was angry with British policy and believed that by mutual understanding and trust they could be brought to see their responsibilities to the coloured races, as he saw them."

A deeply religious man and a lay preacher, Dr. Moody belonged to the Colonial Missionary Society, of whose board of directors he was chairman, and was president of the London Christian Endeavour Federation. From the beginning, he emphasised, as Vaughan noted, ". . . the Christian basis of all his work and never failed to make it clear that the Christian faith was the inspiration of all his interests and effort."

Religion played an important part in the work of the league. This was very much in evidence when every year for many years a league service of worship would be held at Camberwell Green Congregational Church in London, where Dr. Moody was a member and deacon. English dignitaries attended these services, the high spot being the singing of spirituals which moved many white worshippers to a show of emotion.

With Moody's deep Christian beliefs in the brotherhood of man it is no wonder that he found himself in conflict with the revolutionary ideas of many of the members of the league's executive committee. They were young students who had the fire of rebellion in them but lacked experience and the wisdom which age brings with it. The result was that there were "violent disagreements." Eventually, these were gradually resolved but the breach was never fully closed.

Dr. Moody's leadership, strength of character, and the respect which the English people had for him carried the league through many stormy periods and gained it the respect and admiration of white and black alike. In many ways, Dr. Moody's counterpart can be seen in the late Dr. Martin Luther King Jr. They were both devout men with an innate love of mankind and the profound belief that in the end, good will prevail. To many extremists among the Africans and West Indians in Britain in the thirties, Dr. Moody was looked upon as a milk-and-water leader and something of an Uncle Tom—much as Black Power supporters and some extremists looked upon Dr. King in his last years. This in no way detracts from the good that Dr. Moody and The League of Coloured Peoples did for the thousand's of blacks living in Britain between the two world wars.

While no one will dispute Harold Moody's claim to be a symbol of The League of Coloured Peoples' struggle on behalf of blacks in Britain, there were other brilliant young men and women who were no less responsible for the league's success. Two such were Una Marson, Jamaican writer, poet, and publicity secretary and editor of the league's organ *The Keys*, and Arthur Lewis (now Sir Arthur Lewis), the economist.

Una Marson was a leading light among London's black population during the war years. She produced radio programs in which Colonial ex-servicemen and women and war workers broadcast messages overseas.

Una Marson felt the humiliations of race prejudice very deeply. Her best known and most evocative poem "Nigger" is a cry of anguish against white race haters everywhere. It is as meaningful today as it was when it was written in the thirties. Three of the eight stanzas will illustrate the mood:

They called me "Nigger,"
Those little white urchins,
They laughed and shouted
As I passed along the street.
They flung it at me:
"Nigger! Nigger! Nigger!"

What made me keep my fingers
From choking the words on their throats?
What made my face grow hot,
The blood boil in my veins
And tears spring to my eyes?
What made me go to my room
And sob my heart away
Because white urchins
Called me "Nigger"?

God keep my soul from hating such mean souls,
God keep my soul from hating
Those who preach the Christ
And say with churlish smile,
"This place is not for 'Niggers'."
God save their souls from this great sin
Of hurting human hearts that live
And think and feel in unison
With all humanity.

W. Arthur Lewis, a St. Lucian, was editor of *The Keys* from June, 1935, to October, 1936. He was also a member of the league's executive committee. Arthur Lewis came to London in 1933 to enter the London School of Economics. In 1935 he won the Director's Essay Prize, for the best undergraduate essay, and the Roseberry Scholarship, awarded on the Intermediate examination. In 1936 he came second for the Hugh Lewis Essay Prize for the best undergraduate research, with an essay on "The Evolution of the Peasantry in the British West Indies." And four years after entering the London School of Economics he passed the Bachelor of Commerce examinations with first class honours.

Black students of the calibre of Arthur Lewis caused the league to be taken seriously and recognized as a body of responsible opinion. Today, Arthur Lewis has earned a position of international eminence and a knighthood from Queen Elizabeth II.

Another member of the league's executive committee with Arthur Lewis was Hugh W. Springer of Barbados. Today Dr. Springer is a respected scholar and statesman. No less distinguished as a member of The League of Coloured Peoples and a leader among Britain's blacks was Barbados-born Cecil Belfield Clarke. He arrived in Britain in 1914 and in the 1920s, after a very successful academic career, became a doctor. Dr. Clarke was the only black District Medical Officer for the London County Council at that time. On his arrival in Britain he immediately took a practical interest in black people. He was elected first chairman of the House Committee of Aggrey House, a hostel for black students in Britain. From the inception of the West African Students Union and The League of Coloured Peoples, Dr. Clarke helped greatly in their work.

The success of these league members caused Dr. Moody to write:

> The League hopes that young Africans and West Indians coming to this country will discover the wisdom of applying themselves to the work of the League as they seek to achieve success in their own academic career. It is a duty that all of us owe to the future of our race.

Dr. Moody may have practised caution and collaboration with the whites but he was a man of a high principle and stood firmly by the rights of the black race. He fought race prejudice in an uncompromising manner, and no one can deny that it was largely due to The League of Coloured Peoples that blacks in Britain began to gain recognition and rights. Several instances will be cited later on, especially the case of black seamen in Cardiff in the thirties. Even so, Dr. Moody was forced to admit that

> The colour bar, as it operates in Great Britain [in 1934] especially in Cardiff, Liverpool, Hull and London, is getting worse daily. The diffi-

> culty experienced by students of colour in gaining admission to hospitals and medical schools for the study of medicine and nursing is worthy of the attention of the educational authorities.

The league had to contend with the age-old habit of racial discrimination. No hospital would openly admit that there was a ban against black nurses but, said *The Keys*, "after talking to numbers of hospital matrons, secretaries, and governors we learned that a coloured girl has a poor chance of securing a nursing post in the average hospital." Several hospitals, in typical fashion, admitted that while they had no objections because of race or color "They had to consider the feelings of patients, who might object strongly." Even today this kind of excuse is given by British landladies when turning away blacks looking for accommodation.

For once, the English could not hide their true feelings: they did not want black people living among them. It was this feeling which prompted a Liverpool magistrate in 1936 to comment: "It is a damned shame that a coloured stowaway can stand in this public court and say that work will be found for him in three weeks." In its columns *The Keys* remarked:

> We hold no brief for stowaways, but the mentality of this magistrate is interesting. Clearly, in his view the fact that a man is coloured adds to the gravity of his offence. This, of course, is a view common to ignorant whites, and is akin to the view that it is in itself degrading to be coloured: degrading, perhaps, even to be seen in the company of coloured people. We wonder whether this magistrate would have had anything to say if the stowaway had been, not a coloured British subject, but an alien?

The League of Coloured Peoples held conferences, conventions, gave lectures, organized outings for poor black children, made representations to Parliament, city councils and other official bodies on behalf of black people in difficulties. It campaigned zealously and continuously against all kinds of race prejudice whenever and wherever it occurred. This fight lasted well into the years after World War II. Harold Moody died in 1947 but the League of Coloured Peoples continued his good works after his death, in a way similar to the NAACP (National Association for the Advancement of Colored People) in America.

BIBLIOGRAPHY TO CHAPTER TEN

Banton, Michael. *White and Coloured.* London: 1959.

Carey, A. T. *Colonial Students.* London: 1956.

"Colour Before the Law" *The Keys* (April-June, London: 1936).

Cundall, Frank. *Jamaica's Part in the Great War 1914-1918.* West India Committee Circular, February 5, 1920. London: 1925.

Dover, Cedric. *Half-Caste.* London: 1937.

The Keys. Various articles. (London: July, 1933; October, 1933; July-September, 1934).

Little, Kenneth. *Negroes in Britain.* London: 1948.

Lewis, P. C., and Brown, G. W. "We Two Were in Cardiff." *The Keys.* (London: July-September, 1935).

Vaughan, David A. *Negro Victory.* London: 1950.

West India Regiment. Release from the Office of the High Commissioner. London: 1959.

CHAPTER XI

SERVICEMEN AND SETTLERS

Another class of black migrant—the West Indian serviceman—was coming into Britain in much greater numbers. Dr. Little, describing the cause of this migration wrote:

> It was the war of 1914–1918, however, which reintroduced the Negro into England in some numbers. Several thousands of coloured labourers were brought over to do work which would free Englishmen for combatant service. They worked in munition factories, in labour battalions, and also filled the place of many white merchant seamen who were transferred to the Royal Navy. Considerable objections were voiced against their arrival by the labour unions. It was feared that the idea of coloured immigration was the prelude to a substitution of white by coloured labour in wider fields of employment and to a consequent lowering of the wages and standard of living of the working class.

In 1914, black volunteers were coming to help the "Mother Country" in her hour of need. The patriotic feeling in the British Caribbean colonies was well expressed by the small West Indian island of Barbados, known as Little England, which is alleged to have sent a telegram to Britain's Prime Minister of the period, Herbert Henry Asquith, first Earl of Oxford and Asquith, which read: "Do not worry England, Barbados is behind you." This loyalty—misguided, if one is to take into consideration Britain's treatment of her black subjects—is deep rooted, as the Hon. John Fortescue, librarian at Windsor Castle, observed in 1919 in a lecture at the Royal Institute, on the Empire's share in England's wars: "When Britain was at war with Revolutionary France the Government of the day raised twelve West Indian regiments which were formed of Negroes under white officers."

This passionate love of king and country was recognized by Britain because it suited her for the moment. Praise was showered on the blacks of the Empire for rallying to the call of their Mother country when she was fighting the German Kaiser's crack divisions. The most accurate and comprehensive report of the war effort of the British West Indies was given by the West Indian Contingent Committee, signed by Sir Everard im Thurn and Sir Frederick Hodgson. The report read, in part, as follows:

> Immediately after the outbreak of the great European War, all classes of the communities in the British West Indies, British Guiana and British Honduras showed a desire, as spontaneous as it was general, to be permitted to take part in the defence of King and Empire. Many who could afford to do so hastened to England at their own expense, and joined various units of His Majesty's forces; but offers to furnish special contingents for active service were at first discouraged by the Army Council on the ground that the first duty of West Indians was to hold themselves ready to defend their own homes from the expected attacks by enemy cruisers. When, however, the menace became less serious, renewed requests by the West Indian communities to be allowed to send contingents to fight side by side with the Imperial and Dominion troops were gladly acceded to, and recruiting throughout the West Indian colonies began in earnest.

Instead of the two thousand men at first contemplated, 15,601 men eventually joined the British West Indies Regiment. King George V approved the formation of the regiment on October 26, 1915. The men who enlisted in the regiment came from every British owned territory in the Caribbean. Under the auspices of A. Bonar Law, M.P., then secretary of state for the colonies, the West Indian Contingent Committee had been formed on August 30, 1915, in London, "to provide for the welfare and comfort of the men of the West Indian contingents, as well as those who had come over independently, and of others who might come over, to enlist in the new armies." Merchants and estate owners of the different islands donated funds for the contingents.

The regiment served in France, Italy, Egypt and Mesopotamia, Belgium, Holland, and Germany. Many West Indians lost their lives for Britain: 185 were killed or died of wounds, 1,071 died of sickness, 697 were wounded. Distinguished Service Orders, Military Crosses, Meritorious Service Medals, Medailles d'Honneur, and mentioned in dispatches—in all, 129. A much older regiment, the West India Regiment, founded in the latter years of the eighteenth century, took a great part in World War I, acquitting itself very well in Palestine and the Cameroons with the British Expeditionary Force. Brevet Colonel Georges, C.B., who commanded the British contingent in the Cameroons, noted "how well the troops behaved under fire, particularly the signallers, one of whom continued signalling after two enemy bullets had gone through his flag."

Britain had welcomed the help which black servicemen gave her during the war, but when hostilities were ended, a change in attitude towards the black man began to make itself felt. All the black battalions and labor forces were demobilized in Britain. The West India Regiment did not last long after the war; it was disbanded in 1926 and the colors presented to King George V in 1927. (The West India Regiment was re-formed on January 1, 1959.)

A large number of black men who had been brought over to Manchester and other cities to work in munitions and chemical factories stayed on when the war was over. The situation was very much the same in most of the large British seaport cities like Liverpool and London. This meant that large numbers of black men were looking for employment in Britain and had no intention of returning home.

With the closing down of war and other industries many of the black workers traveled to Cardiff where they were hoping to sign on as seamen in merchant vessels. Kenneth Little gives another explanation for the increased number of West Indians and West Africans in Cardiff in the years between the two world wars. He writes that it "was due not only to the laying up of ships during the subsequent shipping depression, but to the more favourable rates of pay available there than by signing on at Liverpool."

There was very good money to be earned during the war years and up to 1919 for those who went to sea. Blacks prospered. With the ending of the war, however, white seamen who were demobilized from the Royal Navy returned to the merchant shipping service. There had been a heavy shrinkage in tonnage making it impossible to find jobs for all. As was to be expected shipowners and shipmasters took the stand "our people first," and there were soon about twelve hundred black men out of work in Cardiff. All they could get in the way of subsistence was twenty-nine shillings a week from the British government as unemployment pay. That was a great blow to them, as Dr. Little noted:

> The coloured seamen had been earning up to £15 per month during the war, and quite apart from anything else, the sudden drop in their economic circumstances was a severe one, particularly as they were in the habit of spending freely what they earned.

Other factors were causing racial friction to increase. The temporary prosperity which black seamen enjoyed had attracted many white women, who consorted with them freely. This, not unnaturally, caused great resentment among white seamen, who, on returning home to Cardiff during the war years found that their army and navy pay placed them at a disadvantage with their own women who preferred the wealthier black men. Also many white demobilized soldiers could not find employment. These appear to have been the prime factors and undercurrents in the serious outbreak of race riots which occurred in Cardiff during that very hot summer month of June, 1919, and which spread to almost every port area of the United Kingdom where black men were domiciled. In Liverpool, Manchester, Hull, Newport, and London, too, there were riots, and the subsequent discrimination against blacks ran high for many years. These riots were the forerunners of the more recent disturbances and were to have a profound and lasting effect on relations between the races in Britain.

In Cardiff the trouble started at about eleven o'clock on the night of June 10, 1919, with a scuffle between some white men and blacks at the end of Canal Parade. A revolver shot rang out, and in a matter of minutes a crowd of about three thousand people collected. After a second shot was fired a series of fights broke out between whites and blacks. These extended from the immediate vicinity, down to Custom House Street, along Bute Street and its side streets. Revolvers were fired repeatedly, and sticks and stones were used in the angry clashes which followed. In attempting to get at the blacks, the mob attacked several shops, and one in Bute Street, where black men lived, was completely destroyed. A report of one of these incidents appeared in the *Western Mail* two days later:

> Hadji Mahomet, the Somali priest, was reported to be living at 1, Homfray Street, and the rioters visited him. In response to the entreaties of his white wife to leave for a place of safety, the resourceful Somali clambered up a drain-pipe at the back of his house. He was immune there from the fury of the crowd while hidden on the roof, and

> with true Eastern stoicism watched his residence being reduced to a skeleton.

Two houses in Homfray Street suffered severe damage, and a fire broke out in one of the black boarding houses. For over one hour white and black men fired revolver shots, smashed windows and fought each other until the fire brigade appeared on the scene and put an end to the rioting. Fifteen people were taken to hospital suffering from bullet wounds and cuts. One of them, a black man, died a few hours later.

A more carefully planned assault occurred the following evening. Very early in the evening a huge crowd gathered near the Hayes Bridge, and the commotion finally settled in Millicent Street off Bute Street. White rioters stormed a house in which eight black men lived and began firing revolver shots. They were hidden in the warehouses of a wholesale grocer who lived across the street. Two soldiers in uniform led the mob. When a party of armed blacks barred the way the soldiers ordered them to drop back. They advanced again, this time holding up a table before them as a shield. Fighting began in the house with the blacks defending themselves with razor blades and a single revolver. A yelling white crowd stood outside exhorting their men and enjoying the onslaught on the besieged blacks. This behavior was recorded in the *Western Mail:*

> There were many brave spirits well out of the danger zone. They had allotted to themselves the task of cheering the invaders and accepting the booty as it was handed out. Old women and slatternly young women shrieked encouragement and it was a sight reminiscent of the French Revolution.

After a considerable time the police and fire brigade managed to intervene. The black men were taken away to the police station in what was described as "protective custody," but the excitement and pockets of rioting continued for some days. The mob was finally held under control and dispersed by "an increased police force and one or two War Department lorries of soldiers in full fighting order, but not before a number of unlucky Negroes had been chased by angry crowds, to find sanctuary just in time, either in a house, or behind the horses of mounted police." Black men who lived in Cardiff at the time said later that during the riots they were compelled to stay in their houses behind boarded windows and barred doors.

The authorities came to the conclusion that these racial outbreaks were engineered by "a relatively small number of persons." It was even stated that a number of men "were deliberately sent into the town for this purpose." That may or may not have been so but the fact of the matter was that white residents joined in eagerly in the fray and some watched with glee while blacks were being beaten. Many of them could not even explain how the trouble started when questioned. Their comments, again, were predictable: "Why should these colored men be able to get work when it is refused us?" "Kill the bastards," or "Lynch the niggers." Always, the black man was hunted; and when he was spotted and unearthed, the mob rushed at him and would savage him.

Official records prove that claims for damage, usually of property, as a result of these race riots cost the City Corporation of Cardiff approximately £4,000, including solicitors' fees.

These riots marked the beginning of hard times for blacks living in Britain; and taught them, too, that they were not exempt from mob rule in this "justice-loving little island," as Anglo-Indian Cedric Dover observed. Already in Cardiff there were fifteen hundred blacks unemployed. About this state of affairs Michael Banton wrote:

> It remains only to observe that relations between whites and coloured men in this country appear to have reached their nadir of disharmony in the inter-war period. Unemployment in the seaports was largely responsible for this; but the racialist doctrine of earlier years may have sharpened the conflict and canalized local resentment.

The situation was deteriorating so fast that some blacks from the Colonies who remained in England took the hint from certain whites and asked the British government to repatriate them. Such a move was looked upon with favor by the English, who actually tried to accelerate matters—largely because of the old fear of racial intermixing. In fact, the *Western Mail* took up the cry immediately. During the Cardiff riots it wrote, June 13:

> The Government ought to declare it to be part of the national policy that this country is not to be regarded as an emigration field, that no more immigrants (as distinguished from visitors) can be admitted, and that immigrants must return whence they came. This must apply to black men from the British West Indies as well as from the United States. In our own country the tolerance which is exhibited towards the problem [of mixture] is due not to far-fetched ideas of racial equality, but to slackness.

Racial attitudes among the British had been very different during the war years. A young clergyman who was in Cardiff at that time, told this story:

> A weak heart kept me from active service, and I was attached to a Labour Exchange in Cardiff. Things were bad then: submarines had turned the sea into a sailor's grave. Just then they transferred two hundred men from the coloured troops in Mesopotamia to work in the Merchant Marine. Jolly nice chaps they were: they all passed through my hands. It was a time of national crisis; and they were jolly brave those coloured sailors. They brought food to Cardiff at the greatest risk of their lives.

After the war the question of repatriation for blacks living in Cardiff proved a difficult one, "partly owing to family obligations and partly to the strong protests of the boarding-house keepers to whom coloured men were in an advanced state of indebtedness." Since the Armistice and the loss of their war-work, blacks had been given food and lodgings by their landlords with the expectation that the government would pay the debts of the unemployed men or help solve their problems. Fearing that they might not receive the money owing them by their lodgers, the boarding-house keepers threatened to eject them. This caused alarm to the black men themselves as well as to the authorities. The position was partially settled by an official grant of money to help out the boarding-house keepers, and by the repatriation of those men who had not been able to to establish domicile in Britain.

Between the years 1919–1938 blacks in Cardiff lived in more distressing conditions than elsewhere in the country, although blacks in every city were to feel the depression years more severely than did whites. An old timer who was in Manchester then reflected:

> Things were hard for we people. After that war plenty of coloured people start to come to Manchester. Them days John Bull will shoot you if he see you with him woman. They like their woman pass God self.

In 1921, according to a comparative study of racial attitudes in England conducted by American sociologist R. T. Lapiere, only 4 percent of the population could claim to be without prejudice. In France the figure was 67 percent.

The very bad race relations in Cardiff during the inter-war years were aggravated by the depression in the shipping industry. The British merchant fleet of out-of-date ships had to face fierce and highly subsidized foreign competition "for fewer and fewer freights, with diminishing profits, and unemployment fluctuating always around a high level," noted Kenneth Little, who further stated that there was consequently bitter competition between white and black seamen for the reduced number of jobs available. The shipping depression coincided with a world trade slump which meant that unemployed seamen in the seaports could not migrate to other areas in search of work. One possible outlet, the South Wales coalfields, in which some blacks had worked previously, were "themselves suffering an unparalleled state of inactivity."

Since the shipping trade was at such a low ebb shipowners who wanted to remain in business decided that they had to keep labor costs to the minimum. They signed on black firemen and stokers—provided that it could be done on board ship—at rates lower than for white seamen. Consequently, black seamen domiciled in Britain were placed at a definite disadvantage. On the one hand their scale of pay by National Maritime rates from all United Kingdom ports meant "that their labour found no more favour in the eyes of shipowners and employers than that of the white sailor." On the other hand, they were viewed by the white unions not as a segment of the working class trying to earn a living in the same way as white union members, but as the representatives of a completely different and competitive category, which "directly or indirectly was responsible for keeping white seamen out of work, and forcing down their standards of living." This attitude has stayed with British trade unions throughout the years although it has gradually been losing support.

The unions fought the issue both inside and outside Parliament as early as February, 1919, and throughout the years of the depression. The basis for debate was always the same! There were increasing numbers of alien workers employed in the shipping industry and British seamen were being displaced by black crews. This point was illustrated by Neil Maclean, M.P., who complained that the British crew of the Brocklebank liner *Malancha* had been paid off and an Asiatic one signed on, with the Asiatic chief cook getting £5 a month while the British one had been getting £20 a month and the rates of pay for the rest of the Asiatic crew correspondingly lower than that of the original white crew.

Various legislative measures were suggested for putting the matter right. For instance, more British seamen could be employed or the wages of black seamen increased. The government could also have replied to the unions and other critics that the number of alien seamen employed was very small since the greater part, although non-European and not born in Britain, was British, born on British possessions in the colonies. Its spokesmen in the House could have stated plainly that it was not the policy of the British government to practice racial discrimination. But the government, taking the view that black seamen were in fact a threat to white labor, introduced tough legislation which crippled the employment chances of black seamen. This legislation was the Aliens Order of 1920, and, more significant, the Special Restriction (Coloured Alien Seamen) Order of 1925, which was an application of the older Aliens Restriction Act of 1914.

The Special Registration (Coloured Alien Seamen) Order of 1925 had wider and more specific powers than the previous one which gave the police power to impose restrictions on aliens, arrest them without warrant, and shut certain clubs and restaurants. Although the main function of the 1925 order was to check the influx of alien seamen into the country, its effect was to put black alien seamen in the same category as other aliens and "obliged them to register in accordance with provisions made under the 1920 Order."

The result of all these provisions was that all black seamen, particularly those based in Cardiff, were obliged, irrespective of nationality and domicile, to register with the police. This stipulation meant that not only aliens but in Cardiff, all black individuals who wanted to establish domicile in Britain and prove their nationality had to carry registration cards. In some cases, therefore, a white alien who had been allowed into the country before 1925 and had in his possession a registration certificate from the police was better off than a black subject who was unable to show documentary proof of his identity; in fact, many could not because they came from parts of Africa where there was at the time no system of registration. Those who needed passports found themselves at the mercy of biased examiners. Their applications were usually turned down. The outcome was that they were classed as aliens, and were not granted certificates until they could prove that they had resided in the country before 1925 when the Order was issued. As aliens, they could then be deported at any time.

Most of the blacks in Cardiff possessed British passports, birth certificates, army and naval demobilization papers from the 1914 war, or other documentary evidence of nationality. The police action in requiring them to register as aliens was obviously a false interpretation of the Act. As Dr. Little wrote: "Satisfied, however, in their own minds that these enactments automatically made an alien of every coloured seaman in Cardiff, they [the police] went zealously to work." Blacks were threatened and victimized indiscriminately, and "threats of arrest and imprisonment were not uncommon if a man refused to deliver his passport on demand." One seaman whose passport had been seized refused to accept an aliens card. He was warned that he would be arrested if he refused to accept it; and when he asked how this could be done, he was told that since he was now without a passport, a continuous certificate of discharge, or an identity card—all of which were in the hands of the police—it would be easy to arrest him outside the police station for being "on British territory without the necessary authority." West Indians in Cardiff were tricked by police who told them that the Acts were not intended for them at all, but rather the Arabs. This deliberate lie gave them an illusion of security, and many registered without protest. Others thought that registration was a mere formality which every seaman was obliged to go through and were tricked into signing. So trusting were these black men and so convinced that the signing of registration certificates did not affect their status as British subjects that some of them who had escaped the notice of the police "voluntarily registered themselves as aliens in order to observe what they thought to be the requirements of the law."

A member of Parliament from Cardiff, Captain Evans, exposed some of these discrepancies in the House of Commons. He declared that through no fault of their own, blacks had now no means of asserting their British nationality. The home secretary's reply did not ease the plight of blacks in Cardiff. He stated that "where passports were out of date or otherwise invalid, the holder had been advised to register in the absence of satisfactory proof of his identity and nationality." He further declared that discharge books were unacceptable, as entries in them were based on facts given by the holder himself. The home secretary also ruled that the marking of registration certificates with the word "seaman" should be enough to distinguish those who held them from persons holding certificates issued under the ordinary provisions of the Aliens Order.

This state of affairs prevailed for several years and was to keep the black British seaman almost permanently out of work. In fact, as the situation of the British shipping industry deteriorated in the years of depression—so did the black man face starving poverty in the British seaport towns and elsewhere in the British Isles. In an *Investigation of Coloured Colonial Seamen in Cardiff* made in April, 1935 by George W. Brown M.A., LL.B., a black American, for the League of Coloured Peoples, these observations were made:

> The decision to employ white British labour exclusively in the shipping industry of Great Britain was not arrived at suddenly or with undue haste. It was the outcome of a mature consideration of the trend of certain events which were ultimately connected with the shipping industry. The Alien Order of 1920, and the Special Restriction (Coloured Alien Seamen) Order 1925, first focused the attention of the public on this organised attempt to displace coloured seamen in favour of white. . . . Unfortunately for the Trade Unions, there were about 3,000 coloured seamen residing in Cardiff who were members of the Trade Unions and their rightful claims to employment could not be easily ignored. The plan of having these men registered as Aliens was devised and put into operation by legislative measures enacted through the influence of the Trade Unions and other labour organisations.
>
> . . . .
>
> As roughly 80 percent of the coloured men have been on the dole, seventy per cent of the year 1934–1935 (April–April), their home life is reduced to a bare subsistence level. The minimum comfort for women and children is obviously lacking in too many instances. A balanced diet is, and in a few cases over four years has been, absolutely impossible. . . .

George Brown's report revealed a scandalous state of affairs and, as English writer David Vaughan observed, it accused "the authorities of willful misapplication of the Alien Order, 1920, and the Special Restriction (Coloured Alien Seamen) Order, 1925. Apparently all colored men were classified as aliens in spite of indisputable evidence of British nationality. The police and the shipowners had the support of the trade unions in this policy."

Blacks were affected in a much deeper way. Color prejudice was practiced not only in employment. It almost entirely prevented social development and cultural advancement. Even church attendance was being denied to black families. Families with black fathers, white mothers, and their children were unwelcome in churches. "From families on all sides," declared George Brown, "one hears declarations of a similar indifference to the churches and missions in the Bay."

The children of black-white unions were the ones to suffer most. Brown claimed that there were no prospects for absorption of these children in "the responsible grooves of the general social order." Secondary education and employment in industry or apprenticeship to trades were denied them. The feeling of the white community was that they were a problem and consequently they restricted and rejected the "half-castes," as they labeled the children of mixed marriages. The League of Coloured Peoples reported this attitude in its comment on current affairs in the January–March, 1936, issue of *The Keys:*

> In a previous issue we appealed for assistance in placing the coloured youth in Cardiff, who are growing up without opportunities for work. The average employer would much sooner have an alien employee than a coloured British one. So of course it is with hotels and landladies offering apartments. Here is another of many problems for lovers of justice to tackle.

Feeling ran so high among the white race supremacists at that time that a Cardiff public official called for legislation to "put a stop to the breeding of such children." Daughters of mixed marriages fared many times worse than sons. They were not even accepted as menials in domestic service, with the result that they were exploited, and some fell into a life of prostitution.

> But [observed George Brown] one wonders why such meagre social opportunities, and cultural facilities do not foster more drinking, rampant gambling, and unrestrained prostitution. These social activities are to be found in every industrial centre, depression or no depression, coloured or non-coloured. Cardiff is far from being an exception. As it now stands, it is decidedly an uninspiring environment for an ever-increasing child population. These general conditions can, and should be improved.

This hope was not to be realized for many generations, and the process has been a slow, grinding, uphill one. To begin with, however, George Brown summarized his report:

If it is criminal and anti-social to tax out of existence a worthwhile enterprise, or ruthlessly to exterminate a helpless community in war, how shall a purposeful policy to drive some 3,000 wage earners out of their sole industry, be characterised? As this report goes to print, CARDIFF is doing just that!

He continued with an indictment of British racial behavior:

Thus a new monument to economic ignorance and racial animosity rises in England. Fresh, vigorous, and dynamic, abundantly nourished by the poisons of the depressions, this tower threatens all intelligent attitudes, and submerges the vital problems still unsettled among shipping labourers. Envious brutality is ever that way. It has recruited as fellow-artisans in this hostile construction, some strange bed-fellows. The Trade Union, the Police and the Shipowners appear to co-operate smoothly in barring coloured Colonial Seamen from signing on ships in Cardiff. The legislative history of this policy has been traced chronologically, and due emphasis placed upon the stipulation to carry only British Seamen which accompanied the two million pound grant to the hard hit shipping industry. These plans and methods were never unknown to the coloured seamen nor did they pass unchallenged by them. Tenseness increased tenseness until on April 16, 1935, a riot broke out at the Cardiff Docks over the flagrant discriminatory actions of a labour delegation in refusing the Chief Engineer of the *S.S. Ethel Radcliffe* the right to repick his coloured crew for a voyage.

Brown accused the British of ingratitude, reminding them that "many of them [blacks] had given of their youth and labour to the industrial and military service of this great nation, and they suffer keenly in their deep sensitive souls, this unmerited assault."

The recommendations, as phrased in his report to The League of Coloured Peoples, were as follows:

(a) That, not one effort be withheld to secure to the Coloured Colonial Seamen in Cardiff, their full and just rights, in the British Shipping Industry as loyal subjects and citizens of the British Empire.

(b) That direct measures be taken to remove immediately such seamen from the wrongful and illegal classification as ALIENS; and that their rightful status and privileges as British subjects be instantly restored.

(c) That direct measures be taken to induce the Trade Union to cease its opposition to coloured seamen sailing on British ships. That all friends of these British workers, the forces of public opinion and the laws of the land be exerted to their fullest capacity in persuading the National Union of Seamen, and its Secretary, Mr. George Reed, to assist in signing Coloured British Seaman on British ships.

(d) That a publicity campaign presenting the facts of the Cardiff situation in their true analysis be released immediately, in order that the public of Cardiff, rich and ignorant, poor and learned, may be honestly apprised of its inescapable responsibility in creating good will and mutual respect among all units of itself for itself. It is well recognised that such social animosities depend not upon factual, biological or cultural differences, but upon individual and community attitudes, not inherited, but consciously imposed or acquired. Thus the workmen of Cardiff must be enlisted as opponents to prejudice in themselves, in their mutual labour activities, and in their common community.

(e) That the seamen's situation in Cardiff be viewed as a feature in the largely domestic and interesting settlements of Tiger Bay, and that cultural and outdoor projects be organised for the children during this summer.

(f) That the League of Coloured Peoples make a thorough Social–Economic Investigation of the indigent problem among Coloured Colonial Seamen in Cardiff.

(g) That the League take the lead in conversations, looking to the creation of some institution or institutions for the development of the children into productive and useful citizens, and the permanent relief of the Cardiff Coloured Community.

These recommendations were quite comprehensive but the league's activities in the Cardiff affair went even further. Dr. Harold Moody got to work straight-away. He contacted the Unemployment Branch of the Board of Trade, and visited Cardiff in order to make strong on-the-spot representations to the authorities. The government set in motion an inquiry into the question of naturalization of the seamen affected. This was brought to the notice of Captain Arthur Evans, member of Parliament for Cardiff, and the details of twelve cases were forwarded by him to the home secretary, who cancelled the alien registration of the men and restored their British national status. It was estimated at this time that there were well over fifteen hundred men who had been forced to carry the seamen's alien registration card around with them and so had been barred from employment on British ships. That was why on June 11, 1936, for example, out of a total of 690 unemployed firemen on the Cardiff Docks Register, 599 were black.

Moody and the league worked tirelessly "to rectify those gross injustices." Discussions were held with Mr. W. R. Spence and other officials of the National Seamen's Union, with Sir Vernon Thomson, chief of the Shipping Subsidy, with Commissioner Lamb of the Salvation Army.

Memoranda were presented to the British Shipping Federation and Mr. G. H. Hall, M.P. (later Viscount Hall); and many questions were asked in the House of Commons. Every effort was made to bring these matters to the attention of the highest authorities in the land and to the British public.

Dr. Moody worked with thoroughness and speed, as the following example will show. On July 8, 1935, he got an urgent telephone call from Cardiff informing him that the officers of *S.S. Eskdalegate*, which was due to sail on Friday of that week, had refused point blank to sign on five Jamaicans, although they had been regularly employed on that ship. He immediately contacted Turnbull, Scott and Company, the owners of the ship, and Sir Vernon Thomson, of the Tramp Shipping Subsidy Committee. The shipowners did not deny that the men had not been signed on. Sir Vernon then assured Dr. Moody that if the men were Jamaicans they would be allowed to join the ship. This fact was proved beyond doubt and the five Jamaicans were re-engaged and sailed.

At that time, 1935–37, the term "Live Register" was used to indicate the active register which had listed on it the names of black and Asiatic seamen either ashore or at sea at the time the register was taken. Some sixteen hundred names which were on it were removed, which was a step in the right direction. Many of these blacks became naturalized British subjects while the greater proportion had their national status restored to them.

The unions continually opposed moves to restore national status to black seamen so that they could work on British ships. Dr. Little made this observation: "From continuous complaints of the unions' spokesmen in the House, and from official and unofficial attacks on the coloured seamen outside, it is difficult to believe that the Aliens Order and its aftermath did not have at least the passive support of the white organizations." The League of Coloured Peoples, in one of its investigations, also indicted the unions, especially the National Union of Seamen: "The most powerful of British Trade Unions is opposed to the employment of coloured seamen."

This discrimination was by no means restricted to Cardiff. Black seamen in Manchester, Liverpool, South Shields, and London felt the blow, though not with such force. In 1937, for instance, nearly all ships leaving the Port of London refused to employ black seamen. The result was that five hundred black seamen settled in London were persistently refused employment, and they and their dependents had no alternative but to live on public assistance. The Colonial Seamen's Association in London tried hard to fight this discrimination but its efforts proved relatively fruitless. Then came World War II. The black man's economic condition took a turn for the better. Competition for jobs between black and white no longer existed but discrimination persisted. By that time, in Liverpool, as elsewhere in Britain, there was a widespread view that the black man was a being of low social status, little skill, and dubious morals. This belief took root because of the adverse publicity given in the newspapers to particular instances of black misdemeanors and, as British sociologist Anthony Richmond observed, "from well-meaning social workers and the like who failed to diagnose certain behaviour and conditions of life as the product of a poor environment rather than inherited defects in the Negro himself."

While these hardships were being suffered by the black population in Britain in the years between the two world wars, the churches played a silent indifferent part. The president of The League of Coloured People was a devout Christian and had advocated Christianity to all black people in Britain as the only way of bringing the races together. Talking about that, Dr. Moody sadly observed:

> I have tried, so far without avail, to awaken the Christian conscience of our organised religion to tackle the human problem of this Coloured Cardiff population. Here is a big opportunity for rendering practical Christian service. I am not asking any Christian Church to go down to Cardiff and dole out money. This would provide no solution to the problem as I see it, nor do I think it would be acceptable to my fellow countrymen there, who, I am glad to say, notwithstanding their poverty, still have some pride left. Neither am I asking anyone to go down to preach the Gospel and tell men "If you join my church I will get you a job." This brings Christianity into ridicule. But I am asserting that, in my opinion, it is an urgent duty of the Christian Church to make a real study of the Spiritual, Social and Economic condition of the Coloured People in this country in conjunction with an organisation like the League of Coloured Peoples with a view to providing an effective solution for the problem of race. The Kingdom of God cannot come on earth until our prayers are more sincere.

The various black seamen's organizations were not powerful enough to cause a drastic change in the discriminatory practices of the shipping companies. The home secretary had restored the national status of black seamen born in the colonies, but the government did not exhibit a general sensitivity to the problems of this segment of the British population or an awareness of the need for legislation to ease them. When conditions were investigated, the seamier, more sensational aspects were highlighted, especially in the press, and this caused tensions to mount on both sides. The investigation by Captain F. A. Richardson is a case in point.

This report was based on a survey conducted by a joint committee of the British Social Hygiene Council and the British Council for the Welfare of the Mercantile Marine in 1935. The captain was intent on producing as graphic a picture as possible of the social ills, lack of amenities, underemployment and destitution common to all contemporary ports, so he chose Cardiff. However, he focussed all his attention on Cardiff's black population, looking at them as a special social problem. His comments on hybridization, as well as disease, caused feelings to run high in Cardiff's white population, already antagonistic to its "alien" groups. The report was quoted by the *Western Mail* and the *South Wales Echo* of July 8, 1935:

> Cardiff has before it a social problem that cannot as yet be solved. Hundreds of Arabs and other coloured seamen have settled in the city. . . . They construct their own places of worship in ramshackle sheds behind their lodging houses, and they mate with the type of women who are willing to accept them because there are none of their own kind to be had. . . . Morality and cleanliness are as much matters of geography as they are dependent on circumstances. The coloured men who have come to dwell in our cities are being made to adopt a standard of civilization they cannot be expected to understand. They are not imbued with moral codes similar to our own, and they have not assimilated our conventions of life. They come into intimate contact with white women, principally those who unfortunately are of loose moral character, with the result that a half-caste population is brought into the world. . . . The half-caste girl is characteristically disinclined to discipline and routine work, and efforts made to encourage and train her have mostly met with failure. By nature and environment, and by the handicaps of colour and common prejudice, these girls have very little chance but to sink to an even lower level.

Statements in Captain Richardson's report about tuberculosis and infant mortality among black people served to inflame matters further. The *Western Mail* reported:

> The problem of the coloured population in our seaport towns demands immediate Government action. Not only the social amenities of the white man's country, but the best interests of the coloured people themselves are in issue.
>
> There is no reason for sentimentality in this matter. Let him who pleads the justice of the coloured man's settlement among us read the report's references to venereal disease and the heavy toll of tuberculosis among our guests. Many of them are citizens of the British Empire; many did fine work in the war. Neither of these considerations should blind us to the plain fact that they do not belong to the social system we have evolved in these islands. Repatriation may involve hardships, and it is our obligation to make it easy for them to return to their homelands, where we will continue to carry the "white man's burden." We can no longer tolerate that burden on our doorstep.

This view was not allowed to go unchallenged. With the controversy over "alien seamen" raging, this attack met with the indignation of the black community of Cardiff. The result was that the uproar died down as quickly as it had arisen; but not before several requests were made by white citizens for an enquiry into the problem of the ports. The government appeared to be quite unconcerned about these pleas.

Not all whites showed hatred for the black community. Several white residents in the dockside areas wrote letters condemning Captain Richardson's report as "misleading," and pointed out its lack of objectivity. In defending himself Captain Richardson said that his aim in the report had been to point out "the serious defects in the social amenities of the district." In a reply in the *Western Mail* of July 10, 1935, he wrote:

> From the Great Western Railway bridge in Bute Street to the waters of Penarth flats there is no form of diversion other than that provided by the Missions. True, there is a cinema which is shewn in the Wesleyan Chapel, but beyond this there does not appear to be any legitimate form of diversion, and there certainly appears to be prejudice in the minds of those dwelling on the city side of the Great Western Railway bridge against members of the coloured fraternity taking their normal places in the cinemas of the city. . . . Therefore, we have this situation of hundreds of men, women and probably worst of all their children being unable to enjoy the normal facilities of everyday life. Their provision of two or three swings and a sandpit in Loudoun Square does not appear to be an adequate means to this end.

It was Richardson's report and the injustices of the Shipping Act, as they became widely known, which caused "a mild revulsion in popular attitudes towards the coloured people," as Dr. Kenneth Little put it. People who visited the black community then said that the black people exhibited stoic calm, were patient and peaceful in these difficulties. A *Daily Express* correspondent reported in his paper in much stronger language about the lack of opportunity and "the degree of colour prejudice which still prevailed in the city." Nevertheless the black population enjoyed a kind of anonymity which somewhat averted the pressure of prejudice. This was due in no small part to the labors of the League of Coloured Peoples in fighting prejudice, no matter where or how insignificant it was. In a report written after the league had been in existence for six years, President Harold Moody traced conditions from the beginning:

> This League was brought into being because of the acute and growing nature of the Colour Problem in England.
>
> When we took up our work it was almost impossible to obtain admission in any hospital in London for a coloured girl who desired to train as a nurse. We have overcome this slightly but the position still stands as indicated by the Colonial Office in reply to our enquiry. "I have written to eighteen Voluntary hospitals both in London and the Provinces, and they all say that they cannot take coloured probationers at present." It therefore remains a fact that our large voluntary hospitals refuse to take as probationers respectable and cultured British citizens merely because they are coloured.
>
> The same state of things obtains with regards to the medical student. One man who studied at Cambridge and had to finish his course in London, unsuccessfully tried half a dozen London Hospitals before coming to me when I was able to fix him up.
>
> In addition I must add that the working class coloured population is at present having a terrible time in this land of the brave and free—they and their children, some ten thousand, are forced to live in conditions such that it is difficult to know how they manage to earn a decent and honest living; they are condemned to conditions of life which should make the moral Englishman blush with shame. . . . We have done a great deal during the past six years to help break down these barriers and remove such horrible blots. . . . In spite of all this we have only just touched the fringe of the matter and there still remains a tremendous lot to be done.

Dr. Moody approached the task with optimism based on his Christian belief in the innate goodness in man. Yet he faced the facts of the situation as he saw them;

> We have proved by many facts and incidents which we have recorded that colour prejudice does exist in this country to a marked degree. We have also proved that the Englishman at his best is aware and ashamed of this fact. He has a keen sense of justice to which one

> can always appeal with confidence. He is prepared to listen to anyone, no matter whence he comes, who is transparently honest, moderate in his views, and genuinely anxious to study the best traditions of English life and character.

The question of black children born in Britain still continued to present a nagging problem and one difficult for the British to resolve. These children seemed to suffer no special difficulties while at school, but on leaving school all avenues of employment and further education were suddenly closed to them. The number of black children leaving school annually before World War II was a mere two hundred, yet, said Dr. Moody, in a population of fifty million they constituted a problem. This certainly did not speak well for the British "keen sense of justice."

When these children left school they experienced very severe difficulties in obtaining suitable work. Neither government nor welfare organizations had much success in solving the problem. The fact that the children were the offspring of white and black caused feeling to get out of hand. There were outcries in some quarters against the "evil of half-caste children in our ports," and the more lurid newspapers published overdrawn articles highlighting the worst aspects.

To tackle the problem a special organizing committee was appointed by the league in 1935, with representatives of other interested organizations. As a result, a National Council was formed with "justifiable hopes of solving this problem." But the league had to face bigotry and ignorance of the worst sort. The committee noted:

> One of the fantastic projects put forward as a solution to the problem was the dumping of these children in their fathers' countries of origin in spite of the fact that in these countries these children would find themselves, in view of their English birth and education, utter foreigners without, in most cases, any ties of family, their parents having been in England for twenty or thirty years. The League believes that the solution of this problem should be found here, in England, or in such a manner that it would involve no unjust hardship on these children.

And there due to the indifference of the authorities, the matter was allowed to remain and lie forgotten.

BIBLIOGRAPHY TO CHAPTER ELEVEN

Brown, George W. "Investigation of Coloured Colonial Seamen in Cardiff. April 13–20, 1935." *The Keys.* (London: July-September, 1935).

"The Coloured Applicant." *The Keys.* (London: January-March, 1936).

The Keys. (London: January-March, 1937).

Lapiere, R. T. "Race Prejudice: France and England." *Social Forces* VII. Quoted in *Negro Yearbook*, 1931–32.

The League of Coloured Peoples. *Seventh Annual Report, 1937-38.* London: March 11, 1938.

Little, Kenneth. *Negroes in Bitain.* London: 1948.

Western Mail and South Wales Echo. July 7, 8, and 10, 1935.

CHAPTER XII

ENTERTAINERS AND WORLD WAR II

So far, this examination of the plight of black people in Britain during the two world wars and the years between has dealt only with seamen and ex-servicemen, settlers and students. But the picture is incomplete for there was a small group of professional men, musicians and actors, who made England their home. Apart from the professional men, mainly doctors, the others scraped a living as best they could from the restricted world of entertainment. They were several expatriate black Americans who had come over with shows at the turn of the century and in the 1920s, enjoyed a measure of success, and remained in Britain. In British films, which had not yet reached a high level of development, blacks played bit parts—Africans dressed in loin cloths and brandishing spears. The only two blacks who made any impact as film actors in Britain in the thirties were Paul Robeson and Guyanese Robert Adams. Writing about this, English film critic and authority Peter Noble said: "Between them they have appeared in about a dozen interesting films, though, unfortunately, opportunities for Negro screen acting occur all too rarely in British studios." What mattered at that time was something of greater significance; as Peter Noble observed:

> It is more than likely that the average Englishman, while holding no particular prejudice against the Negro as an individual, might have certain qualms about allowing a coloured man to marry into his family, and this attitude has been engendered to a great extent by the films he goes to see. And because more than 80 per cent of these films are of Hollywood origin, it may be generally agreed that his prejudices are a result of the anti-Negro bias reflected in American movies.

Many British cinemagoers during those years did indeed regard the black man as "a buffoon and clown" and thought of black actors usually in terms of Rochester, Sleep'n Eat, Rastus, Bill Robinson, Stepin Fetchit, Sambo and Alexander and Mose. Even so, there was a feeling of sympathy, bordering on tolerance, for the black underdog as depicted in films. Some British films helped to spread this more enlightened racial attitude and one actor in particular, Paul Robeson, "made great contributions here [Britain] to a new understanding of the life and problems of coloured people everywhere."

From the early years Paul Robeson was held in high esteem in Britain; so much so that he made his home there, especially after he had been pilloried by the U.S. government for his political beliefs. His greatest success was in Britain; especially the films he made during the years 1935–39. "Every one of those films," wrote Peter Noble, "portrayed the Negro as the dignified central character." Each depicted Robeson against the background of normal British social life, accepted as a part of the English community. Even so, Robeson was to feel the humiliation of race prejudice in the very country to which he proudly boasted that he brought "new understanding of the life and problems of the coloured people everywhere." In 1930 when he played Othello, with the English actress Peggy Ashcroft as Desdemona, there was immense agitation; one woman wrote to a newspaper: "I cannot stomach the idea of a coloured man playing opposite to a woman of my own race, and feel sure there are many who will share my views though I bow to the fact that Paul Robeson is a great artist." Many men and women of her race did suffer agonies watching Robeson kiss Peggy Ashcroft. It was a bitter pill to swallow, and from records of the time it appears that the most hysterical outcries came from white Americans.

Although in the depression years the racial problem was largely economic, the miscegenation issue was, as usual, important. Robeson with Peggy Ashcroft on stage in *Othello* served to give the sex angle greater prominence. Writer Stephen Black lamented:

> For many years white colonials have shuddered at witnessing repulsive Ethiopians intimately, almost maritally consorting with beautiful British girls in streets, in restaurants, in theatres, in night clubs, lodging houses and hotels. There was no concealment of the affectionate attitude of a certain type of white female towards the brown and yellow male.

In fact, it was claimed that black troops were prevented from taking part in the coronation of George V because great attention had been paid to the muscular-looking black soldiers by English women of all classes during the coronation of his father, Edward VII. The same thing happened when contingents of West Indian soldiers arrived in Britain during World War II. At the Wembley exhibition in 1925 when several Africans were on show at an African village, white women would congregate daily around "the great, strong, muscular fellows." These Africans were barred from touring London on their own for fear that English women would "capture" them.

In London's Soho district many out-of-work black men hung about sleazy coffee houses and broken-down cafes waiting for their white prostitute girl friends. These girls would give them money and keep them. It was a well-known saying that but for white women many a black would starve to death in Britain.

In films and on the English stage black actors and actresses in the years between the two world wars could find only bit parts as menials or African tribesmen; as singers, dancers and musicians, however, they were considered to have natural talent and consequently, they could find bookings in the music halls of Britain. In fact, from the latter years of the nineteenth century many black entertainers from America remained in Britain and made names for themselves. Best known and most successful among the early ones were Ed Wallace, Connie Smith, Norris Smith, Ike Hatch, John Payne, and Turner Layton of Layton and Johnson fame. In the thirties came former Blackbirds singer Elizabeth Welch and cabaret artist Adelaide Hall. Those two were well-established and still move in exclusive circles in English society. Another black singer and actor who won fame in Britain during World War II and after was the late Edric Connor of Trinidad.

The first three mentioned (Ed Wallace, Connie Smith and Norris Smith) became firm friends, and for several years they met every Thursday afternoon at Ed Wallace's home in Kensington Lane, Vauxhall, in southeast London. They lived for over half a century in Britain. Ed Wallace, who was born in 1871 in Knoxville, Tennessee, left America in 1899 for Britain. His first appearance there was at London's Middlesex Theatre as a member of the Old Plantation Trio, billed as Novelty Instrumentalists.

The other two partners were Harry Martinett and Ed Roddy. Ed Wallace played alto saxophone, doubling on banjo and cornet. They were so successful that they were booked for a provincial tour. Ed Wallace never looked back after that. He did not reach the fabulous heights which his older black compatriots, Jim and George Bohee, had attained in the earlier years in Victorian England, but even in the lean years of the depression he was seldom out of work.

The same thing could be said of Brooklyn-born Connie Smith. A sort of black Fanny Brice, with a soothing lisp in her Brooklynese voice, she left New York in 1894 when she was seventeen to play the capitals of Europe in Conningham & Dockstader's show *The South Before The War And After*. She joined Augustus Smith of Philadelphia, and they formed a song-and-dance team calling themselves Smith & Johnson. They toured Germany and Scandinavia until Conningham left them stranded in Denmark where they got married. They managed to reach Hull, England, and were booked at the Alhambra Theatre. After a couple of engagements at the Stoll and Moss theatre circuits at the City Varieties Theatre, Leeds, and at the Old Gaiety in Birmingham, the couple moved down to London. There they obtained steady work with the theatrical circuits—Moss, Stoll, McNaughton and William Broadhead. In those days, Connie Smith once said, "We were well known in the provinces. When you were a success with an impresario he booked you up for as long as three years." Smith and Johnson were the most popular song and dance team in Britain. Sickness caused Augustus Smith to retire and soon afterwards he died. Connie Smith was one of the oldest black American artists in show-business. In her very late years she branched off as a straight actress and won much renown in the English theatre. One of her best roles was that of the sorceress, Tituba, in Arthur Miller's play *The Crucible* which ran at the Royal Court Theatre in London in 1955. She died in 1970.

Norris Smith, too, who was born in Columbia, Missouri, in 1881, escaped the humiliating poverty which was the expectation of most blacks in England up to World War II. It was three years after the turn of this century that Norris Smith arrived in Britain to appear in *In Dahomey* with Bert Williams (the immortal comedian whom Norris Smith maintained "was the greatest of all time") and George Walker at London's Shaftesbury Theatre. From London, Norris Smith went to the European continent then returned to America where he toured on the Pantages circuit. Then in November, 1911, he sailed from Hoboken to London as a member of the Four Black Diamonds.

From that time on Norris Smith made Britain his home and show-business his business. He retired in 1954 after appearing in a television play called *Halcyon Days* written especially for him by American actor-playwright Jimmy Dyrenforth. His success in Britain and Europe reached heights which were known to very few black artists at the time. He met and consorted with the British aristocracy and the stars of showbusiness. His first association with royalty was when he sang spirituals for King Edward VII at a Buckingham Palace private party. The young Prince David (later the Duke of Windsor) was nine years old at the time. Norris Smith was to form a lasting friendship with him. One of the high spots in his career was when he understudied Paul Robeson in 1928 in *Showboat* at the Theatre Royal, Drury Lane. Up till his death in 1969 at eighty-eight Norris Smith lived in north London with his English wife, the former Alice McPhearson, sister of the first Labour member of Parliament for Preston, Lancashire. He loved to show friends who visited him signed pictures from those he had known; Peg Leg Bates, Billy Daniels, Leigh Whipper, and the Duke and Duchess of Windsor. A man with wide experience, a deep natural chuckle, and a fund of anecdotes, Norris Smith liked to tell this story.

One night while he was appearing at the Casanova in Paris in 1934 the Prince of Wales sent a request asking him to sing "Old Man River." While he was singing, Michael Farmer, one of Gloria Swanson's former husbands who was occupying a nearby table with a woman companion, deliberately dropped the knives and forks on the floor with a loud clatter, causing Norris Smith to stop for a moment. For a second time Farmer dropped the cutlery. Norris Smith again stopped singing and eyed him icily. In the meantime Major-General Trotter, the Prince's equerry, drew himself up to his full height and walking to Farmer's table he bowed low and asked: "Do you mind remaining quiet while Mr. Smith sings his Royal Highness's favourite spiritual?" No further sound came from Farmer's table. After that, whenever the Prince of Wales visited the Casanova, he used to invite the black baritone to join the royal party.

Black entertainers, by the sheer magic of their talent, had opened white doors while the majority of their fellow blacks in Britain faced the dirty end of discrimination. Other blacks in the entertainment world in Britain who enjoyed privileges denied their brothers were Alabama-born baritone John Payne, for instance, who came to Britain in 1920, settled, and died there at the age of eighty. He was the protégé of Lady Cooke and gained prominence singing spirituals. His luxury flat in Regents Park was once a society meeting place for tea, cocktails, and soirées. When he retired at the outbreak of war in 1939 he moved to Cornwall where he gave piano and voice lessons until his death. One of his best friends was entertainer Mabel Mercer.

Although the age of the "Darling Black" had gone, there was one outstanding exception. He was cabaret star "Hutch" (Leslie Hutchinson). The Grenada-born singer who accompanied himself on piano was always to be seen mixing effortlessly in fashionable society. His lady loves were drawn exclusively from Debrett's *Peerage*, the publication which lists the family trees of British aristocracy. A friend of Noël Coward and many stage stars, he usually attended Coward's first nights with the Mountbattens and their party. Hutch, despite advancing years, had a perennial youthfulness and was still attracting the daughters and granddaughters of those titled ladies he once charmed in the thirties until his death in 1971.

Britain's ambivalent attitudes in racial matters were not able to stifle the growth of talent among its black population. In show business, in theatre, in boxing and in other sports, black talent has always been abundant.

As cricketers, blacks always led the field in Britain. Unfortunately, their popularity on the playing field did not extend to their everyday life among Britain's whites. Several made names for themselves with visiting West Indian teams, with English cricket leagues in the north of England, and later with county sides. Among the greatest in the years between the two world wars were pace bowlers E. A. "Manny" Martindale of Barbados; George Headley from Jamaica, described as the "black Bradman of cricket," and the brilliant fielder, fast bowler and batsman Learie Constantine. In Britain, legends have grown around them and around several other black cricketers like the late Sir Frank Worrell and the greatest all-rounder of all time, Gary Sobers, who has captained Nottinghamshire, an English county side as well as West Indies and International teams.

Reginald Forsyte, London-born of a white mother and black father, won prominence in the nineteen thirties as a pianist-composer for such well-known melodies as "Serenade For A Wealthy Widow," "Strange Interlude," "Southern Holiday," which he wrote for Paul Whiteman, and "Angry Jungle." Just before the coronation of Queen Elizabeth II he received word from the queen herself that his ballad "Importune Me No More"—to words by a sixteenth century Elizabethan lyricist—had been officially accepted. It was used by the queen's own regiment and played at state functions and other court and military concerts, taking its place among the great English folk tunes.

One "half-caste" Negro of talent does not prove that others have the mental capacity of whites, English bigots claimed. Julian Huxley, the noted British scientist refuted this: "There is no objection to mixing the races. Some of the best stocks in the world are the result of racial mixture. The first generation of such a marriage is often superior in vigour."

Two other blacks of mixed parentage who, through their talent only, won positions of respect in England especially in the years before World War II were Avril Coleridge-Taylor, daughter of black composer Samuel Coleridge-Taylor, and Amanda Ira Aldridge, daughter of the celebrated tragedian Ira Aldridge.

Avril Coleridge-Taylor is known in Britain not only as the daughter of a famous composer but as a conductor-composer in her own right. She has written many pieces, for example, *Historical Episode* for chorus and orchestra, *In Memoriam RAF* for orchestra, and a Spiritual "I Can Face it Lord." She has conducted leading orchestras like the BBC Symphony Orchestra and Concert Orchestra and her own symphony orchestra of ninety players. She has also conducted an orchestra and singers several times at the Albert Hall in her father's best-known work, *Hiawatha*. She is still very active in musical circles in London and a few years ago formed a choir of twenty male and female voices called the New World singers. Sixteen of the singers were West Indians and four English.

Amanda Ira Aldridge, a singer and singing teacher almost until her death in 1956 at the age of eighty-nine, was quite a prominent personality in the musical world in England from early in the twentieth century. She sang on the concert platform for several years and later turned to teaching and composing under the pseudonym Montagu Ring. Her most famous pupils were Marian Anderson, Roland Hayes, and Paul Robeson. Miss Aldridge herself won a singing scholarship at the Royal College of Music in 1883 and studied under the Swedish Nightingale, Jenny Lind. Her most successful composition was probably *Three African Dances*. She composed love songs, suites, sambas, and light orchestral pieces. Among her life-long friends were Samuel Liddle, composer of the hymn "Abide With Me," Sir George Henschell, conductor-composer, and Arthur Dulay, conductor of the B.B.C. Bijou Orchestra. Another talented black who made his mark in Britain was Guyanese musician-conductor Rudolph Dunbar, who conducted the London Philharmonic Orchestra at the Royal Albert Hall during the war years.

While The League of Coloured Peoples was operating as a kind of middle-of-the-road black organization, there were other blacks with leftish militant views. They viewed the methods used by the league in its work against racial discrimination, to use the words of one of them, Dr. C. L. R. James, "with at most tolerance . . ." In the early part of 1937 these militant black journalists, writers, politicians, and others met together in London to form the International African Service Bureau, the forerunner of the Pan-African Federation. Principal officers of the International African Service Bureau during its period of formation were Wallace Johnson, the well-known West African trade unionist, general secretary; Chris Jones of Barbados, organising secretary; C. L. R. James, author and journalist, editorial director; Jomo Kenyatta, then the official representative in Britain of the Kikuyu Central Association, assistant secretary; George Padmore, Trinidad-born journalist and author, chairman; and T. R. Makonnen of Guyana, as honorary treasurer. It was mainly through the efforts of Makonnen that the International African Service Bureau and later the Pan-African Federation succeeded in establishing themselves and in launching the *International African Opinion*, a monthly paper of the International African Service Bureau. Makonnen, too, was responsible at a later date for starting *Pan-Africa*, a journal of African life and letters which became the foremost medium through which the ideology of Pan-Africanism was expounded throughout the black world.

The International African Service Bureau was a non-party organization. It owed no allegiance or affiliation to any political party, organization or group in Europe. Writing about the organization in his book *Pan-Africanism or Communism*, the late George Padmore said:

> The International African Service Bureau represented progressive and enlightened public opinion among Africans and people of African descent. It supported the demands of Africans, Asians and other colonial people for democratic rights, civil liberties and self-determination. Although active membership of the Bureau was confined to Africans and people of African descent regardless of nationality, political creed or religious faith who accepted its aims and abided by its constitution, Europeans and others who desired to demonstrate in a practical way their interest in African welfare were permitted to become associate members.

Through lectures, discussions and meetings—all open to the public—the bureau quickly attracted to its ranks a group of brilliant young black intellectuals in Britain. Many of them held Marxist views on economic and political matters. These black intellectuals were never members of the British Communist party, which at that time was engaged in a rush of activities trying to woo West Africians and West Indians to its ranks. It was not successful. Padmore explained this failure in these words:

> Politically minded Negroes despised the opportunism of the British Communists, who during the "Popular Front" period of the thirties, simply looked upon the Africans as "backward, unsophisticated tribesmen." Their legitimate grievances against Colonialism could be easily exploited in the interest of Soviet foreign policy, which at that time was seeking anti-fascist allies against the menace of Hitler's Germany.

So as not to frighten away those sections of the British ruling class which thought Hitler a bigger danger to the British Empire than Stalin, the British Communists adopted go-slow tactics when Africans demanded immediate self-government. Yet, at the same time, they were paying lip-service to Indian independence. Blacks were being bribed with reforms of little consequence borrowed from the Fabian Society and the Liberal Party—organizations which were far from being revolutionary. Turning away in disgust from the hypocritical Communists, leftish members of the International African Service Bureau oriented themselves to Pan-Africanism as an independent political expression of black aspirations for total national independence from white domination, whether it was Capitalist or Communist.

In 1944 in Manchester the International African Service Bureau merged into the Pan-African Federation, becoming the British section of the Pan-African Congress Movement formed by W. E. B. Du Bois in America in 1917, which had held its first Conference in Paris in

1919. The objects of the Pan-African Federation were to promote the well-being and unity of African peoples and peoples of African descent throughout the world; to demand self-determination and independence of African peoples and other subject races from the domination of powers claiming sovereignty and trusteeship over them; to secure equality of civil rights for African peoples and the total abolition of all forms of racial discrimination; and to strive for co-operation among African peoples and others who share the federation's aspirations.

Several issues relevant to black people were openly discussed in the federation's journal, *International African Opinion*—the methods and forms of organization to be adopted by colonial peoples; the tactics and strategy of the national freedom struggle; and the applicability of Gandhian non-violent, non-cooperative techniques to the African situation. The journal was edited by the distinguished Trinidadian historian C. L. R. James assisted by William Harrison, an erudite Afro-American Harvard scholar then doing post-graduate studies under Professor Harold Laski at the London School of Economics.

The Pan-African Federation also published several pamphlets dealing with specific colonial problems: *The West Indies Today; Hands off the Protectorates* (Bechuanaland, Basutoland, Swaziland); *Kenya, Land of Conflict; African Empires and Civilizations; The Negro in the Caribbean; White Man's Problem; The Native Problem in South Africa;* and *The Voice of Coloured Labour.*

Some of the leaders of the federation published specialist studies of the black colonial struggle. Among the best known were C. L. R. James' *The Black Jacobins* (an account of Toussaint L'Ouverture and the Haitian revolution); *Facing Mount Kenya* (an anthropological study of the Kikuyu tribe) by Jomo Kenyatta; *How Britain Rules Africa* (a study in colonial administration) and *Africa and World Peace* (an essay on international politics) by George Padmore. Since that time these black writers and other supporters of Pan-Africanism have made further contributions to the literature on Africa and the colonial struggle. Leading light of the organization was George Padmore. C. L. R. James said of him: "A more tireless leader than George would be hard to imagine: anyone who came from Africa, whether as a member of the government or to escape persecution by the British police, found his way to Padmore's house and received Padmore's advice."

The Pan-African Federation has proved to be of greater relevance to the aims of black people than The League of Coloured Peoples. The former had ideological, cultural, and political implications in the struggle of the black man. It was an important phase in the black revolution. It has become a creed in his search for total cultural, economic, and political independence. As such it holds a lasting place in black history.

In 1945 Padmore invited W. E. B. Du Bois, who had been working for Pan-Africanism before Padmore was born, to go to England as chairman of the Pan-African Federation. One of the members at that time was Kwame Nkrumah, future president of Ghana. During that historic Congress conference in Manchester when the representatives of black and colonial organizations in Britian were assembled, Nkrumah delivered a speech on imperialism which was a masterpiece. This led C. L. R. James to observe: "He [Nkrumah] had learned all there was to be learned from Padmore."

Dr. Du Bois's association with the Pan-African Federation was destined to have the most far-reaching consequences in Africa in the years following World War II. But the Pan-African movement faced serious threats in the years immediately before the outbreak of this same war, and had to fight ceaselessly for survival. Those years coincided with what is known in left-wing political circles as the "Anti-Fascist Popular Front Period." George Padmore in his study *Pan-Africanism or Communism* described what took place then:

> This period was one of the most stimulating and constructive in the history of Pan-Africanism. It was then that Congress had to meet the ideological challenge from the Communist opportunists on the one hand and the racist doctrines of the Fascists on the other, and to defend the programme of Pan-Africanism—namely, the fundamental right of black men to be free and independent and not be humbugged by those who preached acceptance of the status quo in the interest of power politics. It was also at this period that many of the Negro intellectuals who were later to emerge as prominent personalities in the colonial nationalist movements began to make a detailed and systematic study of European political theories and systems (liberalism, socialism, communism, imperialism, fascism), and to evaluate these doctrines objectively—accepting what might be useful to the cause of Pan-Africanism and rejecting the harmful. . . . In this way the younger leaders of the Congress were able to build upon the pioneering work of Du Bois and formulate a programme of dynamic nationalism, which

> combined African traditional forms of organisation with Western political party methods.
>
> A programme of Positive Action, based on the Gandhiist technique of non-violent non-cooperation, was endorsed by the Fifth Pan-African Congress in 1945, and first applied in the Gold Coast in 1950 by Kwame Nkrumah, who had served as one of the joint international secretaries of the Congress.

Dr. C. L. R. James brought the happenings of those historic times into their proper perspective in a talk he titled "From Du Bois to Fanon":

> Kwame Nkrumah was invited to Ghana to work, the Gold Coast it was called then. The story runs that he didn't want to go particularly, because he was busy organising in London and Europe. Padmore insisted that he should go. He went, and while that [the revolution] was going on in the west of Africa, the Mau Mau were carrying on their activities in the east, and I want you to understand that we had no idea that the things which we were fighting for would come with such rapidity. Naturally, we backed Nkrumah, and Padmore worked with him to the end. I did what I could also. But we had not the faintest idea that after it had taken place in Ghana, before ten years had passed, seven-eighths of Africa would be independent.
>
> You know in those days they must have thought Padmore and the rest of us (Jomo Kenyatta was a member, Nkrumah became a member, but most of us were West Indians at the time) were well-meaning but illiterate people talking about the independence of Africa. . . . But it turns out that we were right and they, the learned ones, were wrong. We were able to see it because we were members of an oppressed group of people and knew what was in front of us had to be cleared up. That was what made Du Bois and Garvey the historical figures that they were. Now Padmore went to Ghana when it was established, working with Nkrumah, organising the first Conference of Independent African States and the first Conference of African Freedom Fighters. He worked in Ghana until he died (in 1959), and I was then in the West Indies. Three or four days after I heard the news came a bundle of pamphlets and documents about a conference from Padmore, "We have finished and I send this to you."

In 1939 something of world-shaking significance was to happen. War was declared against Nazi Germany by Britain on September 3. Up to that time the position of the ten thousand blacks (including 261 African and West Indian students) living in British cities, primarily the sea ports, had been unenviable. The majority were relegated to the slums or more dilapidated sections of town: there was little opportunity for juveniles and there were dole queues for their fathers and mothers. This war was to change their lives, as it did the lives of so many others.

As soon as war was declared, the British West Indian colonies rallied quickly to the call of "the Mother country." Their contribution in men, supplies, and money was to be on a far larger scale than in World War I. In a surge of patriotic fervor, many West Indians made their way to London. The Royal Air Force Volunteer Reserve attracted the majority of West Indian volunteers. Eight thousand of them saw war service in Britain. Of that number, less than one thousand were members of air crews and flew in missions in North Africa, Italy, Malta, France, Holland, and Germany.

In the British armed forces, West Indians and other colonials were getting chances denied them in peacetime. On October 19, 1939, just one month after war was declared, the colonial office issued this statement: "British subjects from the colonies and British protected persons in this country, including those who are not of European descent, are now eligible for emergency commissions in His Majesty's Forces." This was one move towards equality but The League of Coloured Peoples campaigned for more. Dr. Moody said: "We are thankful for this, but we are not satisfied. We do not want it only for the duration of the war. We want it for all time. If the principle is accepted now, surely it must be accepted all the time."

Dr. Moody was adamant that all spheres of government service should be as open to black colonials as the armed forces of the Crown. For this purpose, on December 14, 1939, a strong deputation including representatives of India, West Africa, and the West Indies introduced by Mr. Creech Jones, was received at the colonial office by Mr. Malcolm Macdonald. The minister was very sympathetic. He informed the delegation of a new and more liberal government policy in regard to the colonies. He even gave the impression that the government was inclined "to abolish absolutely the colour bar and give every opportunity to Colonials to achieve the highest positions in their respective services."

This new policy was at once put to the test, and Dr. Moody's son Arundel was accepted as an officer cadet in the army. Son Ronald was already serving in the Royal Air Force. Subsequently, Arundel rose to rank of major in the Royal West Kent Regiment, transferred to the Royal

Artillery as a lieutenant. He was promoted to major in the Caribbean Regiment, commanding it on its return to Jamaica after the war for demobilization of its members. Dr. Moody's daughter Christine and his son Harold qualified as doctors and after a short period in private practice in Peckham, London, joined the Royal Army Medical Corps and became captain and major respectively, both serving in India. Garth, the youngest son, was a pilot-cadet in the Royal Air Force. Dr. Moody himself gave more than his full share to the war effort. He was one of the District Medical Officers doing Civil Defense work in Peckham, training first-aid personnel and tending the wounded in air-raid incidents. He was summoned to a big rocket explosion at New Cross which caused Britain's heaviest casualty toll of the war with two hundred people killed and many hundreds injured. Dr. Moody often worked continuous night-and-day shifts in the midst of the bombs dropped on London by Germany's Luftwaffe.

One of the major problems during the war was the evacuation of children from London and other large English cities to the rural areas. Homes had to be found for thousands of children. Black children posed problems which had to be solved by the League of Coloured Peoples. In the league's *Newsletter* for November, 1939, one such case, from Blackpool, was mentioned.

> Among a large party of children which came to our district were two little coloured boys. Nobody wanted them. House after house refused to have them. Finally a very poor old lady of seventy years volunteered to care for them. She gave them a good supper, bathed them and put them to bed. As she folded their clothes she discovered two letters addressed to the person who adopted them. Each letter contained a five pound note.

Black children were not the only ones to suffer from the color bar. An incident is reported in a letter written by an African serving man:

> On December 20th, 1944, there was an ENSA entertainment for His Majesty's Forces. West African nursing orderlies, as well as British nursing orderlies, officers, nursing sisters, ATS and BNCO's had full authority to attend the show. But to my greatest astonishment, the West Africans were turned out from the hall in a disgraceful way. On enquiring the cause of the incident, the only response made by an officer who stood nearby was "Arrest the black monkeys for disobedience of order." Twenty of us were arrested.

Such occurrences were quite common. A West Indian member of the RAF complained on behalf of himself and his West Indian buddies that "Recently the WVS opened a canteen of sorts where everyone can get a drink and a few eats. Even this canteen is unapproachable to us." Matters got to such a pitch that a British minister of government was forced to pronounce against racial discrimination: a color-bar alleged to have been enforced by an RAF medical officer against a young girl who visited West Indian airmen was raised in the House of Commons. Major L. Wilkes (Labour, Newcastle on Tyne, Central), stated that the girl went to the sick quarters of the RAF station at Tangmere, West Hampnett, Sussex. She was ordered to leave the ward immediately by the medical officer, Mr. Wilkes went on to say, who rebuked her saying that her visit to black airmen lowered white prestige.

John Strachey, under-secretary for air, stated in a written reply that the girl visited the station on three successive days, and was ordered to leave on instructions from the medical officer. Previous visits by this white girl had been the subject of complaints by other white patients, the medical officer claimed. Later, the medical officer gave the reasons for this order and added his own personal opinion on the association of black men and white women. In doing that, Mr. Strachey continued, the medical officer undoubtedly exceeded his duty. He had since apologized to the girl. Mr. Strachey wound up the debate by stressing: "Racial discrimination will not be tolerated in the Royal Air Force."

But unfortunately it was. The British authorities maintained that much of the discrimination which was spreading in Britain in the armed forces during the war years was imported by white American servicemen based in Britain. There was more than a measure of truth in this allegation. White U.S. servicemen did discriminate against colonial servicemen as well as against their own black troops in Britain. This led to pitched battles in English pubs and dance halls around the country. Many of these were reported in English newspapers of the day. A victim of this prejudice was Learie Constantine (the late Lord Constantine) who was a welfare officer in Britain during the war. The Imperial Hotel in Russell Square, London, refused him accommodation on the grounds that its white American guests would take exception to his presence. He filed suit for damages in the High Court and won. In summing up, Mr. Justice Birkett said:

> Miss O'Sullivan, the hotel manageress, was a lamentable figure in the witness box. When she could be heard she was so vague and incoherent, and I am satisfied that, on the material points, she was not speaking the truth. She was grossly insulting in her reference to Mr. Constantine and her evidence is unworthy of credence. From the outset she made it clear that the plaintiff could not stay in the hotel, and used the word "niggers" and was very offensive. She declined to receive him and would not listen to reason.
>
> Mr. Constantine bore himself with modesty and dignity and dealt with the question with intelligence and truth. He was not concerned to be vindictive or malicious, but was obviously affected by the indignity and humiliation which had been put on him, and caused him distress and inconvenience which he justifiably resented. I find that the defendants refused to receive and lodge him without any just cause or excuse, and that he did not leave the hotel voluntarily, as alleged.

A stay of execution was refused. Before he died in 1971, Lord Learie Constantine was appointed to the Board of Governors of the BBC.

Prejudice among British and American troops was aggravated, as in peace time, because of that old bogey: SEX. One black American wrote:

> The white girls all over Europe have fallen in love with the black soldier and many of them have cried worse than any American girl ever did when the boys move from a town that they have lived in. I have known the girls to follow them from town to town as far as they could go.

West Indian journalist George Padmore reported a typical incident which occurred in the last year of the war, when black soldiers were to leave Bristol in south-west England:

> "To hell with the U.S. Army colour bar! We want our coloured sweethearts!" shouted hundreds of English girls who tried to break into an American army camp at Bristol when the coloured troops, who recently arrived in this country from Germany, were about to embark for America. British police officers had to be called to protect the coloured soldiers from being mobbed by the hysterical girls, whose ages ranged between seventeen and twenty-four. Kissing and embracing went on for hours until, with a special reinforcement of military police, the couples were separated and the Negroes forced back to their barracks.

These public exhibitions excited passions and were the cause of much friction between black and white servicemen. West Indians continued to arrive in Britain up until the middle of 1944, the majority for service in the Royal Air Force. Several hundreds had already joined the Canadian armed forces. There were girls in the Army Territorial Service. Many West Indians served in the Royal Navy and hundreds of others went in the merchant navy. A forestry unit of nine hundred from British Honduras served for two years in Scotland. Over two hundred technicians from Jamaica, including welders, riveters, fitters, and motor mechanics volunteered from the smaller Caribbean territories to come to the United Kingdom and worked successfully in war factories. About one hundred fifty others were recruited in the British West Indies as trainee-technicians and trained in Britain at government centres.

By the middle of 1944, the British West Indies had also contributed over £750,000 to the United Kingdom for general war purposes, nearly £400,000 for war charities, and more than £425,000 for the purchase of aircraft for the Royal Air Force. Their governments and peoples had lent the United Kingdom over £1,400,000 free of interest. Among the war charities to which the British West Indies contributed, steadily and generously, were the War Funds of the British Red Cross and St. John's Ambulance, King George's Fund for Sailors, St. Dunstan's Aid to the Blind, and Aid to Russia. Mobile canteens donated by the British Caribbean territories operated in London and other cities during the air raids on Britain. They also contributed to the funds for the "Queen's Messengers," the mobile food convoys which helped to feed people in bombed towns. By the end of September, 1943, the British West Indies had mailed to the United Kingdom over four thousand parcels of surgical and hospital supplies, comforts, clothing, honey, and preserves. Jamaica was the first colony in the Empire to send money for aircraft. In less than two months in 1940 the island had given nearly £40,000 to buy bombers.

In men, money, and material the West Indies had contributed much to the war effort; especially those air crew members of the Royal Air Force. Several of the hundreds of West Indians who were members of air crews earned commissions. The majority contributed distinguished service to Britain in "her hour of need," but many gave more than that. They sacrificed their lives. On the one hand, as these stories illustrate, the British people were thankful: A group of West Indian RAF volunteers was walking along Gray's Inn Road in London when several Londoners stopped the men to shake their hands and thank them for coming to help. Women kissed them openly in the streets, at the same time weeping with a kind of open affection the British never normally show in public. On another occasion, a Sierra Leonian in the air force who had broken one of his legs in a crash was spending some leave in London. Taxi drivers would stop when they saw him and offer to drive him to his destination for nothing. Once when he was about to pay the fare a driver brushed it away and added: "I can't take it . . . I must show a little appreciation for what you coloured chaps are doing for us." Although race prejudice was rife, white members of air crew showed no signs of it when fraternizing with their black opposite numbers. In fact, it was well known that English air crew members often wanted to fly in the same bombers as West Indians and Africans, because of a superstition that "Black brings luck."

Many West Indians served with distinction in the Royal Air Force as well as in the other services. They received decorations and were honored for their bravery. One of the most distinguished airmen in the Royal Air Force was Squadron Leader P.L.U. Cross, a navigator from Trinidad. A member of 139 Jamaica Squadron. Ulric Cross flew on eighty missions over enemy territory. Of these twenty-one were over Berlin. For these eighty raids, which ran into four operational tours, Squadron Leader Cross was awarded the Distinguished Flying Cross in June, 1944 and the Distinguished Service Order, November, 1944. The citation for the latter read:

> This officer has set a fine example of keenness and devotion to duty. He has participated in a very large number of sorties, most of which have been against such heavily defended targets as Berlin, Hamburg, Ludwigshaven, and industrial centres in the Ruhr. He is a brave and resolute member of aircraft crew, whose exceptional navigational ability has been an important factor in the successes obtained. His services have been of immense value.

The list of Africans and West Indians who served is long. Many lost their lives. Towards the end of the war the Royal Air Force decided to accept West Indians for ground duties. Thousands were brought to Britain and were trained as fitters, drivers, radio mechanics, and clerks. The majority were stationed at RAF maintenance units in Britain. Several hundreds also served in other spheres of the war effort. Dr. Moody was their counsellor and guide. He protested every case of racial prejudice.

But the league was not entirely successful in stamping out existing prejudice. *John Bull*, an English national journal, published a scathing article titled "These Coloured 'Intruders' ":

> Colonial troops came to this country to help us win the war. But they are bitter because the colour bar still exists in Britain! They are shunned at service camps, banned from hotels and called intruders. They return to their homelands notoriously anti-British. The whole-hearted help of the coloured peoples during the war should have made a difference. You would think the war would cure us of a colour complex. Yet today the colour bar still exists in Britain, not quite so openly as before the war, when it was next to impossible for a coloured visitor to find accommodation at a London hotel, but it was there in the hearts and minds of a lot of people. If you doubt it, ask any of the 8,000 West Indian Servicemen and women stationed in this country. Go and talk to students from West Africa, India and Ceylon. Quietly and soberly, without any exaggerated sense of grievance, they will admit facts that cannot fail to shake the complacency of every thoughtful man and woman in this country.

It was in this climate of intolerance that blacks saw war service in Britain. It may not have been as bad as in the pre-war years but it was there. At the end of hostilities all African and West Indian members of air crew in the Royal Air Force and the Fleet Air Arm were demobilized in England. Ground crew personnel were shipped back home where they were given their discharges. This was done so as to discourage them from settling in Britain. Many of those who actually flew as pilots, navigators, air bombers, wireless operators, flight-engineers, and air gunners were given study grants by the Air Ministry and Colonial Office. Some remained in Britain. Others returned home after their studies. But there were those who had paid the supreme price for the freedom which their compatriots still cannot enjoy in Britain. The master race philosophy of the Nazis was gone but blacks still had to face race prejudice. Black ex-servicemen who were demobilized in England and had exchanged their uniforms for civilian suits were to discover a difference in peacetime Britain. They had "done their bit," received their war gratuities, taken their courses, and were now expected to go back home, to Africa, to India, to the West Indies. In remaining they were to learn the truth: blacks not welcome!

History had repeated itself and the reaction of the British people to black ex-servicemen had reverted to its 1919 form.

BIBLIOGRAPHY TO CHAPTER TWELVE

The B.W.I. and the War. Passed by British Censor No. 446, November 8, 1944. London: 1944.

"Colour Discrimination in the Forces," *Newsletter* (April, 1945).

"Constantine Wins His Case." *Newsletter of the League of Colored Peoples*. (London: July, 1944).

Hooper, Richard (ed.). *Colour in Britain*. London: 1965.

James, C. L. R. *From DuBois to Fanon*. Michigan: n.d.

Noble, Peter. *The Negro in Films*. London: 1948.

"Oldtimers." *Ebony* (Chicago: December, 1956).

Padmore, George. *Pan-Africanism or Communism*. London: 1957.

Richmond, Anthony H. *Colour Prejudice in Britain*. London: 1954.

Rogers, J. A. *Nature Knows No Color-Line*. New York: 1952.

———. *Sex and Race*, Vol. I, New York: 1952.

Scobie, Edward. "Caribbean Wings." *Flamingo* (August, 1962).

———. "Aldridge Family Rule in London." *Chicago Defender*. (March 8, 1952).

"These Colored Intruders." *John Bull*. (January 26, 1948).

CHAPTER XIII

"I COME TO BETTER MYSELF"

"Each immigrant from the Caribbean declares that he has come to the United Kingdom to better himself and then to return to the West Indies and help to build it up."

Donald Hinds
in Journey to an Illusion *(1966)*

By far the biggest wave of black immigration into Britain started after World War II. In June, 1948, 492 would-be settlers from the West Indies—all male with the exception of one girl stowaway—arrived at Tilbury docks on the *S. S. Empire Windrush*, a dirty white troopship. Many of them were ex-servicemen who had seen war service in Britain and had been returned to the West Indies for their discharge and war benefits. Their experience of life in Britain, even though it had been in wartime, had made them believe that they would have more opportunities there for improving their lot than in the impoverished colonial islands of the Caribbean. For the next three years the number of West Indian migrants in Britain remained between five hundred and seven hundred per annum. From 1951 to 1953 the volume increased from 1,750 to 2,200, but in the words of Michael Banton "after this more ships became available to transport migrants and the numbers shot up as fast as the green pawpaw tree." The number was 10,000 in 1954; 27,550 in 1955; 29,800 in 1956; then the numbers fell: 23,000 in 1957; 15,000 in 1958. From 1959 until 1961, the year before the Commonwealth Immigrants Act came into operation, the numbers began to mount again until they reached unprecedented heights: 16,400 in 1959, 49,650 in 1960, and in 1961, 65,300. With the restrictions imposed by the Commonwealth Immigrants Act on July 1, 1962, the numbers began to go downhill, until by the end of 1968, with further strictures added to the Act, there was only a trickle. By then the total number of West Indians and other Afro-Asian peoples in Britain was put at one million—approximately 2 percent of the population.

There were three factors causing this migration. First, World War II. On demobilization most of the colonial ex-servicemen who had not remained in the United Kingdom nevertheless returned in search of employment. Second, in 1952 the United States federal government passed the racially conceived McCarren–Walter Immigration Act. This limited the number of West Indians allowed into the United States to a paltry one hundred a year. Hence West Indians had to turn their eyes to other lands for employment, since the British-owned territories were in a chronically impoverished state. This was nothing unusual for them because as far back as the abolition of slavery succeeding generations of West Indians have been travelling to more affluent countries looking for work: to build the Panama Canal between the years 1881 and 1911; to the United States before stringent immigration controls came into force in 1924 and stopped unrestricted entry; to work the sugar plantations in Cuba; to the goldmines and sugar estates of Cayenne and Surinam; and to the oil refineries of Aruba and Curacao in the Netherlands Antilles during World War II. Dr. Clarence Senior, an authority on race relations, recognized the influence of the McCarran Act on migration to Britain, and explained the British attitude to this Act:

> Resentment against the United States is occasionally encountered in Great Britain for placing the British West Indies under the quota system and assigning them small quotas in the McCarran Act. While the Act is subject to criticism for its racist provisions, . . . it would seem that greater employment opportunities in Britain than in the United States is probably the major factor in diverting from our [West Indies] economy to the British what has been a migratory stream of some importance. The United States has experienced three to four times the proportionate unemployment of Great Britain since World War II.

The third, and probably the most important, factor, as Dr. Senior observed, was Britain's relatively full employment. It was the time when government and industry were claiming that the Welfare State offered full employment for all. So the unemployed thousands of the Caribbean, with other doors closed to them, began the long trek to Britain "to better themselves," even if that meant taking on unskilled menial jobs. As an English journalist said, "obsessed by the need to earn money, many were willing to work ten hours a day, seven days a week."

They came by the boatload, and by chartered air flights to Britain. They sold, bartered, stole and saved to make the journey to their promised land. For the West Indian, as Barbadian poet and novelist George Lamming noted during that period, "England has come to mean opportunity, horizons, success." But West Indian migrants were to find that the journey to those horizons was a rough one, made more uneven by the very fact of color. The West Indian's color was not only "a cage which betrays the bird within it," in the words of Lamming; it was a cage which was to keep him imprisoned in a social and economic strait jacket, denying him equal rights with the host population.

They came in their light-weight suits and straw hats and felt sombreros, teeth chattering, shivering in the draughty, freezing, alien, impersonal, busy atmosphere of the railway stations—Waterloo, Victoria, Charing Cross, or anywhere else they were dumped, together with their cardboard boxes, battered suitcases, and stringtied baskets. London had seen nothing like it before and Londoners were taken aback. A certain annoyance showed on the faces of the cockney porters, waitresses, cabbies, and policemen at this sudden onslaught on their quiet preserve. London's newspaper reporters, columnists, feature writers, and photographers had a field day or, to be more accurate, many field days at Waterloo station and London airport, covering the arrival of fresh contingents of West Indians. Their papers spread front, centre and back pages with an array of pictures, heavily spiced and peppery stories. The banner headlines described West Indians "whose calypso flamboyance could not be chilled even by the frosty air of an English winter." Actually, those gay West Indians, were cold, hungry, miserable, and frightened.

Most extreme in his denunciation right from the start of this black migration into Britain was Oswald Mosley, whose paper *Action*, cried "Blacks Invade Britain," and "Send the Coloured Immigrants Home." The newspapers of the popular press, on the look-out for sensational copy in their race for big circulations, played up this influx of West Indians to the hilt, although not with the virulence of Mosley. Their press reports served to instill more apprehension, even fear, in the minds of the British people, who began to look at these black strangers to their shores as invaders who would disrupt their stable pattern of life. They saw, with minds conditioned by highly colored press reports, their standards, their customs, even their morality being impaired. Resentment of those "unwelcome" guests had already started to set in and do its ugly work. Kind welfare officers and harassed colonial office staff members with their cups of tea and sandwiches and pats on the back could not do much to cheer up those bewildered migrants. Eyes searched everywhere for relations and friends who were supposed to be there to meet them. Some were disappointed and lost, and had to depend on the bounty of British officialdom. Spivs, wide boys, and "sharks" of both races circulated in the crowd waiting to prey on the unfortunate ones. Many an innocent West Indian girl found herself caught up in London vice almost as soon as she left Waterloo station.

Nothing stopped the flow, as year in year out West Indians, and afterwards, Indians and Pakistanis, settled in Britain. The big blow to this migration came with the Commonwealth Immigrants Act in 1962. However, even before that black immigrants had to contend with many serious problems of integration into the host society, the most pressing being that of housing.

Jobs of a sort were relatively easy to find. Coming from an area which had always suffered from chronic unemployment West Indians were grateful for even the lowest paid jobs—porters, street cleaners, washhouse and lavatory attendants, building site laborers, laundry maids, and other unskilled jobs which whites thought beneath them. As time passed they found themselves moving into the higher paid and semi-skilled jobs. They became railway guards, conductors and even drivers. Some of the better educated gradually became accepted in white collar jobs.

From the very beginning of the post-war migration to Britain, black people have been concentrated in the big industrial cities where it was easy to get unskilled and semi-skilled jobs: in London, Liverpool, Nottingham, Leeds, Sheffield, Wolverhampton, Bradford, Coventry and Glasgow. However, they also settled in smaller numbers in several other towns. It could be said with much justification that there is scarcely a market town in the whole of the British Isles where one would not come across black settlers.

The housing problem has always been one of the main causes of racial friction in Britain. Blacks have always been blamed for the overcrowding and shortage of houses but the housing situation was serious before the war and slum clearance schemes had to be postponed at the outbreak of hostilities in 1939. Moreover, during the war 223,000 homes were totally destroyed by German bombs and rockets.

The influx of West Indians, and of Pakistanis and Indians must be seen in that context. There has always been a long list of people waiting for borough or county councils to house them. The arrival of black migrants from 1945 caused increased and sometimes bitter competition for the limited accommodation available. Many people did not realise that black migrants were usually at the end of such queues and that there was a general unwillingness in Britain among white landlords and landladies to take black tenants. It was commonplace to see advertisements for accommodation in the British newspapers which said "Coloureds not wanted," "Whites only," "No blacks accepted," etc. There is scarcely a black man or woman who has not experienced the humiliation of having an English landlord or landlady bang his or her front door shut when approached for accommodation.

George Lamming explains one of the ways the English have of dealing with this situation:

> People [English] who were ashamed of the conduct of their army in Kenya or the Caribbean found themselves unprepared for a black stranger, whose skin made class irrelevant, and who had read that there was a room within which he would like to rent. Could he have it? You knew that the answer had to be given there and then. And the answer was often long, circuitous, a marathon of courtesies that ended with a regret that the room, like a bird, had just gone. Of course, it was still there, and empty, too.

This treatment was quite typical of the British national character and West Indians have encountered it, not only when looking for rooms, but also when seeking employment. One is charmed and put completely off guard by cosy smiles and polite, mild-mannered language, as one hears the word "No," dressed up in the habit of the English gentleman. It is this kind of ambiguity which West Indians found difficult to understand or accept.

In the early years of West Indian migration to Britain, certain rapacious landlords would rent their substandard slum houses to blacks. They would let rooms on an "around-the-clock" basis; one set of tenants by day and another by night. Yet these very landlords and landladies would accuse West Indians of living in crowded conditions, with too many in a room. For this kind of "cattle shed" accommodation they were charged exorbitant rents, from thirty-five shillings to two pounds weekly. No wonder that it became an obsession with West Indians to save their money and buy houses as soon as they had accumulated enough for a down payment. Even so, the houses sold to them were usually those condemned for slum clearance.

This "fleecing" of immigrants looking for rooms was also practiced by some black landlords, although it was not widespread. One Jamaican journalist working in London exposing this, wrote: "Those West Indians who are engaged in this racket are as much moral criminals as the English housing racketeers."

As the years went by rents were raised. The price of a single room went up from £2 a week to £3. 10s. and then to £5. This rent was fairly typical of the big industrial cities of Britain. To stop this type of racketeering rent tribunals were set up by local councils and many were firmly on the side of the tenant against the racketeer landlord. In 1964 Councillor Tom Agambar, Vice-Chairman of the Deptford Housing Committee, in one of the South London boroughs said:

> There must be hundreds of cases in the borough where landlords are taking advantage and forcing people to pay high rents because they can find nowhere else to go. This type of landlord thinks he can get in on suffering and shortage to make an easy penny. . . . The Housing Committee knows that house after house, as it comes up for sale, is being bought, filled with people, and turned into a seaside boarding house.

Not many migrant families qualified for council flats and those that did were usually at the end of housing queues. If they were housed by the council when their turn came, there would be outcries that they were given preference over whites.

The housing situation in Britain, instead of easing as more houses were built, was, if anything, worse in the declining years of the sixties. West Indian immigrants cannot be blamed for this because the Commonwealth Immigrants Act of 1962 their numbers have been severely reduced. The English writer Elspeth Huxley gives a realistic picture:

> Our housing situation is a jungle but the basic facts are plain. Despite the addition of some 300,000 new dwellings annually—the Government's target is now 400,000—we are not keeping pace with the demand. Of the seventeen million houses on this island (Britain) nearly half were built before 1919, and of these a majority have become, or are becoming obsolete. Nearly three million of them have stood for more than a century. The official estimate that 600,000 actual slum dwellings are due for demolition is almost certainly an underestimate. Into the middle of this really brutal situation steps the immigrant clasping his cheap little suitcase and hoping to be greeted as a welcome guest. He hasn't created any new problem by arriving—we'd have a housing shortage anyway—but he certainly makes matters worse.

However, old prejudices still remain and West Indians are made the scapegoats for the persistent shortage of accommodation in Britain. They are blamed for the depreciation of the value of property; accused of living in packed unsanitary conditions in slum areas, of playing their radiograms at full volume at midnight, of having wild parties, of cooking highly spiced foods with strange smells, and a host of antisocial habits. If one West Indian kept his garden in a weed-choked condition and did not clean his windows, then all West Indians were lumped together as dirty.

One English observer remarked, however: "In fact, in some parts of the Midlands, Indian and West Indian households can often be picked out in a drab grey suburban street by the fresh and bright paintwork on the houses." Even that was a bone of contention with some whites. One man in Birmingham said pointing to the vividly painted gate and railings of a West Indian's house, "Why do they want to be so different?"

Although black migrants have found relatively little trouble in obtaining employment in Britain, their problems with white workers, trade unions and management were more serious.

When the early batches of black migrants began arriving on the British labor market, certain sections of the press reported that they were living on the country's National Assistance and not working. After a while this story took root and was accepted by those who saw black people as a threat to their way of life. An Anglo-Indian writer Vernon Naresh Nath Waughray made an observation on this point which should have been obvious to anyone not confused by racial prejudice:

> Many of the coloured immigrants in Britain have sold their land and other possessions, or borrowed heavily, to come to this country. Bearing this in mind the extent of the indebtedness of most of the immigrants it is very unlikely that they come here to draw National Assistance.

Precisely so! But there are still people who cling to this racial cliché, and yet will say in the next breath that immigrants take away houses and jobs.

It is generally accepted, however, even in the most conservative circles in Britain, that in certain services migrants are serving a useful purpose. From the early years of the postwar migration, thousands of West Indians went to Britain to work for London Transport, British Railways, and hospitals under special employment schemes between their island governments and transport and hospital authorities in Britain. In the case of transport workers this was particularly true of Barbados. Hotels, too, have entered into agreements with West Indian authorities and have taken on increasing numbers of black workers, mostly as kitchen hands, maids, waiters, laundry assistants, and cleaners. Some have taken catering courses and have reached higher positions as chefs, cooks, head waiters, and other responsible catering posts.

As far back as 1961 it was generally agreed that hospitals provided a good indication of the migrant's contribution to Britain's well-being. Donald Chapman, then the member of Parliament for the Northfield division of Birmingham said in a debate on the Immigration Bill:

> In Summerfield Hospital, thirty-four State-enrolled nurses out of ninety-six are immigrants. Fourteen porters out of forty-three are immigrants. At Marston Green Hospital, six ward sisters out of twenty-two, with a turnover of 50 percent, and forty-seven pupil midwives out of seventy-two, with a turnover of 60 percent are immigrants. At Heathfield Road Maternity Hospital, twelve staff midwives out of thirteen and twelve pupil midwives out of eighteen are immigrants. . . .

To this list hundreds more hospitals could be added. In the last years of the sixties Britain's health services depended to an even greater extent on migrants. Black nurses were by then being called "dark angels of mercy."

Britain's entire structure of hospital staffing would collapse if black doctors, nurses, orderlies, and catering workers withdrew their services. In some hospitals, particularly in London, Liverpool, Birmingham, and

Manchester, the number of hospital staff below the senior registrar grade was as high as 90 percent black. In 1964, a breakdown of the main hospital regions showed that in Liverpool 36 percent of the doctors were from overseas. In Newcastle it was 51 percent, Leeds 50 percent, London 37 percent and Manchester 49 percent. The term "overseas" in these instances included doctors from West, East, and Central Africa, India, Pakistan, Persia, and the West Indies. Approximately fifteen thousand girls from the West Indies left home every year to train as nurses in Britain before the severe clamp on West Indian migration was applied in 1962. The medical authorities claimed that two-thirds of the hospitals in the United Kingdom would be forced to close if all the black staff left.

Although hostility from white patients still exists it is decreasing since black doctors and nurses are an everyday sight to whom whites have slowly grown accustomed. Grenada-born Dr. David Pitt, a county councillor and race leader who has a large London practice, explained the black doctors' point of view:

> The practice of medicine is something which transcends national and colour barriers. In our language an infected tonsil is an infected tonsil in London, Lagos or Lithuania. They are all the same colour. If they have to come out then they have to come out. A black doctor takes them out in just the same way a white doctor does.
>
> Any Negro nurse or doctor must realise that to them the patient comes first, no matter if he suffers from warped thinking.
>
> Britain should be proud to have so many young coloured doctors and nurses. It is a tribute to the great tradition of British medicine.

Many young doctors and nurses have performed brilliantly in their professions in Britain. In 1964 the first Gold Medal to be awarded to a nurse at Rush Green Hospital in Essex was won by Nurse Catherine Mitchell, twenty, from Gros-Islet, St. Lucia, West Indies. The Gold Medal award is based on the work and overall performance of the nurses during their entire training. The list of medal awards to West Indian nurses is a very long one and bears out testimony (if any is needed) that black nurses can hold their own, and in many instances, better their British counterparts. Blacks are to be found as senior staff medical officers, specialists, consultants, senior house officers, senior registrars, ward sisters, and matrons in British hospitals.

However, a report published by *The Sunday Times* in October, 1968, showed that black doctors were having a very tough time, and that in some instances they were being exploited, and made to do "menial jobs." The result of this, stated the report, was that Britain would lose nearly five hundred doctors to the United States and Canada. Some black doctors had already gone directly to the United States, leaving Britain's health service, already undermanned, severely crippled. The medical services started to feel the pinch, and the British government tried very hard to get as many black doctors as possible into Britain, quickly.

What has been said of the black migrant's contribution to the economic structure of Britain in transport and hospitals can be repeated in other spheres of employment. The late Claudia Jones, editor of the pungent London-edited *West Indian Gazette* made this point: "Throughout Britain, the West Indian contribution to its economy is undoubted. As building workers, carpenters, . . . in factories, West Indians are easily evidenced."

Seeking justification for their increasing prejudice, the British people turned to the problems of crime and disease, claiming that the coming of black migrants has caused an upsurge of the former and greater incidence of certain types of the latter. Again, facts and figures disprove both these allegations. Official figures published in 1959 disclosed that 118 out of 156 cases of serious assault involved whites only; and prosecutions for living on immoral earnings showed that out of 97 convictions, 37 were Maltese, 18 West Africans, 11 were from Eire, and 31 from the United Kingdom. In 1961 the Minister of State at the home office said that there was no danger to the nation's health from migrants, or evidence that they brought any particular disease into Britain.

In September, 1968, the allegations were refuted at an official level. David Ennals, a home office official with a special responsibility for immigration, denied emphatically the suggestion that violence was increasing in Britain because of the presence of black people. He said that crime among black migrants was "below national level." (There were fifty million whites and one million blacks in that year.) He maintained: "It is a view commonly held that there is some link between colour and crime. There is absolutely no evidence to substantiate this claim." He cited a recent study in an area of the city of Birmingham which has one of the largest black communities in Britain, and claimed that:

> Fewer than 5 percent of all arrests in a significantly coloured neighbourhood were coloured people. They comprised only 2 percent of the

offenders against property, by far the largest class of crime, 4 percent of arrests for drunkenness and similar offences and 18 percent of those arrested for crimes of violence—insignificantly over the population. Only a tiny proportion of offenders placed under the supervision of probation officers or committed to reform schools over the past three years were coloured. Only in offences related to drugs were coloured immigrants over-represented.

On the question of health, reports have shown that West Indians have a lower tuberculosis incidence rate than the white population. A survey of tuberculosis in Birmingham was taken in 1956–57. There were 1,620 notifications among the white population of 1,100,000 born in England, Scotland, and Wales. Among the Irish, whose population was estimated between 45,000 and 70,000 there were 225 cases. Of the Indian and Pakistani population of 8,000–11,000, there were 123 notifications. There were only 21 cases among West Indians, whose total population was believed to be between 20,000 and 25,000.

Venereal disease is common to both host and migrant communities. Cross-infection is likely to occur in this field and so public interest tends to concentrate on that illness. There is no evidence that the influx of black migrants brought with it an increase in either tuberculosis or venereal disease. The allegation that conditions of employment, housing, and climate tended to increase the risk of tuberculosis to the migrant was disproved by the figures published in a World Health Organisation report in 1964. Although up to eight years ago medical knowledge of venereal disease was patchy and incomplete, the available evidence showed that the incidence rate, particularly for gonorrhoea, among West Indian migrants was higher than among the white population. In 1965 there was a disturbing increase in the number of cases among teenage white girls. The problem was that of a pool of infected promiscuous white girls trading, many of them exclusively, with black men. Explaining this incidence of venereal disease among migrants in 1965 Dr. W. D. Dolton, Deputy Medical Officer of Health in Bradford wrote:

> The effects of sexual behaviour of coloured immigrants on the host population are relatively small. Allegations of rape and seduction are more likely to be based on resentment than fact. The first gesture of hospitality to many a coloured man in this country has been a girl on his doorstep, offering her services for the night. It is not surprising that many accept and that some are subsequently unable to distinguish between those who wish to offer their services and those who do not. It

> is disturbing too to find cases among men who will be reunited with their wives in the very near future. After months or years of abstinence, they sometimes, misguidedly, visit a prostitute to test their potency, and come away with gonorrhoea.

In more recent times, with the arrival of the wives of migrants, this hazard among males has virtually disappeared and with it the relatively high incidence of venereal disease.

Up to 1968, however, groups of whites agitating for a total ban on migrants were making allegations which had been disproved by official figures years before. One Sunday at the end of September of that year several hundred demonstrators marched through central London and delivered a seven-page document to the Archbishop of Canterbury, Dr. Michael Ramsey, stating that immigration should be halted as it posed a threat to the health of Britain. A spokesman of the group, the Immigration Control Association (ICA) said:

> We are concerned at the spread of disease which is brought in by immigrants. Tuberculosis has been a particular problem and one case of leprosy is reported each week.

The boiling point for growing race prejudice was bound to come. It was something which the authorities should have foreseen but did not. As *West Indian Gazette* editor Claudia Jones put it, in 1964 "Extreme manifestations which underlie the present status of West Indians in Britain were graphically witnessed in late 1958, when racial riots occurred in Notting Hill and Nottingham." But there had been several minor racial eruptions which produced enough smoke to have shown those concerned that the fire was being stoked for a mighty conflagration.

For instance, in May, 1948, a crowd of about two hundred fifty white men besieged and stoned a house in Birmingham where a number of Indians had been living. On the August Bank Holiday in that same year there was a fight outside an Anglo-Indian cafe in Liverpool. This triggered off a succession of violent attacks on black people which continued for another two nights. At this time there was a marked increase in the number of colonials living in Liverpool, and unemployment among black seamen had reached its peak. The prime causes of this outbreak of violence, nevertheless, were Bank Holiday drinking and quarrels over women. West Africans and whites fought pitched battles with knives, bottles, and stones. About sixty blacks and ten whites were arrested. On most occasions the white men involved ran away from the scene as soon as they saw the police, but the blacks tended to stay and fight it out, even with the police. In the majority of cases, the blacks were convicted for assault and given short terms of imprisonment or made to pay small fines. In a couple of cases the decisions of the court were reversed on appeal, and a few were dismissed at the magistrate's court.

This incident created more racial tensions in Liverpool. Blacks remained convinced that the police were biased against them, a conviction shared by most blacks in Britain. Anthony Richmond, a lecturer in social theory at Edinburgh University said of this disturbance, "the fact remains that West Indians and other coloured people in the south end of Liverpool remember the incidents with bitterness and claim that this was another confirmation of the basic hostility between English people (the police in particular) and the coloured community." The reaction of the English people was no less bitter. Richmond wrote: "The attitude of white people . . . who knew no more than they had been able to read in the press appear to have been confirmed in their view of the coloured population as an unruly element, dangerous and hostile, which should be punished firmly and discouraged from coming to England and disturbing the peace." Richmond did, however, add that some white people who were aware of the facts of the case "were appalled at what they considered to be injustice against the coloured community."

Racial clashes were a regular part of life in Britain. In London, a fight between whites and blacks in Deptford Broadway in July, 1949, set off an evening of rioting. There had been sporadic fighting for several nights before. The police escorted the black men to their hostel and kept them indoors. By that time a hostile crowd of about one thousand white people gathered outside the hostel, and although a police cordon had been drawn across the road, the crowd continued its siege and made persistent efforts to enter the hostel. The black men threw bottles and cups, saucers and plates from windows to keep back the crowd. Two black men were seriously injured and three policemen hurt. Seven white men and eight blacks were later tried on various charges.

Five years later in another part of London, in a small street of terrace houses in Camden Town, racial warfare was waged for two days. Both whites and blacks were very militant. Crowds soon joined in, and skirmishes with bottles and axes were started, culminating in some bloody incidents. One black man was chased by a crowd onto a bus, where the fight continued. Youths set on two black men and beat them up. On the evening of the second day the white crowd became so hostile that fifty policemen stood by and sealed off the streets at both ends. Firemen had to be called in, as there had been threats of arson. As the evening wore on and it became quieter the firemen returned to their station. Soon afterwards, however, a petrol bomb was thrown into a house occupied by black men and two white women. The house quickly burst into flames.

People soon began to forget, except the few who were directly or professionally concerned. Nor did any of the intermittent brawls and fights in London and in several provincial cities such as Nottingham attract much attention. Anthony Richmond said of this: "The coloured people themselves and their immediate neighbours, social workers and anthropologists were well aware of these troubles. But public opinion, in general, did not take much notice."

BIBLIOGRAPHY TO CHAPTER THIRTEEN

Banton, Michael. *White and Coloured.* London: 1959.

British Broadcasting Corporation. *Going to Britain?* (booklet) London: 1959.

"Britain's Problem Children." *Mother and Child* (November, 1947).

Carey, A. T. *Colonial Students.* London: 1956.

Davison, R. B. *Black British.* London: 1966.

———. *West Indian Migrants.* London: 1966.

Egginton, Joyce. *They Seek A Living.* London: 1957.

Glass, Ruth. *Newcomers.* London: 1960.

"Gold Medal Nurse." *Flamingo.* (London: September, 1964).

Hinds, Donald, *Journey to an Illusion.* London: 1966.

Hooper, Richard (ed.). *Colour in Britain.* London: 1965.

Humphry, Derek. " 'Menial Jobs Only' for Our Commonwealth Doctors." *Sunday Times.* (London: October 27, 1968).

Huxley, Elsepth. "Blacks Next Door." *Punch.* (London: January 29, 1964).

Institute of Race Relations. *Coloured Immigrants in Britain.* London: 1966.

Jones, Claudia. "The Caribbean Community in Britain." *Freedomways.* (Third Quarter, Summer 1964.)

Lamming, George. *The Pleasures of Exile.* London: 1960.

Lewis, E. R. *The Whites and the Coloureds.* London: 1962.

McAlpine, Eric. "Housing in Britain." *Flamingo* (September, 1964).

Morris, Mervyn. "A West Indian Student in England." *Caribbean Quarterly 8,* No. 4 (December, 1962).

Naipaul, V. S. *The Middle Passage.* London: 1962.

Patterson, Sheila. *Dark Strangers.* London: 1963.

Richmond, Anthony H. *Colour Prejudice in Britain.* London: 1954.

Row, Robert. *The Colour Question in Britain.* London: 1954.

Ruck, S. K. (ed.). *The West Indian Comes to England.* London: 1960.

Scobie, Edward. "White Life in Black Hands." *Flamingo Magazine.* (London: February, 1964).

Senior, Clarence. "Race Relations and Labour Supply in Great Britain." *Caribbean Quarterly* 5, No. 2 (February, 1958).

———, and Manley, Douglas. *The West Indian in Britain.* London: 1956.

Waughray, Vernon. *Race Relations in Great Britain.* A Peace News Phamphlet. London: 1960.

CHAPTER XIV

THE NOTTINGHAM AND NOTTING HILL RIOTS

By the late fifties the numbers of black immigrants had increased tremendously and white people began to view this growth with alarm and to talk of it as a black invasion. When the headlines in the national papers told of race riots in Nottingham in late August of 1958, the British public saw it as something of national importance. Ugly and primitive emotions, long suppressed, came out into the open and black people, many of whom remembered the race riots of 1919, prepared again for an intensification of prejudice.

The Nottingham riot began, as riots usually do, with a small incident. On Saturday, August 23, 1958, a fight started between a black man and a white man outside a public house called The Chase, at closing time. This alehouse was in a decaying district of Nottingham where between two and three thousand black people lived. The exact reason for the fight was never determined, though various versions were given. In a short space of time, however, the fighting spread. Several white men and women clashed with black men. Dozens of people were injured by knives, razors, palings, and bottles. It was estimated that nearly fifteen hundred people gathered and formed themselves into an ugly, riotous crowd. Many black men, with cuts and bruises, were removed by the police for their own safety. Eight white persons were taken to hospital. After about an hour and a half, order was restored and by midnight the crowd had dispersed.

That was not the end of the matter because deep down feelings of hate were still festering. Black people had been hounded, humiliated, and beaten in the streets by whites before that Saturday. These assaults became more and more frequent until the riot outside The Chase.

When Monday came, a surface calm seemed to have descended on the residents of that district and *The Times* of London reported: "All Quiet Again in Nottingham." Other national newspapers were less optimistic and less restrained; they had picked up stories from white youths (teddy boys) that other such teddy boys far and near had invaded the district waiting for the next Saturday night. (Teddy boys were white delinquents who hung around coffee bars and clubs looking for trouble.)

The scene was well set. The rendezvous was kept in St. Ann's Well Road, where the disturbances had taken place the previous Saturday. The road was crowded with teddy boys, sightseers in cars and on foot, reporters, some local whites, policemen, but very few blacks. They had been advised to remain indoors. Police patrols kept the large crowd, which by that time had grown to four thousand, on the move. When a car with blacks in it tried to pass through the crowd shouted "Let's lynch them," "Let's get at them." Teddy boys who poured out of a public house tried to smash their way into the car. They beat on the windows and tried to overturn it. Finally, policemen managed to force their way to the car and said to the black men: "Go like hell." They did.

Later on, more trouble started, sparked off by a cameraman who lit a magnesium flare to "film a scuffle between a small party of youths." The crowds, which had already begun to disperse, hurried back to the scene thinking there was a fire. There was a great commotion and shouting, "Find some niggers." By that time the black men had vanished from the streets. Finding no blacks to attack, a gang of white ruffians turned on the police, but no policeman suffered serious injury. Twenty-four white men were charged the following day. The Chief Constable held a press conference at which he said:

> This was not a racial riot. The coloured people behaved in an exemplary way by keeping out of the way. Indeed, they were an example to some of our rougher elements. The people primarily concerned were irresponsible teddy boys and persons who had had a lot of drink.

On the following Saturday night crowds again converged on the district and set about "nigger-baiting." A siege of some black people's houses developed into a battle between the tenants who hurled milk bottles from the upper floors and a white mob below who bombarded the houses with bricks and bottles, breaking several windows. In a dark alley blacks were chased by whites and five of them were set upon and assaulted. When police vans arrived on the scene people started to disperse and all became quiet.

No further anti-black demonstrations took place after that in Nottingham, but as a strange footnote a bus company in a nearby town advertised coach tours to see "the terror spots of Nottingham."

Most of the 3,000 blacks in Nottingham were pretty sure that there had been "a racial riot." A Jamaican, Lawrence Phillpotts, who lived in Nottingham for fourteen years after his demobilization from the Royal Air Force, said at the time: "For over a year an anti-coloured feeling has been growing up in the St. Ann's Well Road district where over 2,000 coloured people live. . . . The worst type of English working-class people live there, too. They're very ignorant and pick on coloured people. Teddy boys stand around the streets in groups and abuse coloured people who walk by."

An Englishwoman, Mrs. S. Barton, who ran a cigarette shop at the corner of Peas Hill Road and St. Ann's Well Road at that time, gave another reason for the trouble. She said: "Some white people see these coloured men rolling about in large sleek cars and they get worked up about it because they haven't got the same themselves."

Yet a third explanation for the flare up came from Claudius Stevens, a miner. He believed that the cause was even more basic. "There is jealousy because white men don't like to see their girls going with my countrymen."

That was not the end of the story. An English butcher in St. Ann's Well Road district admitted: "The coloured people are not bad, but they get humiliated. I have seen a group of Teddy boys stop a solitary coloured boy and not let him go until he had forked out four or five cigarettes to keep the peace."

He went on to say: "In a pub I saw a coloured man needled by a group of whites so much that he got fed up with it. When he said something to them they took him outside to report him to a policeman for starting a fight."

Nottingham was only a foretaste of events in Notting Hill in London. The extreme manifestations of racial unrest which editor Claudia Jones observed were very much in evidence. The British authorities seemed unaware that further disturbances were imminent even though there had been sporadic outbursts before the violence of Notting Hill. It continued non-stop for several days and had spread over a much wider area from Shepherd's Bush and adjacent Notting Dale to other pockets in Notting Hill, Kensal New Town, Paddington, and Maida Vale. In Nottingham the trouble had been in the middle of a district heavily populated with black people, but in London the main explosions occurred along the borders of relatively concentrated black settlements and even further afield. By far the most hostile elements came from the housing estates and districts which were and still remain white. North Kensington, which has a considerable cluster of black residents, a shady reputation, and blacks and whites living in close proximity in substandard conditions was comparatively quiet.

Although, as in Nottingham, the riots were preceded by a series of assaults, in London it was not the retaliation of those blacks who had been attacked which triggered off the crowd outbursts. Nor was there a set chain of incidents, like fights after pub closing time, during those turbulent days. What happened, was that "nigger-hunting," and "nigger-baiting," as the English newspapers described them, spread like wildfire. It attracted an increasing number of whites as active participants and passive spectators in several districts of London simultaneously.

Concrete evidence of this "nigger-hunting" came in July and August, 1958, when gangs of white youths were roaming around making specific attacks on anyone with a dark skin. For example, in mid-July a pack of fifteen "teddy boys" raided a black-owned cafe in Shepherd's Bush. These youths came from a large housing estate in nearby White City. They reduced the place to a shambles and ran away before the police could arrive. Again, twelve days after this incident, some twenty or thirty white youths attacked this same cafe. Six of them, whose ages ranged from eighteen to twenty-three and who came from Shepherd's Bush, Fulham, and Notting Hill, were arrested. Five were found guilty of causing "malicious damage" and were fined. In evidence at court the cafe owner said: "It was like an earthquake. I didn't try to stop them because

I would have been killed if I had." Three weeks after this last raid, on Saturday August 11, another gang of "teddy boys" besieged a house full of black tenants in Shepherd's Bush, smashing windows and doors. A laughing, jeering crowd of white people gathered, enjoying the spectacle and not making any attempt to stop the youths or summon the police.

This was the mood of the white populace in West London. They were after the blacks. Incidents which occurred over a period of weeks had an ugly, malevolent twist. Blacks were afraid to walk the streets for many reasons, one of them being a weekend sport practised by white car drivers. Such drivers, young teddy boys as well as respectable businessmen would drive their cars at black men and try either to kill them or run them off the streets. All over London, particularly in the western districts, slogans on walls began appearing out of nowhere; slogans painted in white; slogans which displayed the worst forms of fascism and which were not restricted to the "lunatic fringe" of race-haters, like the Mosleyites and the White Defence League; slogans blazoned with such phrases as "Keep Britain White," "People of Kensington Act Now," "Niggers Go to the Jungle," and "Blacks Go Home. You Have Been Warned." Not only were these anti-black signs sprawled across walls in the Notting Hill, Westbourne Park, and Ladbroke Grove areas; extremists like Oswald Mosley's Union Movement, Colin Jordan's White Defence League, John Bean and the National Labour Party (in no way associated with the British Labour Party), Andrew Fountaine's British National Party and a strong group called The League of Empire Loyalists were busy whipping up race hate and poisoning minds with continuous meetings, at which there would be this land of rhetoric:

> Boycott the Sammy Davis Show. We have no need for half-castes here. This one-eyed Jewish nigger should go home and give decent white artistes a chance.
>
> There are plenty of cages in the zoo. Failing that, go back to the jungle where you belong.
>
> The National Assistance Board pays the children's allowances to the Blacks for the coffee-coloured monstrosities they father. Material rewards are given to enable semi-savages to mate with the women of one of the leading civilised nations of the world. We must keep Britain White.

With passions inflamed by these extremist groups and feelings already at an explosive pitch, the battles of Notting Hill which started in earnest on a Saturday night August 23, 1958, did not surprise the black population. The strange thing about it was that those in authority seemed unaware that a racial cauldron had boiled over. British sociologist R. B. Davidson of the Institute of Race Relations in London, explained this attitude: "The official policy of the British Government was that the best way to deal with the problems that were arising was to leave them alone in the belief that the problems would solve themselves in time."'

They did not. On the Saturday night when the racial explosion took place, there was an air of acute tension and public exhibitions of aggression in many parts of West London. Before and after closing time that night there were several attacks on black people and the few houses they occupied. Then in the small hours of the morning, a gang of nine white boys aged between seventeen and twenty, most of them from the Shepherd's Bush area, cruised around the district in a car. They were, they said, "nigger-hunting," and were armed with iron bars torn from street railings, starting-handles, table legs, pieces of wood, and knives. As soon as they spied a black man walking along the street they would pounce on him and attack him mercilessly. Five black men were taken to hospital, three of them seriously injured. One was brought to the magistrate's court in a wheelchair to give evidence later. Another who had suffered a severe chest wound was taken into court on a stretcher, causing the magistrate to remark: "I have never before seen a man in that state brought into court. I don't think he is fit to give evidence."

This was the incident which the newspapers tagged the notorious case of the "nigger-hunting" youths. They were tried at the Old Bailey three weeks later and sentenced to four years' imprisonment each. In passing sentence Mr. Justice Salmon expressed feelings of revulsion.

This judgment became news around the world and it seemed to soften the savage blows which were struck at Notting Hill's black residents. Right-thinking English men and women were appalled, yet very few recognized the blatant, obvious signs of growing racial discord. However, one could not help but notice the fear and suspicion which showed in the faces of black people as they went about their daily business. No more was there any friendly banter between black people and whites in the markets or shops. More often white faces could be seen transformed into masks of sullenness whenever they had to move in and around black districts like Brixton, Paddington, Westbourne Grove, Ladbroke Grove,

Notting Hill, Portobello Market, Shepherd's Bush Market, Goldhawk Road and the Hammersmith area, all in south western London.

Newspapers were still more concerned with the incidents which had very recently taken place in Nottingham. The *Manchester Guardian* reported favorably on the stand of the British police in the Notting Hill area.

> Police have shown in this area that they are determined to be firm and have arrested some of those believed to have been involved in the incidents with complete impartiality. This, they believe, may prevent future outbreaks of violence.

The question of police impartiality has, however, remained in doubt. It was said and generally believed that some of the young police officers on duty in the Notting Hill area had served in Kenya during the Mau Mau trouble. The truth of this was never confirmed or denied at official level, but nearly all the black people who resided in the Notting Hill district during that period of unrest will tell—with one voice—that the British police were certainly not impartial. If anything, they adopted rather strong-arm, fascist dealings with blacks and white journalists who showed sympathy to blacks. In fact, one reporter was arrested and charged with a minor violation, and was acquitted by the magistrate.

The supposition that police impartiality would prevent further recurrence of racial violence proved false; three days after the story in the *Manchester Guardian*, shortly before midnight on Saturday, August 30, violence erupted on a far larger scale at Bramley Road in the neighborhood of Notting Dale, where, curiously enough, relatively few black people lived. Several of their houses were attacked: one house was set on fire; two others were bombarded with bricks and milk bottles; and a bicycle was thrown through the window of a fourth. An aggressive, angry crowd of about two hundred collected in the streets and rowdyism and fighting broke out, people arming themselves with iron railings, axes and some with bicycle chains. Two policemen were slightly injured in the fray, and thirty more were called in to clear the streets and restore a semblance of law and order. An incident which took place in Powis Square in the heart of the riot area is indicative of the general pattern of police behaviour:

A group of West Indians had gathered on the square outside a cafe owned and frequented by the West Indians and their English friends. The men stood around two BBC reporters who were on the scene taping on-the-spot interviews. Suddenly a Black Maria police van came to an abrupt stop nearby. A howl of delight came from a white crowd who had been standing on the other side of the square jeering at the West Indians. The police rushed towards the West Indians, began searching them and bundling them like sacks of coal or dirty clothes into the back of the Black Maria. One of the West Indians being searched, a bearded Jamaican called the Baron, a race leader and militant spokesman at meetings in the square and in Hyde Park, was being manhandled to such an extent that one of the BBC interviewers on the scene, Commander George Villiers, could not contain his feelings any longer. He exclaimed angrily: "Today, as an Englishman, I have been made to feel ashamed of British justice."

But the police went on with their rough handling. One of the officers asked "Have you any weapons on you?"

The Baron replied: "Yes . . . My weapons are pen and paper." And with that he proceeded to remove his fountain pen, with a flourish, and hand it to the police officer. Angered at the Baron's cool indifference three or four of the police officers grappled him by the seat of his trousers and his collar and pushed him into the Black Maria, banging his head on one of the back doors. As the police van drove off to the police station in Notting Hill, the Baron was seen to be bleeding.

Commander Villiers and the other BBC reporter (the writer of this book) on the scene went to the police station and were allowed to see and talk to the Baron. He was eventually granted bail. Both Commander Villiers and his BBC colleague agreed to come to the magistrate's court and give evidence. When the case was called the magistrate found it necessary to call only one witness, and even before Villiers could finish his evidence the magistrate stopped the case. He spoke in strong terms condemning the police officers involved for their behavior.

It would be no exaggeration to say that the attitude of the British police in the Notting Hill area during those days of riot and violence was unsympathetic and anti-black. The few policemen who were not prejudiced did not count for much in helping to stop the carnage and destruction which took place in that hot summer week of September of 1958.

The attitude of the criminal courts and the magistrates and judges is another matter. They acted justly, sternly, and treated those whites who beat up blacks with fairness and severity.

To go back to Notting Hill, on the Sunday morning of August 31, there were similar scenes in Bramley Road. Crowds of as many as four to seven hundred whites were involved in the fighting. The shouts of the white mobs of "nigger-hunters" sounded sharply against a background of row houses.

"We'll kill the black bastards."

"We'll castrate those black ponces."

"Lynch those black f . . . . . s."

There were pitched battles with iron bars, dustbin lids, knives and bottles between white and black, and between the "mob" and the police. Several people were severely injured and taken to hospital. Two police cars were systematically wrecked. All this took place even though the police had taken extra precautions and were patrolling the area in pairs. Disturbances then spread like wild fire in several other areas. A gang of one hundred youths arrived with sticks, iron bars, and knives gathered under the railway arches near Latimer Road Station. Almost within ear-shot, there were other skirmishes—in Harrow Road and in Kensal Rise, areas thickly populated with blacks. The report of the trial of some of the ringleaders involved in the Bramley Road fighting that evening was fully covered in most of the British national papers, the story in the *Manchester Guardian* being the most exact and unsensational:

> Ten white and three coloured men were later charged with making an "affray" and tried at the Central Criminal Court. Five men were sentenced to terms of imprisonment ranging from eighteen months to two years; eight others, including the three coloured men were found not guilty. A charge of making an affray has been seldom brought in the recent period. (There was one previous case in February 1957.) An affray is an ancient misdemeanour at common law, defined as "a fight of two or more persons in a public place to the terror of Her Majesty's subjects." The Recorder in sentencing the men said: "By your conduct you have put the clock back nearly three hundred years and disgraced yourselves and your families. As a growing menace, street warfare has made it necessary to revive the law and it must be sternly enforced if society is to be rescued from the miseries of the Middle Ages." He characterised their case as one of "street brawling sharpened and intensified by racial jealousy."

The situation was, in fact, alarming. Blacks remained hidden indoors as much as possible, showing themselves only when it was absolutely necessary—shopping when their supplies ran out and going to work in gangs or with police protection. Attacks on blacks were made by white youths and men indiscriminately—women, children, the aged were not exempt. Molotov cocktails, hand-made bombs, flaming rags soaked in petrol and lighted sticks were hurled through doorways and windows where black people lived.

From that Sunday there was an uninterrupted, chaotic, senseless, repetitive sequence of rioting and arson, day and night, over wider areas which threatened to spread and envelop whole sections of the metropolis where black people were resident or known to frequent. Crowds grew to pregnant sizes; tempers keenly edged; threats more insistent; and fears swelled to irrational proportions. This virus spread and so did the human failing of curiosity as more and more sightseers watched greedy-eyed for the sight of bashed-in black heads and the flow of blood. Although most of the more realistic black people remained indoors, realizing that the weight of white numbers was heavily tipped against them, the more militant and indignant, primarily Jamaicans, came out of doors ready to defend themselves against any attacking "Nordic." These black militants collected empty milk bottles, rocks, and some hand-made bombs; and around Blenheim Crescent, Powis Square, Powis Terrace and nearby spots shelled the baying, jeering white mobs in the streets from vantage points on the rooftops. These houses were bombarded with petrol bombs and bricks. There were attacks and counter attacks. After a while even black women joined with their menfolk in fighting the white hooligan mobs. The Jamaican women were in the forefront of this battle, but other West Indian women joined in. The Notting Hill Riots were race riots, and cannot properly be described otherwise. (This writer was a witness to the whole series of events.)

The climax to the Notting Hill riots came on Monday and Tuesday, September 1 and 2. Violence and all forms of disturbances broke out at all hours of the day and night and were widespread. Marauding whites came from all over London looking for "a punch up," ready to do grievous bodily harm to blacks. They continued in several places for many days. There were sporadic outbursts, too, similar to those of late August, and these continued until mid-September in Notting Hill, Notting Dale, Paddington, and also in a few scattered, more distant London districts.

Even the more popular of the national newspapers could not hide the horror and increasing fear and violence of the Notting Hill outbursts at the time. Top reporter commentator and writer Mervyn Jones, a colleague of this writer on Labour's Independent Weekly newspaper, *Tribune*, wrote for the issue of Saturday September 15, 1958, what has been described as one of the most penetrating reports of the "fascist activities in Notting Hill."

> I have seen fear—the fear of mob violence and race hatred—dominate a part of my native city.
>
> Fear . . . I try to interview a Labour Councillor in North Kensington, and am told he won't be at home. He has moved his family to stay with friends elsewhere for the time being. "You see," the explanation goes, "he lives right in the danger area."
>
> Fear . . . The barman in a pub tells me: "The women are petrified. You should have heard them scream last night. And it's starting again—we don't expect anyone to stir out of doors after dark."
>
> Fear . . . A woman peers cautiously out of her cafe and says: "Oh, dear, there they are gathering again. Can't anybody stop them?"
>
> Fear . . . I walk down Portobello Road with a Negro. Two young women of his colour stop him: "Can you fight, man? Come round where we live tonight. We're still alone—the rest of the house is white folks. Just passed four Teddy boys on the corner. They didn't say anything, just showed us their knives."
>
> Fear . . . A pub landlord relates that, in the dinner hour, he heard a gang deciding on the night's plan of campaign. He heard them say: "We're starting up Westbourne Park Road tonight." (So they did.) Then: "We'll do old . . ." and he mentions the name of a Councillor known for friendliness to coloured people. At this point he sees me make a note and exclaims: "Mind you don't print the name of my pub. The brewers won't send flowers if I go into hospital with twenty stitches."
>
> So I knew what to expect when darkness fell. The only thing I hadn't bargained for was this: people gathered in little groups on every corner, under every archway, not to take part in the terror, but to watch.
>
> As the mobs race down the road and an ambulance whirls past clanging its bell, I stop to talk to an elderly lady standing in her dressing-gown under the flaking porch of her once respectable house.
>
> She smirks with all her false teeth and says: "I'm just watching the fun, that's all." And I remember the Labour Party agent, Tom McGregor, telling me a few hours earlier in his Scots burr—"I'm thankful to say I'm not English."
>
> The "fun" begins. Five black men, grimly silent, stand warily in the yard of their house. A white boy rushes from a side-street, yelling: "They're all in the area, they can't get out."
>
> Another shouts: "Come on, let's go down there!"
>
> All at once, Westbourne Park Road is full of running screaming

people. All white: age, sixteen to twenty; quite a few of them girls, though I hear one lad tell his girl: "Will you bloody well stay there till we've finished!"

The darkness is bright with small, sudden fires, which burn harmlessly in grimy front gardens or are stamped out in the street when the police arrive. Someone phones the fire brigade and two engines roar up, but aren't needed.

A reporter takes lavish notes as a hysterical woman a block away from the trouble swears that the fires were started by the blacks.

A kid whose voice hasn't broken, but who insists he is sixteen, heads down the street with absurd determination. I advise him to go to bed. He calls me a foul name and pipes: "We're going to scare the hell out of the niggers."

The missiles were inexpertly thrown; some were not even used. I pick one up—a beer bottle half full of petrol, with a wad of felt jammed in the neck.

Later, at the police station, I see the haul of confiscated weapons. A butcher's meat hook; a spiked railing; the wooden bar of a starting handle; a file; an expensive adjustable spanner, probably stolen from the user's place of work.

The police seem to be few. But nothing much happens, because the gangs don't stand and fight. When the first squad car comes, they scatter and make for somewhere else—and they all seem to know where. Police and reporters prowl round, guessing.

We move down to Talbot Road, where the largest force of police I've yet seen—maybe twenty, with two Black Marias—rings a Negro club. Coloured men come out and yell: "What have we done? Why don't you chase up the gangs?" With them, scared and sulky, is a white girl. She is arrested.

The district seems to have gone mad. But I remember some of the sane, decent talk I've heard earlier in the day.

In a cafe, a white factory worker puts it like this: "I always say there's good and bad in all sorts. We're a mixed lot—English, Irish, Scotch, Welsh, Jews—so why not coloureds? Got some of them where I work. Some I like, some I don't."

He adds with satisfaction: "One girl we got there her boy friend is mixed up with the gangs. His old man slung him out of the house. That's the stuff."

In a pub argument, a customer declares that the Negroes ought to learn good manners. The landlord takes him up. "Manners? It's always please and thank you when I serve them, and a pleasant good morning if I meet them in the street. Some local lads drink with them. The decent sort, I mean, not these thugs."

The barman adds: "I've never seen a fight among the coloured chaps —not once." I ask if the white men start fights. He stares at me: "Are you kidding?"

A Jamaican who has worked for six years as a tailor and now owns property explains to me: "The people who started this are below average intelligence. I try to ignore people I can't reason with. I blame the newspapers and the television for the way they present this. The headlines call this a race riot, but it's just hooliganism."

Another says: "I respect most English people. We understand this is the work of a tiny minority. As I read in *The Times* today, they've got to have someone to attack. But what can it lead to? They can't kill us all. We won't yield. The Government can't deport us—it would be un-British."

He worked in an engineering factory till his hand was crushed in an accident. When it was mended, his job was gone. He thought of going back to Jamaica. "But not now. We've got to stick it out."

Roy Johnson, a railwayman, has been in Britain for seven years. He hasn't been to work since Monday. "They'll know why," he says. "I've got three children. I intend to protect them."

Fred Williams works in a barber's shop. The windows have been broken six times recently. "White people never see it happening," he tells me bitterly. "I can't figure out why they get this way. You say good morning, they don't answer. My wife knows she gets overcharged in the shops, but it's no good saying anything."

No, they can't figure it out. I hear the phrase repeatedly from black and white. Various explanations are advanced.

"Enviousness," says the woman in the cafe. "It all comes down to sex," declares the man in the pub. "Parents don't control their kids nowadays," says the landlord.

North Kensington is badly housed and overcrowded. Negroes have bought houses and forced out white tenants—but white landlords exploit the immigrants too.

Negroes walk out with white girls. "Can't help it if they like us," says the engineering worker with a grin. "Man, we're only human."

Someone tells me about unsavoury clubs. Then he digresses into an anecdote about "the worst club in the borough." It turns out to be run by whites.

Everyone criticises the police. "Half asleep . . . always there when it's all over" is the general verdict. Among the gangs, the assumption is that "the rozzers look after the niggers."

But the coloured men point to the large number of their people—obviously not the aggressors—among those arrested. One man tells me he was arrested while he was running away from twenty thugs, some of whom were caught. When he was taken to a cell, he says, a plainclothes detective said "Get inside, you black bastard."

The conviction is growing that someone is behind it. "The first two days, I thought it was spontaneous," says Tom McGregor. "Now I'm not so sure."

Several white people told me: "You see older men sit in cars and give

> directions." Nobody can identify them. I looked for them at the flash-point but in vain.
>
> I did see one man in obvious authority in the Kensington Park Hotel, rallying centre of the gangs. About fifty, with a brutalised red face, he wore a leather jacket and a peaked cap modelled on the old German Army pattern.
>
> The gangs certainly have a plan of campaign. People had heard shouts of "Oxford Gardens next!" I saw obvious messengers on fast motorcycles. Gangs arrive in cars from other parts of London.
>
> There are signals, too. As a packed car drove by, one young thug said to another: "It ain't them. Hasn't got its indicator out."
>
> "I reckon it's the Mosleyites," declared a young policeman.
>
> Their paper, ACTION, is sold vigorously in the riot area. And on Monday they held a meeting just where the clashes had been worst, in a place where meetings have never been held before. Nobody can understand why it was allowed.
>
> The speakers declared that only the Union Movement can keep Britain white. They tried to organise a march to the Labour Party office and made strong attacks on George Rogers, M.P.
>
> He is hated by the gangs because it was reported that he phoned Scotland Yard and demanded extra police when the rioting began. The march didn't come off; chasing Negroes was more exciting.
>
> What will happen now? It will die down, most people think. The gangs are cowardly and lack staying power; Negroes are grouping for self-defence; it might rain.
>
> But the harm will remain. There is a wary coldness between neighbours. North Kensington has no interracial clashes that I could hear of . . . "It will be a long time before good feeling is re-established," says Tom McGregor.
>
> And unless the fear can be broken, he will be right.

Up to this day the fear still remains. And, in any case, Tom McGregor was off reckoning when he spoke about the re-establishment of "good feeling." In the first place there was no "good feeling" in Notting Hill, an overcrowded, festering section of West London were the worst elements of the minority groups lived cheek by jowl; where one's Saturday night's brawl belonged to the couple in the next room or flat; where one couple's sexual idiosyncrasies were common property to the couple in the next room and vice versa.

Mervyn Jones's report was typical of those which appeared in most of the English newspapers of the time except that it was descriptive and did not try to cover up the ugliness of the situation.

The Times even, noted for its rigid objectivity, could report at that same time and occasion:

> A crowd of youths went through Oxford Gardens . . . smashing windows in houses where coloured people live; "They didn't miss a house," said one white resident.
>
> In Ladbroke Grave a well-dressed coloured man was kicked in the back as he was leaving the Underground Station. At once crowds started to gather and groups of youths fifty to one hundred strong rushed from the streets near by where they had been marching, shouting and throwing stones.
>
> It appeared they had been called to the scene by occupants of large cars, some of them containing eight or ten people, which were cruising round the area.
>
> A coloured man with a girl companion walking down Lancaster Road was chased by a crowd of screaming youths and girls. Saucers, cups, and bottles were thrown. The couple took to their heels pursued by the crowd crying "Let's get the blacks."

The *Manchester Guardian* of September 2 reported:

> It comes as a shock to hear the ugly phrase "Lynch him!" on English lips. But it must be reported that these words were used not once but a dozen times yesterday afternoon . . .

The *Manchester Guardian* report leaves no doubt about the motivating factors behind the Notting Hill debacle:

> Into this ugly situation stepped an outsider who had no inkling of what was in store for him. Mr. Seymour Manning is a twenty-six-year-old African student who is at present living in Derby. He had come down for the day to see friends in Notting Hill, and though he did not know it he was under close observation from hostile eyes from the moment he stepped out of the Latimer Road Underground Station.
>
> In the four hours that I had been in this area he was only the third coloured person that I had seen venture out of doors. I watched him disappear up Bramley Road. A few minutes later there was an outburst of screams and jeering and I saw Mr. Manning sprinting back towards the Underground, his tie and blazer streaming out behind him. As his three pursuers closed in, he turned in desperation and flung himself into the doorway of a greengrocer's shop, turned, and slammed it shut. A moment later, the shopkeeper's wife . . . appeared in the doorway, locked the door behind her, and turned to face the trio of thugs. She had two friends with her—a housewife of her own age and a boy in his teens.
>
> She kept them at bay until the police arrived a few minutes later. Soon after the first two constables came to her rescue, a radio car

> arrived, and after that came full reinforcements. It was during the interim period, before it was clear that the police were on their way in force, that people on the opposite pavement called out for a lynching. I went up to one of the young men, who looked to be about twenty-five, and asked him what he had against the African in the shop. "Just tell your readers that Little Rock learned us a lesson," was the reply.
>
> Another youth, who had also been calling for a lynching, turned to me and said: "Tell them we've got a bad enough housing shortage around here without them moving in. Keep Britain white."
>
> Half an hour after he had taken refuge in the store, Mr. Manning was rescued by a squad of policemen who held back the crowd and escorted him to a car. He was taken to the home of his friends, where he was treated for bruises and shock.

This violence ran unchecked as the tempers of the large crowds increased. Though the efforts of the police were strengthened they were of no avail. The member of Parliament for North Kensington, George Rogers, toured the area in a loudspeaker van, appealing to the people for "common sense, decency and tolerance in this matter of race relations." To the white mobs yelling murder and mayhem at every black man they saw, Rogers' words ran like water off a duck's back. Yet the tenacious M.P. kept asking people "to remain calm, to stay indoors in your homes tonight and to obey the police." Five white men who were subsequently fined in court were said to have been driving around in their sleek cars shouting "Stir them up," and other unprintable exhortations. When night descended on the district, the Union Movement, Oswald Mosley's group, set up a stand outside Latimer Road Underground Station. The purpose could only have been to add fuel to an already smoldering race fire and cause more violence and destruction. The following incident, reported in the *Manchester Guardian* of September 2, 1958, illustrates the intense racial feeling which prevailed in those days:

> A boy of fifteen appeared before the Juvenile Court. He was said to have approached a coloured man in a railway compartment at Liverpool Street Station and shouted: "Here's one of them—you black knave. We have complained to the Government about you people. You come here, you take our women and do all sorts of things free of charge. They won't hang you, so we will have to do it." The coloured man was frightened and moved to the other end of the compartment. Another passenger called the guards and the boy was put in the guard's van.

Scotland Yard issued an appeal to the public, declaring that the Metropolitan Police "will continue to carry out their duty to preserve the Queen's peace without fear, favour or discrimination." They stressed that "at incidents of unrest the situation is seriously worsened by the presence of sightseers." In spite of this Scotland Yard appeal, the incidents of the previous day were repeated. Most black people remained indoors, though some were indignant and took up more militant attitudes. Black bus conductors, however, who lived in the North Kensington area, were escorted home by police at the end of their working day.

The scene there at this period was described by a report in *The Times* of September 3:

> A dark face against the light of a lamp post in Bramley Road went by. "Look, that's a wog going along," said one of the many pale boys that stood about hawking *Action*, the Union Movement paper. But nobody stirred. Too many police were hovering about in the still warm air. The man went out of sight, the only dark face I saw.
>
> A big crowd of youths chanting, "Down with the niggers" assembled in Lancaster Road and a youth leading one group held up a banner with the slogan: Deport All Niggers.
>
> Racial feeling is not confined to the gangs of youths, many of them from the Elephant and Castle and other distant tough districts, who cause the trouble in the evenings. In one street where some of the ugliest fighting has taken place your Correspondent found a group of men in a public house singing "Old Man River" and "Bye Bye Blackbird," and punctuating the songs with vicious anti-Negro slogans. The men said that their motto was "Keep Britain White," and they made all sorts of wild charges against their coloured neighbors.

In all about fifty-five people were put under arrest on that day, more than on any of the previous days. They were held on a variety of charges: using insulting or threatening behavior, obstructing the police, or being in possession of offensive weapons. Curiously enough, firearms were not used. Weapons included broken milk bottles, dustbin lids, iron bars, and loaded leather belts. These were placed in a box marked "Exhibits" at the magistrate's court and to them were added flick knives, stilettos, razors, a bicycle chain, choppers, a club, and a huge carving knife.

The police and the peace-loving citizens in the area were hoping for rain to dampen tempers. When it did rain, on September 3—after four of the most violent days Londoners had ever witnessed—the crowds melted away and unrest became more localized. But the next day burnt hot and dry again and an air of tension returned. Petrol bombs were hurled at the houses of black people in Notting Hill and Paddington. The familiar "anti-Nigger" taunts followed by flurries of bottle-throwing started up again. The most trivial and harmless encounter between black and white raised tempers to race-hate heat. When a black mother's baby carriage brushed against, and became entangled with, a white mother's stroller at a road junction in North Kensington, a hostile crowd of about 150 people instantly collected on the spot, and the police had to be hastily summoned to disperse them and restore order.

The authorities, both British and those from the high commissions of the migrant countries, plus the myriad racial and other organizations, could not and had not done anything tangible to avert either Nottingham or Notting Hill. The pattern with the British government was to allow black Commonwealth migrants to enter the country unchecked. But once they were in, they were left, in the main, to their own devices and had to fend for themselves. They were apparently expected to get lost in a sea of white unwelcoming faces. Integration was never more than a word bandied about by the social historians and writers of the time. This is not meant as a slur on the hard, grinding, almost pioneering work which the Migrant Services Division of the Commonwealth High Commission in London—still young and groping for direction—was performing. They were tackling this complex traumatic mass arrival of black faces on a white scene against great odds.

So on September 5, 1958, only two days after a downpour of rain had eased the tension, the late Norman Manley, then chief minister of Jamaica, and Dr. Carl La Corbinière, the deputy prime minister of the now defunct West Indies Federation, presented their dignified, calm selves at the hot Notting Hill scene. A third peacemaker and nerve-soother, Dr. Hugh Cummins, the then prime minister of Barbados, arrived shortly afterwards. The sum total of their efforts has been described by the English writer Ruth Glass, an urban sociologist.

> They [Manley, La Corbinière and Cummins] held talks with the Government, addressed meetings of their countrymen and visited the critical areas in London and Nottingham. . . . Gradually the coloured people in the troubled districts of London went outside again. But unrest and fear were still acute until mid-September.

The police, not without police dogs, were still patrolling the area with reinforcements and dispersing any groups that formed in and around public houses and street corners, particularly black groups. When Mr. Manley was touring Paddington on September 8 with his VIP colleagues, he was ordered by the police to "move along" while he was in conversation with four other West Indians in the street. Irritated by the incident, Mr. Manley remarked later: "As there were fifteen to twenty people at the time on the opposite side of the street, I felt it was a discriminating act and indicative of the attitude of the people in the area to our people, which I can only hope is not general anywhere else."

During that period, calls from all quarters for calmness and tolerance fell on unheeding ears. Attacks on black people and their homes continued not only in the Shepherd's Bush to Paddington belt, but in several other places in Greater London. "Nigger-baiting" and sporadic attacks on blacks and their property never did stop, although there was a brief lull which some people thought due to Mr. Justice Salmon's controversial and severe sentence on the nine youths on September 15. What was noticeable in the riot area, however, was that standards of "normalcy" had changed. It could even be said that there were degrees of "normalcy," varying from a kind of coldeyed muted hostility to outbreaks of quarrels and minor skirmishes. Ruth Glass summed it up with these words:

> Since the riots sporadic aggression against coloured people in those marginal parts of West London has become routine, though it does not follow a regular curve. It has been an uneasy truce.

Mr. Justice Salmon may have been perfectly right when he said to those nine "nigger-hunting" white boys:

> It was you men who started the whole of this violence in Notting Hill. You are a minute and insignificant section of the population who have brought shame upon the district in which you lived, and have filled the whole nation with horror, indignation and disgust.

This view was current in England at the time. There was widespread agreement that a very small group of hooligans was responsible for the racial troubles in Nottingham, Notting Hill, and elsewhere. Subsequent events which are still very much embodied in the deep core of racial attitudes in Britain do not corroborate this reassuring view of the 1958 race riots.

Racial conditions in Britain in 1969 and 1970 proved to be as explosive as they had been over a decade before. Right wing "Keep Britain White" groups, extremist members of Parliament, and, indeed, the majority of the British people in spite of the welfare work of societies, race relations boards, and race acts and laws, have kept race hate on the boil; and it would not surprise even moderate thinkers in Britain if another Notting Hill flared up. It is now apparent that the "trouble makers of Notting Hill" gave violent manifestation to tendencies which were latent in the social strata of Britain. One might say that they were shouting what others were whispering when they saw black people living and working and laughing and loving in their midst. This very quality in the British national character clouds the whole race problem in ambiguity and danger, as George Lamming has noted:

> But this kind of ambiguity can produce the most disastrous consequences; and its worst example, in my experience, was the racial violence of Notting Hill. Here all the niceties of cricket came to an end. I don't think that we have heard the last word from Notting Hill.

The pervasive British ambivalence toward color, which was illustrated so sharply in 1958, remains unchanged.

BIBLIOGRAPHY TO CHAPTER FOURTEEN

Jones, Mervyn. "The headlines call it a race riot . . ." *Tribune.* (London: September 7, 1958).

Lamming, George. "After a Decade." *West Indian Gazette* (February, 1962).

Scobie, Edward. "The Lunatic Fringe." *Flamingo Magazine.* (London: September, 1961).

———. "A New Scar on the Face of Britain." *Tribune.* (London: September 5, 1958).

"On the subsequent repercussions . . ." *The Times.* (London: September 16, 1958). pp. 142–43.

"Trial of Bramley Road Men." *Manchester Guardian.* (London: September 20, 1958).

CHAPTER XV

NOTTING HILL AFTERMATH

Tension lasted for nearly a year after the Notting Hill riots. People were afraid that the coming summer months would be a repetition of the last. The British government, sad to say, was not really aware of the powder-keg which was still there, and which could be ignited and cause another race riot. And something did indeed happen—not a race riot but the senseless, brutal murder of a quiet West Indian, Kelso Benjamin Cochrane, from the island of Antigua.

It was about one o'clock on Sunday morning May 17, 1959, when the tall, lean Cochrane, bespectacled and soberly dressed, was walking along Southam Street, Notting Hill, to his furnished room a few streets away. On the sidewalk at the corner of Goldborne Road just about twenty yards in front of Cochrane were six white youths, all aged about fifteen or sixteen. They were lounging against a derelict shop window when they saw the West Indian walking in their direction.

Suddenly, the six of them rushed across the pavement and barred his way, shouting: "Hey! Jim Crow"—a favorite racial insult with the Notting Hill street toughs.

Then they began to attack Cochrane. One of them tried to rip out an iron railing to use as a weapon, but failed. The black man, whose left thumb had already been broken and was in plaster, tried as best he could to ward off the knife attacks, but was outnumbered.

In just under sixty seconds the fight was over. Kelso Benjamin Cochrane was left on the sidewalk, bleeding to death from a knife wound in his chest.

The six white ruffians scuttled away from the scene of their crime to the back-street, crumbling and over-crowded row houses which bred them and which, in a shroud of stubborn silence, hid them and has hidden them ever since from justice.

Not long after, two black men and a taxi driver found Cochrane, barely alive, on the sidewalk at the corner of Goldborne Road and Southam Street. Ironically, only a few yards behind him stood a blue police box complete with telephone. It was empty and there was not a policeman in sight.

The two black men and the taxi-driver lifted Kelso Benjamin Cochrane up from the ground, then took him to St. Charles Hospital. It was too late. He was already dead!

The most important witness of the crime was twenty-two-year-old Mrs. Joy Okine, the English wife of a Ghanaian boxer. She was sitting sewing in her home, only twenty yards from the spot where Cochrane was stabbed to death. She said:

> When I saw what was happening, I tried to get downstairs. My mother stopped me as she had heard the boys call out "Jim Crow" and we know what that means round here. . . . There was a fight. The coloured man was sticking up for himself. He went down and the others gathered around. . . . Then it was all over and the boys vanished. The coloured man was left on the pavement. I didn't look after that. I mind my own business around here. The boys were around fifteen or sixteen. . . . They were smartly dressed, but I thought they had been drinking.

After telling the police what she said, Mrs. Okine became so afraid of reprisals that she had to be guarded by policemen on twenty-four-hour duty outside her home. And there was justification for this action: one white youth who would not disclose his name boasted: "The gangs around here would take their revenge on any white person they thought had given information."

From the very beginning the search for Cochrane's killers has proved difficult. The day after the murder the police made this statement: "We are checking on various eye-witness reports of the fight, but most of the statements are conflicting. We have not made much headway up to now." The weapon—a stiletto-type knife with a six-inch blade—could not be found, despite the fact that detectives and council workmen searched thirty street drains near the spot where Cochrane was killed. A knife said to be the murder weapon was sent in the mail to Harrow Road Police Station, but on examination this claim proved to be false.

All the elements of the Kelso Cochrane murder case have been conflicting. The police claim that the motive was robbery. Others are sure that it was a race crime. To back that up, a white youth came forward to say that he had been approached by fascist elements to murder a black man —any black man—for £200. Joy Okine, who witnessed the killing, maintains that Kelso Cochrane died "because he was coloured." The forty-five-year-old taxi-man, George Isaacs, who saw three youths running away from the murder spot said: "I'd recognise the killers anywhere," but the police never managed to bring the Cochrane killers to justice. In May, 1959, an announcement was made that the police knew the killers, but no one was charged. Detective-Superintendent Ian Forbes-Leith made this statement: "We are still very much concerned with the case and are actively engaged in finding Cochrane's killers. The files on the case are certainly not closed." Most blacks in Britain, however, believe that the investigation of the crime was half-hearted, and the bad taste left in the mouth by this wanton and senseless murder has not become less bitter with time.

The belief that Cochrane was killed because he was a black man has been accepted by every black person in Britain. The attitude of white youths in Notting Hill over the Cochrane murder supports this view. It was summed up by one of them when he declared arrogantly: "Just one less of the blacks, I say. We've got too many of them here anyway."

The week after the murder of Kelso Benjamin Cochrane, the situation in Notting Hill was certainly no better, and, if anything, rather worse than it had been during the race riots of the previous year. It was common practice, then, for English youths to hurl bricks at black people's homes, breaking their windows, and to insult them in the streets. In a period of four months, Roy Lando, a hairdresser from Jamaica, had his salon in St. Mark's Road damaged half a dozen times. Finally, he boarded up the windows and doors with planks of thick wood because he felt that it was pointless repairing the damage again and again. There was precious little police protection for the property of blacks in that neighborhood, and no one would come forward with information about the incidents. Trinidad-born Macdonald Moses, who was public relations officer of the Coloured Peoples Progressive Association, talked about the worsening of relations between blacks and whites:

> After the riots last year there was a sign that coloured and whites were willing to get together and put differences right.
>
> But while this progressive work was going on, fascist elements set to work suggesting compulsory repatriation of coloured people. That bad housing and unemployment could be blamed on coloured people and that if they were sent home things would be put right. In the past few months the White Defence League and Mosley have intensified the anti-Negro campaign with the result that tension is mounting.

Donald Chesworth, London County Councillor for North Kensington, who was in the thick of things, a tireless worker for better race relations in the Notting Hill district, shared this view:

> Of course, Mosley's presence in the area and his desire to stand as a Parliamentary candidate is causing unrest. And I'll tell you why.
>
> People in Notting Hill for some reason or other seem to be dissatisfied and unhappy. Mosley tells them that coloured people are taking their homes away from them, that mixed marriages should be made illegal, and that all Negroes should be sent back to their own country. Naturally, that breeds hatred of coloured people. This hatred leads to acts of violence being committed.

One of the architects of race hatred was Colin Jordan, a former schoolteacher, whose offices were at 74 Princedale Road, Notting Hill. He was the man behind the White Defence League. His organization published a newspaper called *Black and White News,* which was being hawked around the Notting Hill area along with similar propaganda pamphlets. Among its reasons for "Keeping Britain White" were that "the coloured invasion increased the housing shortage enormously; that the employment of British workers was in danger; and that Negroes promoted vice."

Not a day passed without the residents of Notting Hill finding anti-black pamphlets in their mail. English families were being urged to "stop the coloured invasion." Spokesmen from the West Indies high commission in London sent pleading messages to West Indians to keep tempers cool. But these West Indians were losing faith and had taken more than they could stomach; people like Peter Fryer, editor of *The Newsletter,* and the Trotskyites made more sense to them. Black organizations and black people were urged to join in patrolling the streets, protecting the more timid blacks who remained in their homes expecting violence to enter their front doors.

Other black organizations also felt that "the law-abiding agencies" failed to give them adequate protection. These organizations were not given to hysterical shouting and extremism; but they, too, were prepared to organize protection groups. At the head of this move was Aloa Aka Bashorun, chairman of the Committee of African Organisations in Britain, which included representatives from twelve organizations working for the welfare of black people. Mr. Bashorun demanded "adequate, unbiased police protection," but, failing that, his committee had pledged itself to try to get "full permission to organise our own defence."

Several other groups, both white and black, were working along what they termed "constructive" lines to ease the feeling of ill-will and tension which the Mosleyites, the White Defence League and other fascist bodies had been spreading in Notting Hill. In July, the Institute for Group and Society Development, led by Dr. Richard Hauser and his wife Hephzibah Menuhin, held a Goodwill Week in the neighborhood. There were essay competitions for black and white children; cricket matches between English and West Indians; exhibitions of African art at Leighton House; special films with black actors in tolerably dignified roles; steel band concerts; dancing and drama presentations by black artists in the London parks; and finally a dance for whites and blacks at Porchester Hall in Paddington.

Welfare organizations, borough council bodies, government agencies, and liberals and citizens of all races went all out to heal the sores of Notting Hill and Kelso Benjamin Cochrane. At that time those involved believed that these efforts would bring quick results. Donald Chesworth, who established on-the-spot headquarters in Cambridge Gardens so that he could work quickly and get things going was very optimistic: "Let's look on the bright side. In every case of discrimination all the public bodies and the general public have opposed them and won. We have made progress in other directions, too. Every school in the area has coloured children and coloured teachers."

Chesworth, with unfounded optimism, looked upon this "so-called progress" in race relations in Notting Hill as only a beginning. More plans were put into operation for improving these conditions. In conjunction with Dr. Donald Soper (later Lord Soper) and certain other organizations, Chesworth planned to open a community centre for all races near Ladbroke Grove. He claimed that there was "a shocking lack of social amenities in the district which must be put right."

Another group which had already joined hands in this "let's get together and love each other" brotherhood of racial goodwill was the Stars Campaign For Inter-Racial Friendship (SCIF). A three-point plan was elaborated by SCIF's secretary Peter Leslie:

> First, SCIF militants are to go around the streets distributing copies of our pamphlet *What the Stars Say.*
>
> Second, well-known stars are to write letters to the press deploring acts of racial intolerance as they occurred.
>
> Third, sympathisers and members of SCIF in the press, radio, television, theatre and films are to go to all lengths at their command to expose publicly and protest more strongly against race prejudice whenever this became necessary.

One of the many duties of the office of the Commissioner in the United Kingdom for the West Indies, British Guiana, and British Honduras was to see about the welfare of West Indians in Britain. This office set in motion a Community Development Centre which brought together seventeen white and black welfare organizations in London. Regrettably, these scores of estimable groups working towards racial harmony had scant success.

Out of the racial hatred and mob violence there did emerge one organization with high ideals, the Standing Conference of Organisations concerned with West Indians in Britain. The need for and the birth of such a body was explained by Jamaican writer Eric McAlpine very graphically:

> So Notting Hill, though shameful to Britain, unconsciously served as a stimulant to mould togetherness among West Indians in Britain. Hitherto, West Indians wended their individual ways, not caring about each other, and the problems of discrimination and injustice with which they were faced. Notting Hill, to use a Jamaican expression, "put fire under Quaco tail" and made him see that his individualistic way of life only meant that he could die without a friend to attend his funeral.

The need was felt for an organization to act as "a bridge between the English and West Indian communities." The founders wanted to meet and discuss common problems affecting their relationship in the community, and to take collective action to ensure that tragedies like Notting Hill would not recur. The Standing Conference, they argued, could not be a completely West Indian organization as far as individual members were concerned.

Right from its inception in that tragic year, 1958, the Standing Conference of West Indian Organisations, which had executive officers of both races, stated that it would not abuse everybody with a white skin. It maintained that as far as it was concerned "Unity is the first prerequisite of the West Indian in Britain; plus having friends who can argue his case in certain quarters." It recognized that the West Indian Community was in Britain to stay and that the Standing Conference would have to act soberly in what it set out to do and, at the same time, be a militant voice against injustice. By the time it became well established it had sixteen interracial organizations affiliated to it in the London area alone.

The primary task with which the Standing Conference concerned itself was integration, a task which was made doubly difficult because of Britain's hidebound attitude to class which becomes even more rigid when extended to racial barriers. The Standing Conference stood little chance of succeeding in its objective. This was not apparent at the time and was best explained by the retired Trinidad politician and former federal minister Albert Maria Gomes, who went to settle in Britain. He said: "The Englishman's real trouble in his difficulty in accepting us."

However, the Standing Conference has succeeded in bringing before the public some of the problems of West Indians living in Britain: relations between West Indians and the police; bad housing conditions, and the other problems of discrimination. By bringing these matters before the authorities, the Standing Conference gained recognition at both local council and government levels. Members of the three main political parties in Britain—Conservative, Labour, and Liberal—have been regular guests at all meetings of the Standing Conference. In a reciprocal manner, Standing Conference members have been invited, from time to time, to attend political meetings. The Standing Conference has also been acting as policymaker and guide to member groups carrying out the field work. Speaking of those early days of the Standing Conference, West Indian Chairman Clem Byfield said that "The original idea was that it should be concerned with the training of leaders of West Indians in Britain. But this idea was quickly put aside. . . . Now we go about and address many English groups on the West Indian way of life and problems of West Indians in Britain. Now no one is doing that from government level."

The problems which the Standing Conference considers important are social security and economic development. The members felt that when economic development was attained the West Indian would get social security and integration. Byfield put forward the view:

> Because we have made a study of minority groups all over the world we are convinced that when you have got economic strength, you are more easily accepted in society. The Standing Conference has been working towards that end. Integration has so far been the main thing that we have pushed. It has not been the success we hoped for originally; we are now going to try and get that through the strength of our pockets.

The Standing Conference of West Indian Organisations has not been successful in integrating the races. In its early years the most that could be said of its achievements was that it helped West Indians to demand in a frank way the same hospitality in Britain that they gave to Britons in the West Indies. The English members of the Standing Conference were no less zealous in their efforts at integration than their West Indian colleagues. They worked tirelessly to break down the barriers. Like their West Indian counterparts they dreamt of "a West Indian centre in London; somewhere to meet, and where our host of English friends can come and meet us."

The years have shown that race relations in Britain instead of improving have become worse. The Standing Conference is not to be blamed for this. Its efforts have met with a growing wave of white extremist propaganda. Perhaps this accounty for its changed approach to the problem. It has become a more militant, aggressive group, much in keeping with the mood of the black man everywhere in the world today, particularly in the United States.

The British government itself decided to examine what positive steps it should take to prevent further racial violence and avoid inviting what one newspaper writer called "Birmingham, Alabama," to its shores.

The flood of reports, comments, and articles first caused by the riots, continued non-stop for twelve months. The opinions of official institutions and their spokesmen began to be made public and to be clarified. Week after week, radio and television programs, local and national conferences were devoted to the subject of the black population. Prominent personalities, organizations of all shades of social, economic, and political color, political parties, trade unions, voluntary bodies and even the soapbox speakers of London's Hyde Park gave voice to their views on the problems of black and white in Britain. The British Council of Churches and many ministers of religion and their congregations spoke out. After the deed there was no shortage of condemnation for the "dastardly attacks."

The Labour party in a statement on racial discrimination said:

> The Labour Party utterly abhors every manifestation of racial prejudice, and particularly condemns those instances which have recently occurred in this country.

The Bow Group, an independent research society of younger Conservatives said:

> The foreign reputation of the United States has suffered severely as a result of Little Rock. For the U.K. to be laid open to similar charges would disillusion many who look upon Britain as a tolerant corner in an intolerant world.

A warning came from the Conservative Commonwealth Council:

> We cannot retain the integrity or the cohesion of the Commonwealth unless we can solve and eradicate colour prejudice here in Britain.

When the Notting Hill disturbances occurred, the House of Commons was in its summer recess. But as soon as Parliament reconvened, debates were held in both Houses. Opinion polls were carried out on racial conditions. The Queen in her 1958 Christmas Day message made a friendly reference to people from the Commonwealth living in Britain, obviously alluding to black migrants.

Many solutions for racial tension were proposed. Some of the measures suggested included more housing for low-income groups; better methods of educating people in the responsibilities of citizenship; and improved mutual exchange of information on British and Commonwealth affairs; legislation against racal discrimination and group defamation.

The government felt that these proposals did not get to the root of the matter. Public opinion maintained that the "colour problem" was aggravated by the growth of the black minority, and, as they wrongfully claimed, especially by "undesirable" black immigrants. Certain members of Parliament backed by several right wing newspapers, not forgetting the extremist "lunatic fringe" demanded that immigration of black people into Britain be controlled. They went further, proposing that migrants from the Commonwealth who were convicted of criminal offenses should be deported. That was the beginning of the Act which was to put the brakes on black immigration from the West Indies and other parts of the British Commonwealth. Entering the British Isles without let or hindrance, visa or work permit, or any other entry certificate or voucher was to be stopped.

It was immediately after the outbreak of violence in Nottingham, that two members of Parliament, one Conservative (Nottingham Central), the other Labour (Nottingham North), called for a partial closing of the "open door" policy which Britain had always operated for migrants from the British Colonies and Commonwealth. They were sternly rebuked by the liberal independent *Manchester Guardian* which wrote: "It is deplorable that they should have spoken as though the entire onus rested on the coloured community and talked of restricting immigration to the country as if this might be the prime remedy."

But the views of those two parliamentarians found many supporters and the happenings at Notting Hill intensified the demand for curbing immigration made by several other M.P.s and elder statesmen, and in particular by some of the previous advocates of the "quota" system of entry. This pressure was shown very clearly in this last paragraph of the government's statement issued on September 3, 1958.

> As regards the wider aspects of policy, Her Majesty's Government has for some little time been examining the results of this country's time-honoured practice to allow free entry of immigration from Commonwealth and colonial countries. While this study of major policy and its implications and effects on employment will continue, Her Majesty's Government do not think it right to take long-term decisions, except after careful consideration of the problem as a whole.

The first part of the text reads:

> The Home Secretary, Mr. Butler, has reported to the Prime Minister on the incidents involved in racial disturbance in Nottingham and Notting Hill. Those incidents have an immediate and a long-term importance.

English sociologist Ruth Glass made this observation:

> It could hardly be denied that the demand for restrictions did not refer to the majority of immigrants from the Commonwealth—to those who are white—but to the minority, those who are coloured. It had already been estimated in 1956 that about one in four of all immigrants from Commonwealth countries in the United Kingdom were coloured. Immigration control was a polite term for some sort of colour bar.

The Conservative party in power, the opposition Labour party and the Liberals then began a see-saw game, with the government thinking of modifying its views on immigration restriction. This change of attitude was caused by reaction in the Commonwealth and also in Britain. As a result, and as a palliative to this strong criticism the British government reported in December, 1958, that it "did not see the necessity for any general control of immigration. The Government are considering very carefully the possibility to deport criminals."

The government admitted, however, that such an action would give rise to great complexities. Hence when the issue was further discussed, a cool attitude was adopted toward suggestions for the deportation of criminals. This was by no means the end of the matter. Some members of the opposition Labour party, right from the beginning, supported the idea of controlling immigration. Others went as far as to back proposals to deport undesirables. But the party line was of a different nature:

> We are firmly convinced that any form of British legislation limiting Commonwealth immigration to this country would be disastrous to our status in the Commonwealth and to the confidence of the Commonwealth peoples.

The Liberals were of the same mind. The Labour party's policy was to change when it came into office.

There were more hypocritical assurances from other quarters. The Conservative Commonwealth Council, for instance, speaking for the anti-immigration wing of the Conservatives, gave the assurance that it would be wrong to "deny Commonwealth citizens their traditional right to come to Britain"; adding: "It is our view that if we were to legislate against colour we would in the end bring about the disintegration of the Commonwealth."

Members of both political parties, Conservative and Labour, who were in favor of immigration control, were always anxious—in the beginning, that is—to say that they did not intend "to legislate against colour." As the public debate on the issue continued some Conservative M.P.s showed their true motives. Such a one was Mr. Cyril Osborne, who came out as a knight in shining white armor and boasted:

> I realise that our motives might be misrepresented overseas, but it is time someone spoke for this country and for the white man who lives here, and I propose to do so.

Mr. Osborne went on to list the potential dangers—imagined—that black people would bring into Britain: tuberculosis, leprosy, prostitution, drugs, crime, etc. His speech was received with some dismay on both sides of the House of Commons. Some M.P.s showed anger and embarrassment at his lack of tact. A number of members were inclined to support the idea of deporting criminals. A Labour M.P. made of braver stuff than the rest, Dr. Horace King, replied to Mr. Osborne immediately:

> Having just returned from the Deep South, I may be pardoned if I make an observation or two on the distasteful remarks we have just heard . . . remarks which almost made me feel I was in the South again. . . . I believe it is almost a sin against the Holy Ghost to equate crime with the colour of the skin.

The debate was to assume national proportions. In fact, it affected the whole of the British Commonwealth of Nations and the future of Britain's role in a multi-racial Commonwealth whose population was four-fifths black. There was nothing the British government could do which could erase the idea from the minds of most people that the question of control of immigration in Britain was inspired by race prejudice. In fact, Mr. Martin Lindsay, a Conservative M.P., in seconding a private member's motion "to restrict immigration" was quick to say:

> We all know perfectly well that the whole core of the problem of immigration is coloured immigration. We would do much better to face that and discuss it realistically in this context. . . . We must ask ourselves to what extent we want Great Britain to become a multi-racial community.

The climate of opinion on the government and opposition front benches was such that it would be politically unwise to restrict immigration from the Commonwealth. It was felt that this would have an undertone of race prejudice if pursued. This feeling was shared by the Upper House. Lord Salisbury made it quite clear:

> I know that it would only embarrass them [Her Majesty's Government] if we were to do that at the present time, and the last thing we want to do is to embarrass the Government on this particular issue. It would be far better, if possible, to settle this matter by agreement.

Wisely, the government shelved the idea of restrictive legislation on Commonwealth immigration to Britain, though it was taken up again in a relatively short space of time. For the time, being, anyway, a suggestion was made to explore the possibilities of coming to an agreement with Commonwealth countries.

Coinciding with this mood, another line of thought was taken up by some members of Parliament; talk of anti-discrimination bills began to be heard. In the House of Lords, Lord Silkin said "We are all against discrimination, just as, in theory, we are all against sin." No one, however, could agree how to fight the sin of racial discrimination: should discrimination against people because of race, color or creed in employment, housing, hotels, restaurants, and other places be made illegal? Like the issue of control of immigration this was nothing new. Discrimination had been practised against the Jews for decades; in World War II black troops in Britain and other theatres of war had experienced many of its ugly manifestations. There had been a number of cases brought to the attention of the public by the press; and one in particular, the Learie Constantine case (p. 188), received wide publicity. It took pride of place in the paper at the time in spite of the fact that it happened in the heat and action of the 1939–45 war. In Parliament in the late forties and fities several questions on the legal aspects of discrimination had been put before the House on a number of occasions. Many private members' bills to make discrimination an offense punishable under the law had been presented but none of these gained a majority. Neither the postwar Labour governments nor the successive Conservative governments showed any inclination to introduce such legislation. They put forward the usual threadbare arguments which were to be used *ad nauseam* until the sixties.

These arguments were based on three main contentions: first, it was claimed that such legislation was unnecessary because "some of the sanctions implicit in existing common and criminal law were relevant and adequate." Second, members of Parliament held stoutly to the view that "discrimination was not a fit subject for legislation because it was difficult to draft an Act defining the offences, and to enforce it; and to do so, moreover, without interfering with certain common law privileges of individual freedom." Third—and by far the strongest argument—was that discrimination could not be removed through "the majesty of the law" but only through the influence of "enlightened public opinion."

There were those, too, who said that there had been legislation against racial discrimination in the United States and it had not brought any better conditions. In fact, they said, it had only inflamed the already strained relations between blacks and whites. They did not want such a state of affairs to exist in Britain. But the Nottingham and Notting Hill riots served to throw these groundless claims back in their faces and prove to them that the "certain privileges" in the common law were woefully inadequate to stop the racial animosity which was mounting everywhere in Britain. The Labour party recognized this danger and soon after the disturbances in September, 1958, issued this statement:

> The Labour Party urges Her Majesty's Government now to introduce legislation, making illegal the public practice of discrimination. In any case, it pledges the next Labour Government to take an early opportunity of introducing such legislation. . . . It will use the full weight of Government influence against all such discrimination.

As can be expected the Conservative party and its government members in both Houses disagreed. The same antediluvian arguments trotted out previously against legislative proposals of this nature were echoed again more loudly. Another argument was that discrimination would be increased rather than diminished by any formal legal prohibition against it. One government spokesman in the House of Lords, Lord Chesham, in an extensive debate on the question, argued:

> The Act of Parliament would run a risk of recognizing the existence of discrimination in a way which might draw attention to it and would tend rather to foster it than to do away with it.

Prejudice however, could no longer be kept in the background; incidents of racial discrimination were occurring with increasing regularity and always made news. People began to take sides in a very positive way; and as the back alley agitation by the less educated among the English working class became increasingly ugly in character, the cry for countermeasures by friends of the black man gained momentum and would not be ignored.

Already in that year a group of twelve Labour M.P.s led by Fenner Brockway (later Lord Brockway) had made an abortive attempt when they sponsored a private member's bill to make illegal "discrimination to the detriment of any person on the grounds of colour, race and religion in the United Kingdom." Actually, it was the third attempt by Mr. Brockway to introduce such legislation. The bill defined discrimination:

> . . . a person exercises discrimination where he refuses, withholds from or denies to any other person facilities or advantages on the ground of the colour, race or religion of that other person.

It then described the public places as lodging houses, restaurants, and dance halls in which discrimination should be made an offense under the law. It also made proposals "that restrictive covenants or provisions in leases, relating to the use or occupation of premises, should be void; and that restrictive practices in employment should not be allowed." The bill was framed so that if it became law it would have an educational rather than a punitive purpose. The proposed penalties were slight, with a maximum fine of five pounds for a first offense, and of twenty-five pounds in the case of a second offense and conviction. Another stipulation was "that anyone in charge of a licensed (or registered) public establishment who practised discrimination (as defined) may be refused a renewal of or deprived of his license or registration."

This bill suffered the fate of most private members' bills: it did not even get a second reading in the House of Commons. After the riots these same twelve members of Parliament came back with a similar bill, only to meet with the same disappointment. Those in the House who favored an anti-discrimination law were too few to have their wishes accepted by the majority. Similar proposals were later put forward, both formally and informally. In the summer of 1959, a deputation of Labour and Conservative M.P.s discussed their moves for an "anti-colour bar" legislation with R. A. Butler, the then home secretary. Following a pattern already dictated by the government Mr. Butler by implication repeated the Conservative view that such legislation would serve no useful purpose:

> Racial discrimination has no place in our law and responsible opinion everywhere will unhesitatingly condemn any attempt to foment it.

This view forced Sydney Silverman, a Labour party member, to ask:

> Will the Rt. Hon. Gentleman bear in mind that while it is perfectly true, as he said, that racial discrimination forms no part of our law, there is nothing in our law to make racial discrimination itself illegal? Does he not think that the time is rapidly approaching when there ought to be?

It was apparent to everyone that government was in no way prepared to make racial equality a part of British law. For, at that time, the press also brought to the notice of the government and the people of Britain that the government had not ratified an International Labour Office Convention "to pursue a national policy designed to eliminate any discrimination on the basis of race, colour, sex, religion, political opinion, national extraction or social origin in respect of employment or occupation," and to introduce the appropriate legislation whenever it was found necessary. The government reply was a White Paper of June, 1959, saying that "while fully sympathetic to the spirit of the two Instruments," they did "not propose to ratify the Convention or to accept the supplementary Recommendation."

This smelt of hypocrisy. Sympathy with the ILO Convention and the minority voice in the House of Commons in favor of anti-discrimination was not enough. It only created more tension in race relations and gave the white extremists more reason to stoke up racial hate. The Kelso Benjamin Cochrane murder was a grim manifestation of this active racial hatred which was polluting the minds and lives of all peoples in Britain, particularly the whites who interpreted the government's reluctance to make any bold move on the issue to mean that the government supported their resentment of the presence of black people in Britain. The immigrants themselves realized that their position was more and more insecure and that they were in a position where every basic liberty and freedom which existed in the constitution of Britain, could very well be denied them because of race and color. This situation bore a certain similarity to the James Somersett case (see chapter V) where the law took no notice of blacks.

Little wonder that the "Keep Britain White" groups came out openly and with strong fascist-toned expressions:

BLACKS INVADE BRITAIN
REDS COUNT ON BLACKS
BLACKS SEEK WHITE WOMEN
BLACKS MILK THE ASSISTANCE BOARD
AMERICA POURING NEGRO TROOPS INTO BRITAIN

were the headlines emblazoned on the lead page of *Black and White News*, published by Oswald Mosley's White Defence League, who were joined in their racist campaign by the National Labour Party and by a British branch of the Ku Klux Klan whose headquarters was in Waco, Texas.

On April 15, 1959, just before the Kelso Cochrane murder, the propaganda of these hate groups had reached such a pitch that the British Caribbean Association of the Conservative Commonwealth Council issued a strong warning:

> In the atmosphere which still exists in the Notting Hill neighbourhood, the presence and propaganda of Sir Oswald Mosley and his followers with the "Keep Britain White" slogans could easily start off new outbreaks, especially during the summer months when it is customary for both white and coloured residents to congregate in groups in alley-ways or on street corners. It is hoped that the police will watch the activities of this fascist element, which we regard as disruptive and dangerous, especially in that part of London.

Three weeks later Kelso Benjamin Cochrane was murdered.

In 1960, a shot was fired through the window of the editorial offices of *Tropic* magazine, presumably intended for the editor (the author) who had only just left the room. An editorial comment in the magazine noted that although the incident was reported to the local police, no result of the investigation was ever reported.

The government was still playing a weak, indecisive role in tackling the race problem, and by 1961 the hate organizations had achieved a kind of national notoriety. Secretly, large segments of the silent British people supported their views. The Ku Klux Klan began a wider campaign issuing threats to prominent blacks in the racial conflict in Britain. Their threats and invectives were aimed particularly at black newspapermen and editors in Britain. During the period of the Notting Hill flare-up the editor of the Brixton-based *West Indian Gazette* caught the attention of the Ku Klux Klan, who must have thought it the right moment to add to the ferment and create more tension, fear, and violence. Although they held no meetings in Trafalgar Square or on the London street corners, mysteriously their literature began appearing. One Britisher appeared on television claiming that he was a member of the Klan and that the organization was growing and indeed had already started intimidating blacks.

The year of Kelso Benjamin Cochrane's murder was a general election year, and hate groups used the question of race on their platforms with impunity. In fact, some of the less scrupulous contestants for seats in Parliament took stands against immigrants in their vote-catching antics. They acted in the belief—not unjustified—that black immigrants were not wanted in Britain; and to make repeated reference to the problems attendant on uncontrolled immigration of black people into Britain was a sure way of winning seats. Mosley jumped into the fray very early; he made his first election speeches in April when he stood as a Union Movement candidate for North Kensington. Throughout the summer and autumn, Mosley's Union Movement held outdoor and indoor meetings, and eagerly canvassed from door to door, using the telephone, pushing provocative publications into mail boxes and interfering at the meetings of other parliamentary candidates. All these high powered pressure tactics did Mosley little good. He did not come close to gaining a seat in Parliament, getting only 8 percent of the votes, but that did not in any way diminish his fervor.

Others, too, were out in full battle array. In 1961, when the writer was editing the London-based magazine *Flamingo,* he came to the notice of the Ku Klux Klan because of an article written in the September, 1961, issue of the magazine. Two letters were the result, the first dated October 4, 1961:

> My dear Black Savage:
>
> I have here before me a copy of *Flamingo* dated September 1961 in which the Aryan Knights Ku Klux Klan of Britain has received mention. You have little idea just how much. Many groups have turned to us for help, and we are training them with patience for that DAY when

by combined effort, we will drive the black brothel crawlers from the shores of Britain. It is said that fire purifies, and we intend to purify. Perhaps your office is high on the list. Have you heard of one black bas . . . called Kelso Cochrane? Unfortunately, he attacked a Klansman but did not get far enough away to tell the tale. What did the police do? They did not help the foul-mouthed Mau Mau oath taker. They turned the other way. You have been warned—Black Jungle Brute. We act fast.

Very Aryanly Yours,
Horace Sherman Miller,
Box 5062,
Waco,
Texas.

The British national newspapers took up the issue and Scotland Yard protection was sought. Papers which circulated in the Caribbean with headquarters in London also carried the story:

KU KLUX KLAN SENDS THREAT LETTER TO SCOBIE

Scotland Yard To Give Protection . . .

Forty-three-year-old Edward Scobie, of Dominica, editor of a magazine for coloured people which is being printed in the United Kingdom, has asked Scotland Yard for police protection following a threatening letter from the Ku Klux Klan in Texas, U.S.A. Scobie a 6ft 4in former wartime RAF officer is married to a 29-year-old English girl and has two young daughters. He said: "I'm more worried about the children than anything else. We live in a fairly isolated region in Surrey. There's no one for miles around."

Police have kept the letter and promised Scobie protection and that the matter would be investigated. . . . And the directors of the magazine he edits have lodged a complaint against the American Embassy in London.

The Klan letter was published in a subsequent issue of *Flamingo* and brought a reply from Horace Sherman Miller:

9th December, 1961
My dear Jungle Ape:

I have here before me a copy of *Flamingo*—December issue, and on page 2 a copy of my letter is printed, and followed by the following remarks: "We have no comment other than to say the matter has been placed in the hands of the police."

No doubt the jovial Inspector pretended to be most sympathetic, but White Coppers have no sympathy for black niggers, and they are most unlikely to walk from Whitehall to Waco to show that they are favor-

able to your cause, when at heart, they despise all pox-ridden blacks. When Kelso Cochrane was eliminated, did they question any Klansman? Did they even pay a visit to 93 Iverna Court and protest to Sir Charles against any deed or Act? We are immune to Mau Mau.
Aryanly Yours,
Horace Sherman Miller.

This second letter was also taken to Scotland Yard. Investigations were carried out, particularly with referrence to the murdered West Indian, Cochrane but these drew a blank.

But that was not the end of the Klan's activities. In an article headed "The Ku Klux Klan Burns in Britain," published in one of the most popular weekly picture magazines, *Today—The New John Bull*—the writer began:

> A bottle smashes against the wall of a neat terrace house in Balsall Heath, Birmingham. Flames leap up the front, scarring the woodwork. . . . A mile or two away in the suburb of Handsworth, people run from their houses at two o'clock in the morning, to find a cross ablaze in a front garden. . . . In a city where seventy-five thousand coloured people strive to live, play and work in harmony with their white neighbours, the Ku Klux Klan, that sick, hate-crazed, race-baiting hangover from the darker days of Dixieland, are on the rampage again. . . . Crude posters, plastered on to walls in the secrecy of the night and quickly replaced when they are torn down, proclaim: "Blacks go home. You have been warned. . . ." They are signed: "Ku Klux Klan." Turned out by the hundreds on the Klan's private presses, they do not bear the printers' imprint which the law demands. For that would lead the police to the fanatics behind the Klan. That is why they operate at night. But the petrol bombs, the flaming broomstick crosses, the bricks through windows . . . these outrages are increasing. . . . The police do not know the full extent of the Klan's operations, because most coloured victims keep quiet in case of reprisals. . . . The Klan is the most active of several organisations deliberately fostering race hatred in Birmingham.

In 1961 Scotland Yard claimed to know the identities and numbers of Klansmen in Britain, and to be keeping a close watch on them. No British Klansman, to the knowledge of the author, has ever been prosecuted for any bomb or other kind of criminal outrage. But from time to time they make news in the national papers when they wreck the car of a black man, or attack blacks in dark city streets.

It was obvious to all that if the British government did not step in to stem the mounting tide of race hate, trouble lay ahead. As the *Today* writer summed up:

> If the riots come, it will be the attitude of Mr. Collet (arch race-hater), the Rook (a former RAF officer and cloak-and-dagger race hater), the KKK and the other white-skinned propagandists who bring them about —not the coloured people.

The black people had by then been reduced to a state of fear and confusion. A recurrence of rioting was feared if something was not done to counteract extremist racial hatred. The government had been indecisive, groping, dilly-dallying, "arguing the toss" and arriving at nothing practical, nothing that showed promise of clearing the air. Black organizations themselves were going off at many different tangents, not seeing a path clear before them. In any case, fear of violence still lurked in their minds. They were not anxious to have their skulls cracked open again or their property destroyed.

By December, 1961, more than 90 percent of the British supported the idea of controlling immigration, according to a Gallup Poll which had been conducted during the third week of November. Yet only one in three persons revealed that they were actually hostile to immigrants, especially black people; one-third were neutral, and one-third would actually welcome schemes for absorbing black people into their local communities. However, the Tory government did not pass the Immigrants Act quickly and quietly to appease the British public. Delay was first caused by backbench insistence that the committee stage should be taken by the whole House, and not by a handful of members in an upstairs room. The queen's ministers reluctantly gave way. More trouble lay ahead from both Conservative and Labour amendments calculated either to destroy the whole purpose of the Act, or, farcically, to reduce its life-span from five years to one. Other amendments would exempt citizens of the Irish Republic from immigration control. These amendments were tabled in order to force the government to defend, or at least explain, by what special set of circumstances and privileges were Irish immigrants exempt from the Act; and that they should also be included. Home Secretary Butler's retort, speaking on the second reading of the bill, that "Irish problems were only solved by maintaining or creating an anomaly," only served to prove that this immigration control was aimed primarily at the non-white Commonwealth migrants.

The delay caused in Parliament over the passing of this Act was not a bad thing. It gave the public a chance to air their views at great length on immigration in Britain, particularly the entry of black people, because, as already noted, the figures had risen sharply between 1959 and 1961.

Members of both parties in Britain's House of Commons around November–December, 1961, held opposite, clearly defined views on this question. Hugh Gaitskell, leader of the Labour party opposition, declared his belief in unrestricted immigration. On the other side of the House, Tory members, said one political weekly magazine, "have made it pretty clear that the fewer black faces they see on the streets of Britain the better they will be pleased." They displayed a remarkable reluctance to quote hard facts and figures, a failing which was shared by their home secretary. Mr. Butler, did not know, for instance, that more people left Britain to settle overseas than were going there to work and live. It seems unbelievable that a home secretary would not have such information readily available.

Members on both sides of the House allowed emotional attitudes to prevail. Nigel Fisher, Tory member for Surbiton in Surrey, and, in fact, one of the more enlightened opponents of the Act, pointed out that "what people feel eventually becomes what they do." It was argued that if the average man or woman in Britain feels that black people will have an increasing effect on his way of life; will lower his living standards; debase his moral values and sensibilities; or, as one politician said bluntly "create a coffee-coloured society"—then nothing on earth could prevent public opinion from becoming racist. But what parliamentarians, and indeed the thinking man and woman were reluctant to face or accept was that Britain could not, realistically, expect to rely on black people to keep hospitals or transport services going, and at the same time, wish that they were not on the scene.

There were those who maintained that although the government could not find a solution overnight, it was right in saying that the British people were not prepared to accept black people, even if they were also British. It was this ambiguity, already discussed, which was again creating a tug-of-war within the British national character and preventing the government from decisive action. To take up the attitude of not wanting black people in Britain, apart from being blatantly racist, would hurt the country economically, morally, and in the long run as a leader in world affairs. There were those who were clamoring for government education of the British people about the migrants from British colonies.

Newspapers from Land's End to John o' Groats, covering all inclinations and representing almost nearly every political and other view under the sun, entered the controversy. Organizations of diverse aspirations were not slow to move in and have their say. Most bitter and outspoken about immigration control were the black publications. Among those foremost in fighting the Act were the *West Indian Gazette* and *Flamingo*—both published in London. Claudia Jones was the dedicated black editor of the *West Indian Gazette* (and *Afro-Asian Caribbean News*). Born in Trinidad, Claudia Jones lived for many years in the United States where she was active in youth work and civil rights activities. She was deported under provisions of the McCarran Act and went to live in London. She died in her middle forties a few years ago. During the height of the debate on the Commonwealth Immigrants Act, the front page lead story of February, 1962, *Gazette* carried this story:

> ANTI-COLOUR-BILL-LOBBY
>
> Feburary 13th
>
> The newly-formed Afro-Asian-Caribbean Conference representing nearly 200,000 coloured people residing in Britain will implement plans for a COMMONWEALTH Lobby on February 13th, 1962, in protest against the British Government's colour bar legislation—officially known as the Commonwealth Immigrants Bill. Chief demand will be to urge the Government to withdraw the Bill.
>
> In a call to thousands of Afro-Asian-Caribbean citizens the Conference summoned nurses and medical staff from hospitals in their uniforms; bus, train and transport personnel, factory, canteen and municipal workers in overalls or uniforms and others in their national costumes to converge on the House of Commons to lobby their Members of Parliament.

The Conference action followed intense activity in the preceding month. Demands to replace the current color-bar Commonwealth Immigrants bill with legislation against racial discrimination was made at a mass demonstration in Trafalgar Square, London, on January 14. Participating in the earlier march from Hyde Park, organized by the Movement for Colonial Freedom, were 2,000 persons, including members of Parliament, members of the British Labour Movement, Young Communists, Young Socialists, West Indians, Ceylonese, Indians, Pakistanis, and Irish workers. Mr. John Stonehouse, Labour M.P. for Wednesbury, declared that the bill should in fact be termed the "End of Commonwealth Bill." He maintained stoutly: "If it is passed it will mean the virtual end of the Commonwealth Association of which we have all been proud." Mr. Stonehouse went on to say that he deplored the way some Tories were taking advantage of recent smallpox cases to promote agitation against the entry of Commonwealth citizens and made specific references to the devoted work of nurses from Africa and the West Indies in British hospitals.

The demonstrators carried banners bearing such slogans as:

NO COLOUR-BAR ON IMMIGRATION
WEST INDIAN STUDENTS BILL
NO COLOUR-BAR FOR BRITAIN
CONDEMN COLOUR-BAR IMMIGRATION

and others of like nature. Resolutions were passed condemning the Immigration Bill, after various speakers had delivered addresses. Mr. Maurice Orbach, a former M.P. who was chairman at the rally, said: "The Bill before Parliament is morally wrong and economically insane." Mr. Orbach also read a message of support from Hugh Gaitskell, parliamentary opposition leader of the British Labour party.

Commonwealth heads of state had been contacted by the Afro-Asian-Caribbean Conference and several deputations conferred with representatives of the high commissions of Ghana, Canada, India, the West Indies, Nigeria, and Malaya, as well as the embassy of the United Arab Republic. The high commissions of three Commonwealth countries, India, Nigeria, and the West Indies, issued statements. India maintained:

> Any kind of control based on race or colour discrimination would be objectionable to the Indian Government and public opinion would be so strong that the Government of India may have to contemplate reciprocal action.

Nigeria did not go as far as the Indian government and threaten "reciprocal action." However, it voiced concern over the British government's proposals:

> Nigeria deplores the racial overtones of the bill and the encouragement which it may and in fact has given to racialist and fascist elements in the country.

Sir Garnet Gordon, C.B.E., the commissioner of the Federation of the West Indies, British Guiana, and British Honduras (dissolved later that year, 1962) said that "the Federal and Unit Governments of the West Indies had taken on an unequivocal stand against the Bill."

"Our Government," he said, "had urged Commonwealth consultation." Sir Garnet envisaged the bill, already causing tensions, as further indication of "a change in U.K. policy towards West Indians in Britain which would encourage harmful incidents."

The Afro-Asian-Caribbean Conference treated the proposed debate on the bill as a matter of urgency and to set in motion the protest Commonwealth lobby against the introduction of what it termed "legislation apartheid" into Britain. A forty-eight-hour vigil was posted and this was followed by a public protest meeting. Support came from a number of British organizations such as the Movement for Colonial Freedom.

Equally outspoken on the proposed bill was *Flamingo* magazine. Its position was crystal clear. It was opposed to what every black man in Britain believed to be a racist measure. When in mid-November, 1961, Prime Minister Harold Macmillan pushed his Immigrants bill to its final and inevitable stages with all haste a Labour M.P. jeered: "What a way to run a Commonwealth." This feeling was shared by nearly all blacks. They argued that had the influx of immigrants to Britain consisted of Canadians, Australians, or New Zealanders, the demand for such a bill would never have arisen. Stepney Councillor Solly Kaye, writing in *Flamingo*, stated flatly:

> There is no doubt that the Commonwealth Immigrants Bill will encourage every racialist and fascist in Britain and abroad. Negroes will be dismayed and angry—as will every person who loves peace and brotherhood of man. . . . So powerful is the poison of racialism that even in Stepney I have heard the children and grandchildren of Irish immigrants, who came to England to escape famine, repeating race-hate policies. I have even heard some Jewish constituents voicing the arguments of Mosley fascists. Could tragic irony go further? Britain will bar citizens of the Commonwealth—except when they are needed for the armed forces of course. . . . Of course the Bill is one that will

> hit the coloured worker. It is designed to do that. It is introduced in response to those who demand that.

To justify its mood, the British public trotted out all the old stories that blacks took away their homes, etc., which were given ample space in the British press. The government did nothing to set the record straight since this Immigrants Act was calculated to win political favor, to appease the national conscience. It was flagrantly apparent that throughout the debate on the bill by the press and public, facts about immigrant life in Britain were lacking. The British government had nothing concrete to put before the House. Members of the opposition were in the same plight. It was for this reason, and to help eliminate prejudice, preconceptions and misconceptions and to brush away many fallacies about black people, that *Flamingo* magazine asked one of the leading market research organizations to prepare a survey on West Indians in Britain.

The facts unearthed showed that West Indians in particular have a high standard of living and have been well absorbed in the community. They are a vital part of Britain, despite the pressures and subterfuges of prejudice that they continuously suffer.

The period covered in the market survey was around 1961–62. Based on samples from London, Manchester, and Birmingham where the majority of migrants lived, the survey showed that the average West Indian household's weekly income was £15. 10., 66 percent of the average family's income. In only 2 percent of households where there was a male at the head was £8 or less earned. More than 19 percent of households with males at head had an income of £20 per week.

West Indians could be found in various walks of life. In employment nearly 62 percent of the heads of households interviewed had semi-skilled or skilled occupations—bus drivers, conductors, machine operators, fitters, electricians, etc.; 18 percent had unskilled jobs—porters and laborers.

The problem of accommodation, also a sore point with the British, was shown up in the survey in a hopeful light. For instance, 17 percent of informants owned their own homes; 4 percent of those interviewed in the London area owned their own accommodation as compared with 8 percent of all households in the London County Council area; 31 percent of the informants in the Manchester and Birmingham areas owned their accommodation as compared with 37 percent of the households in conurbations covered by the Rowntree Trust Housing Study in 1961. About one half of these immigrants paid an average rent of £2. 10., per week. Most West Indians tended to live in small units of one or two rooms. Ninety percent had a private bathroom or shared one; 92 percent had the use of a separate kitchen.

On the question of expenditure the households were spending up to £4. 10. per week on food eaten at home but 27 percent or more were exceeding that amount, allowing as much as £6 or more per week on food. Nearly one half of the informants (47 percent) were buying a commodity on hire purchase. Half the buyers were paying more than £3. 10. per month. One of the noticeable points was that 44 percent of those interviewed said they managed to save some money from the weekly pay packet regularly. About one half of these said they put away in savings more than £2 per week.

When interviewed about education, 90 percent claimed that they had started their full-time education between the ages of five and seven, and continued until they were fifteen years or more; 13 percent were educated beyond eighteen years of age while 20 percent were taking part-time educational courses in the U.K., 14 percent of these attending evening classes. Of those under thirty years of age, 30 percent were taking part-time educational courses, and 20 percent of these were enrolled at an evening school.

These facts proved of some value in the House of Commons. When the Commonwealth Immigrants bill was being debated, Mr. C. Royle, member of Parliament for Salford West, in Lancashire, said:

> There was put into my hands today a summary of a document which has been prepared by the British Market Research Bureau for *Flamingo* magazine. The Bureau has been carrying out some careful researches into the circumstances and living conditions of the West Indian population in this country, and I want to quote one or two figures from the report.

The quotations were favorable ones but even so, even at this stage, it was obvious that it was going to be a losing battle, in spite of the fact that the British government was being put wise to the fact that black immigrants were not lowering the standard of living, or guilty of the other imperfections attributed to them because of race. However, on February

17, 1962, the Commonwealth Immigrants bill faced its final passage in the House of Commons. It went through this third reading by a majoity of 107. Thus the Conservative government had given way to the prejudices of the British. Only a dozen Conservative M.P.'s abstained. With the exception of about twenty Labour members who also abstained, the Labour Opposition in the House voted against the bill. Talking about Labour's attitude, Mr. Dennis Healey (Labour, Leeds East) claimed that the changes brought about in the bill showed "the Commons at its best". He said that the opposition voted against the bill because it felt that it was unnecessary and irrelevent to the poblems it purported to solve. The bill, he felt, struck at Britain's traditional attitude towards immigration; at the preservation of good Commonwealth relations and the belief that Britain was "without original sin over colour discrimination."

The irony of the passing of this bill was that while free entry of foods and people from members of the Commonwealth was being restricted, Britain was granting privileges to prospective white European partners in the Common Market. But the opposition Labour party did not commit itself to repeal the bill if it came into power. With the usual flexibility that politicans achieve when they do not want to have to eat their words and fall back on promises made, Labour promised only that if after it conducted serious surveys, it was found necessary to control immigration, it would consult with Commonwealth governments. This, Labour claimed, was to find out how control could be achieved without damage to their interests and confidence in British loyalty. This did not deceive the more realistic leaders of the Commonwealth countries or black leaders in Britain. To them the roots of the Commonwealth Immigrants Act, as it was officially designated when finally passed through the House of Lords and given Royal Assent, were steeped in racial discrimination. Claudia Jones made no bones about this, writing: "Its passage [through the House] was accompanied by the most foul racialist propaganda perpetrated against West Indians and other Afro-Asians by Tory and fascist elements." The government stipulated that the Act would come up for review after a period of twelve months, and that an advisory council and appeals tribunal would be set up. But these acts of appeasement did not, could not, cloud the Tory government's intention and make it acceptable to blacks. Neither did the Act achieve what it was alleged to do. Claudia Jones made these points:

> The pious and hypocritical sentimentality accompanying the Bill's passage was further exposed when the Tory legislators removed the non-Commonwealth Irish Republic from the provisions of the Act, revealing its naked colour-bar bias. The result, following a year of its operation, showed that 80 to 90 percent of all Indian and Pakistani applicants were refused entry permits; and West Indian immigration dropped to a little over 4,000 qualifying for entry. The latter occasioned cautious queries, whether West Indians had either turned their backs on Britain or had become bitter with the Act's passage.

This accusation of "pious and hypocritical sentimentality" was not without foundation if the interpretation of the Commonwealth Immigrants Act is examined. In issuing instructions to Immigration Officers with regard to the exercise of their functions, the home secretary declared that they must carry out their duties "without regard to the race, colour or religion of Commonwealth citizens who may seek to enter the country." No one in his right senses believed that, since, in the first place, the main blow fell on the black Commonwealth citizens.

Yet, the Commonwealth Immigrants Act stated:

> Immigration control applies to citizens of *all* Commonwealth countries and to *all* other British subjects—except those born in the United Kingdom or holding a United Kingdom passport. It also applies to British protected persons and citizens of the Irish republic, but control is not imposed on persons travelling between Ireland and Britain.

Those who suffered most under the Act were immigrants from black Commonwealth countries; and the clause of the Act which directly affected them was the one dealing with Ministry of Labour vouchers. It stipulated:

> All people subject to control who wish to enter the United Kingdom for the purpose of taking or seeking employment, must possess Ministry of Labour vouchers. Applications for vouchers are dealt with in three categories:
>
> Category A. Commonwealth citizens who have a specific job to come to in this country.
>
> Category B. Applicants who possess certain special skills or qualifications.
>
> Category C. All other applicants—i.e. unskilled workers with no jobs to go to.

Since most black immigrants came under Category C, their entry into Britain was severely restricted. The issuing of entry vouchers was strictly controlled by a committee of British government ministers whose duty it was to meet and decide how many vouchers should be issued. Factors which they took into consideration when issuing vouchers were the employment and housing situation, pressures on the educational system, and, what they would not openly admit, the prevailing mood of the British press and public on the race question. Only the bigoted would argue that the system of immigration control in the Act was not conditioned by color bar. But the British refuse not only to admit this fact, but to see it. Claudia Jones made the point adroitly: "There is a reluctance on the part of virtually all sections of British public opinion to assess the fundamental reasons for the existence of racial prejudice."

The Commonwealth Immigrants Act covered other aspects involving the entry of immigrants into the United Kingdom. One of the more important of these was the entry of wives and children (under eighteen) of voucher-holders or Commonwealth citizens already resident in Britain. These would be freely admitted. Fiancées wishing to come to marry someone already in the United Kingdom were not allowed to enter until they had satisfied the Immigration Officer that the marriage would take place within a reasonable time (normally three months).

The refusal of admission to immigrants into the United Kingdom was left to the decision of an Immigration Officer. He could refuse admission to anyone who did not qualify under the conditions previously mentioned. In addition, there was the general power to refuse admission on the grounds of health, criminal record, or national security. This power could not be used against anyone who qualified for admission as a wife, as a child under sixteen, or as a returning resident.

There were flagrant cases of abuses of power by many immigration officers. Several of them were suspect in their feelings and attitudes to black immigrants. Their positive action some years later in backing the views of Enoch Powell, a Conservative member of Parliament who wanted to stop black immigration totally and repatriate those already in Britain, gave ample evidence of how unsuited most of them were for discharging their duties without prejudice or bias. A very militant anti-black group of immigration officers operating at London airport were to cause the Labour government of Britain much embarrassment in 1968.

The Commonwealth Immigrants Act came into force on July 1, 1962. As already shown, the numbers of migrants coming to Britain in search of employment reached its peak in 1961 with overflowing boatloads arriving every month until the Act became operative. The question then was did the Act do what it was intended to do: stop overcrowding in the already overpopulated cities of the United Kingdom? It did not. Conditions in the majority of English towns and cities are much worse today than they were in the early sixties. New towns have been created to absorb the overspill of the large industrial towns and cities, but still with the growing population (in spite of increased family planning and the use of "The Pill") the problem continues to be acute. In 1962, a survey was published by the *Economist* Intelligence Unit which revealed some interesting facts about immigration. This survey did not get wide publicity in the British press. It pointed out that although 650,000 immigrants came to Britain between 1951 and 1960, they did not swell the population, for almost as many emigrated in the same period. The survey concluded: "It is likely . . . that the net [immigration] movement over the period has been virtually negligible, at little more than 0.01 percent of the population."

If, therefore, there has been an overspill of population in Britain since the time that control was put on black immigrants under the Act then immigrants are not to blame. For every time the Act has been reviewed in Parliament more stringent controls have been imposed and the numbers drastically reduced. When the Act came into force the number of Commonwealth immigrants who applied for employment in Britain under the voucher system under Category C of the Act was approximately 30,000. In 1963 there were 28,000 labour vouchers taken up from the new Commonwealth, in 1964, 14,000; in 1965, 12,000; 1966, 5,000; in 1967, 4,700; and in 1968 there were further changes contained in the Commonwealth Immigrants Act. This brought under immigration control citizens of the United Kingdom holding United Kingdom passports who have no substantial connection with Britain by birth or paternal parentage. This legislation not only aimed at controlling the influx of Asian immigrants from East Africa, but was to affect persons in other parts of the world who had hitherto been similarly exempt from United Kingdom immigration control. The allocation for such persons was a mere fifteen hundred vouchers a year. During the Lords debate on the bill the Lord Chancellor, Lord Gardiner, said: "I do not like this Bill. I do not suppose anyone likes it." Lieutenant-Commander S. L. C. Maydon (Conservative) said in the Commons that the bill should be thrown out and one substituted which would prohibit all immigration except for six-month permits for visitors of good character, students on limited permits, and specially qualified persons with limited permits subject to renewal. The Archbishop of Canterbury said in the House of Lords that the government should be asked to remove the figure of 1,500 as being quite inadequate. Whatever might be done to retrieve the situation, much harm has been done by the bill. In the House of Commons Ben Whitaker (Labour) maintained that had the immigrants been white the bill would not have been drafted. Most people agreed with him. At the time racialism was rife in Britain. Some claimed that it was not yet deeply rooted, but the future was to prove them wrong.

BIBLIOGRAPHY TO CHAPTER FIFTEEN

"Coloured People and the Police." *Flamingo.* (London: September, 1960).

"Flamingo Fights the Bill." *Flamingo.* (London: January, 1962).

"The Ku Klux Klan Burns in Britain." *Today: The New John Bull.* (London: October 20, 1962).

Labour Party Statement on Racial Discrimination. (London: 1958).

McAlpine, Eric. "Standing Conference." *Flamingo.* (London: April, 1964).

Parliamentary Debates, Commons. series. (London: December 5, 1958) col. 1588.

Parliamentary Debates, Commons. series. (London: June 4, 1959) cols. 369, 371.

Parliamentary Debates, House of Lords. series. (London: November 19, 1958) cols. 672, 673, 718.

Scobie, Edward. "The Road With Soiled White Hands." *Tribune* (London: May 29, 1959).

West Indians in London, Manchester and Birmingham. British Market Research Bureau Report. (London: November, 1961).

White Paper on Ratification of ILO Convention to Eliminate Discrimination. Parliamentary Command Paper No. 783. (London: June, 1959).

"Who Killed Kelso?" *Tropic* (London: June, 1960).

CHAPTER XVI

BLACK POWER REACHES BRITAIN

Political expediency can change both politicians and their motives, and that is precisely what happened to the Labour party in 1964. For the General Elections in Britain in that year produced two unpleasant shocks for the West Indians, Africans and Asians living there. The first was the failure of the Labour party to live up to its pledges in the House of Commons when it opposed the Immigrants Bill, and the second was the way immigration became an election issue in several areas. To the dismay of immigrants, the Labour party completely changed its policy for the election. Perhaps it is not surprising that Labour either lacked the courage to stand by their convictions or had second thoughts about immigration control. For one of the issues which appeared in that 1964 election was what the British press termed "the colour question." The immigration issue centred in the Birmingham area and especially at Smethwick, where the Labour foreign secretary lost his seat to his Conservative opponent, Peter Griffiths, a blatant white supremacist. (Mr. Griffiths lost his seat in March 1966 when the Labour government called a snap election in a successful bid to increase its extremely slender majority.)

From the time the Labour party came into power informed political circles repeated that Prime Minister Harold Wilson's Cabinet had intended to impose a permanent ban on entry into Britain of unskilled immigrants who had no jobs awaiting them. And, in practice, no immigrant of this kind was allowed into Britain after the Labour government took office in October, 1964, although more than twenty-five thousand were admitted in the two years before that. The reason for the Labour government's toughness towards black immigrants was the fear of losing votes in the future elections. This attitude persisted right up to June, 1970 General Election, which the Labour party lost. Blacks have, in consequence, lost their faith in Labour and, in fact, blacks in Britain are losing trust in whites. They will not even ask their unions to make representations, for, as they not unreasonably claim, the unions are prejudiced against them. They do not participate fully in trade union affairs because they are made to feel unwelcome. This is particularly true of the black workers and unions in the Midlands areas of Wolverhampton and Birmingham. When it comes to blacks, trade unions in those districts "are infested with the bug of prejudice." The condition of black-white worker relationships in 1969 is illustrated by the following cases:

In Wolverhampton, the city represented by Enoch Powell in the House of Commons which has become pathologically sick as a result of Powell's anti-black mouthings, a black factory worker was asked to change his job, with no apparent reason except that he was a militant organizer. He refused to obey the order and was fired. All black workers came out in sympathy. But the white workers did not: they advised the management strenuously to "keep out the wogs" and offered to work overtime to maintain production. The management fired 180 black men.

A black bus driver, also in Wolverhampton, with fourteen years' service and a Lancashire accent, very integrated, applied for promotion to the position of inspector. He was unsuccessful, though some white recruits trained by him were promoted over his head. The management quietly ignored his application, but the white union secretary declared to him with brutal frankness: "White employees will not take orders from coloureds." Black nurses voiced the same complaint about promotion. This seemed to have been the accepted pattern of affairs in trade unions, and by 1969 black workers were being repeatedly victimized, even though the union bosses had made grandiose claims that British trade unions did not practice or recognize a color bar.

In other areas with few black workers there were some black shop stewards, secretaries, and presidents of trade union branches, as well as delegates to Trade Councils. There are also cases where black people have come up through the ranks of their trade union branch and local Labour party and been elected to the local council. But these are minority instances and have occurred less frequently since 1967 when the situation of race and color began to show marked deterioration.

As far back as 1963 the Transport and General Workers' Union had been trying—for a long time, and as quietly as possible—to persuade its own workers to accept black colleagues on the buses in Bristol. The unions have always found that their main task has been to convince their members that the risk of unemployment would not be materially increased by the employment of black workers. Signs of improvement can be expected only when the racial climate in Britain improves. It was at rock bottom in 1969 and the laudatory proclamation made by the General Executive Council of the Transport and General Workers Union on September 21, 1961, reaffirming that "discrimination on the grounds of colour and race is contrary to Trade Union principles" sounded just as meaningless to black workers in Britain in 1969 as it had eight years earlier. The unions' campaign for the creation of a social climate under which race prejudice could not survive, did not prosper. Racial prejudice was more apparent in trade unions and other sectors of the British population in 1969 than it has ever been in the past.

Churches in Britain do not seem to have risen to the call. They have not been able to make any significant contribution to the improvement of race relations in Britain. This is not entirely surprising since many ministers of religion are themselves racial bigots and have been at pains to give wide publicity to their unchristian, uncharitable attitudes. Rev. G. H. Nicholson of the Church of St. Mary the Virgin, Burghfield, near Reading in Berkshire, some years ago published *Some Problems of Race* which included some most objectionable declarations, for example:

> While "racial discrimination" has a bad name, and can be used in an evil way and for evil purposes we have to face the fact that the Bible, from beginning to end, sets forth God as being in a beneficent way, The Great Racial Discriminator. . . .
>
> I have at the Rectory an Indian work of art in the form of an ornamental shield. Every scene has to do with fighting and the centre piece depicts the delight of the victor in digging out the entrails of his dead opponent. . . . Every year some hundreds are murdered in the native areas near Johannesburg alone, and this, in matters that have nothing to do with the white man.

Other English ministers followed the same vein: the Rev. P. E. Blagdon-Gamlen of St. Bartholomew's Church, Derby, in 1962 started a strong race-hate campaign in his parish. He wrote an article in which he declared that "sentimentality has run riot," and inferred that liberal-minded and left-wing groups in Britain are turning Britain into a black man's land.

The following year Blagdon-Gamlen stated: "Now that Jamaica is independent, let the Jamaicans return home and keep England for the English. . . . Prevention is better than cure. We do not want a Congo situation in this country. Signs of witchcraft and Mau Mau are not lacking." Quite apart from the fact that both Reading and Derby have become home to thousands of black people, that kind of talk from a minister of religion shows that racism must be deeply ingrained in the Church of England. Of course, there were outraged cries from genuinely God-loving clergymen. (The then Archbishop of Canterbury and his successor have always spoken fearlessly against racial discrimination and have endeavored to be examples to their clergy.) It would not dawn on the minds of Rev. Nicholson and Rev. Blagdon-Gamlen that the moral standards in Britain disillusioned West Indians and other black immigrants, who had expected higher standards from the Mother Country. Whatever the moral behavior of West Indians in the Caribbean they are good churchgoers and they took the habit with them to Britain. There they found that the English are not a churchgoing people and that little respect or leadership could be obtained from the church. Some West Indians inevitably fell quickly into the English habit. Others, who were Baptists or belonged to the Pentecostal Church or less orthodox sects, turned their basement rooms or front parlors into places of worship where they could follow their religion in the free, unrestricted, uninhibited style to which they were accustomed back in the Caribbean. They could sing lustily, clap hands, and move in evangelical ecstasy to the compelling rhythms of spirituals and gospel songs and hymns thumped out on tambourines, cymbals, guitars, electronic zither and piano. As more and more West Indians came to Britain the following among these sects grew. However, in the many Catholic, Anglican, and Methodist Churches where blacks were tolerated and sometimes even welcomed, staid English worshippers got used to the natural sincerity with which the former expressed their faith.

From the very beginning the only party in Britain which opposed the system of "quotas" and "controls" for Commonwealth immigration was the British Communist party. In 1964 the Executive Committee of this party issued a statement declaring its opposition to all forms of restrictions on black immigration; declared its readiness to contest every case of discrimination; urged the repeal of the Commonwealth Immigrants Act; and called for equality of opportunity for employment, rates of wages, promotion to skilled jobs, and more openings for apprenticeship and vocational training. The British Communists came out openly on the side of black people and challenged and fought all forms of racial prejudice which cropped up. The party did not succeed in attracting many immigrants to its ranks, in spite of the strong stand it adopted on their side. In fact, most immigrants were politically apathetic.

When the Commonwealth Immigrants Act was passed in 1962, the British government set up the Commonwealth Immigrants Advisory Council. Its primary function was to advise the home secretary on matters which he might refer to the Council from time to time affecting the welfare of Commonwealth immigrants in Britain and their integration into the community. The Council's terms of reference were:

> To examine the arrangements made by local authorities in whose areas substantial numbers of Commonwealth immigrants have settled, to assist immigrants to adapt themselves to British habits and customs, and to report on the adequacy of the efforts made;
>
> to examine whether the powers of local authorities to deal with matters affecting the welfare of immigrants are sufficient and whether any further action can usefully be taken by the Government to stimulate action by local authorities; and
>
> to examine the relationship between action by local offices and Government Departments and local authorities on the one hand, and the efforts of voluntary bodies on the other, in furthering the welfare of immigrants.

By 1964 the Commonwealth Immigrants Advisory Council had published three reports of its work. They dealt with housing, education of of Commonwealth immigrants in British schools, and immigrant school-leavers. The council's findings on housing, though suggesting some ways in which this problem should be tackled, did not uncover anything which was not well-known to the British government and to welfare organizations concerned with the well being of immigrants in Britain.

The second report, on immigrant children in British schools, dealt with the situation as though the structure of education in certain schools with large numbers of immigrant children would be adversely affected. It admitted that there were some cities, including ports, where there have been immigrant children in the schools for many years who have been well-integrated into the school community life. No practical differences had arisen over these children yet the report assumed an attitude of undue pessimism in the case of areas where immigrants had only recently settled:

> Children from different backgrounds are, at least at first, going to make heavy demands on the time of their teachers. The presence of a high proportion of immigrant children in one class slows down the general routine of working and hampers the progress of the whole class, especially where the immigrants do not speak or write English fluently. This is clearly in itself undesirable and unfair to all the children in the class. There is a further danger that educational backwardness which, in fact, is due to environment, language or a different culture, may increasingly be supposed to arise from some inherent or genetic inferiority.

English teachers, when asked about immigrant newcomers to primary and secondary schools, all admitted that the black child was "amazingly adaptable" but took a little while to settle in at school. As one mistress put it: "They are a bit shy and quiet to begin with. I believe it has much to do with the discipline at home which is much stricter than in an English home. The coloured child always minds his manners. But once he's 'tested out' his new environment he soon becomes friends with his classmates and enters with spirit into all the school activities." The curriculum in West Indian schools is patterned on that of Britain. The language spoken is English, even though West Indians have added their own inflections, their own variations, their own colloquialisms and national idiosyncrasies to it. Many are the stories of mothers and fathers in the Caribbean chastising or correcting their children for not speaking the standard English taught in schools. Customs and behavior do not differ greatly between English children and immigrant children for a very sound reason: English patterns of life have been imported wholesale in the colonial countries and are not alien to non-whites from these territories. Whether they are to be used as the barometer by which the culture and behavior pattern of the black man should be measured and judged is something else.

Today much of this colonial brainwashing, or whitewashing, is being discarded and an awareness of black beauty, black pride, black heritage, is sweeping through the peoples of African descent scattered throughout the lands of the world—from Africa, through Europe, the Americas, and the Caribbean. It is a movement which cannot be dismissed lightly—a reversal of all that is Uncle Tom in the black man, of all that has been imposed, injected, into his brain and thinking by the white man. This feeling of black pride has engendered a state of intellectual revolt against all that is racially servile, cringing, and cowardly. The black man will come to terms with his worth and importance as a human being equal on any terms with the white man. He will have been instrumental in creating a world where white does not mean a superior status. It will be a world where, as Jamaican author Andrew Salkey has said, "We will all be soul brothers and sisters."

Problems in housing, problems for immigrant children at school, and problems when they leave school. In an investigation carried out by the Institute of Race Relations in 1960 it was found that:

> When coloured children leave school—the present coloured "bulge" is still in the primary schools however—they leave a cosy world where they are judged by their skill at games or the colour of their blazer and enter the adult world where the colour of their skin may be more important. Youth Employment Officers have found it difficult to find apprenticeships for coloured youths. This was particularly commented upon in Birmingham, Coventry, London, Manchester and Newcastle. Employers prefer white boys whose background they know. Some firms believe that coloured boys will not stick at their training or, if they do, that they will go back to their own country at the end of their courses. It is difficult also to place coloured boys and girls in clerical jobs even if they hold the General Certificate of Education. Some girls had to take up factory work after looking fruitlessly for office appointments.

In 1964, when the Commonwealth Immigrants Advisory Board carried out its investigations on immigrant school-leavers the position had not improved. In 1965, a year later, A. Roy Truman, district inspector of the Inner London Education Authority wrote:

> Vigorous government, university and local authority action is needed to overcome current difficulties. Planning policies and city redevelopment schemes must aim at preventing the emergence of "coloured" schools. The growing number of well-qualified coloured school-leavers must be helped to secure the posts for which their educational achievements fit them. All employers and employees should accept some responsibility for this.

Far from impeding progress in education, immigrant children increased the scope of awareness and gave a wider, broader, more progressive approach to English school teachers with multiracial classes. Most English schools saw the process as one of "integration"—which meant respecting the different cultures, diets, and ways of dress, but expecting all pupils to conform to the general pattern of school life.

The presence of overseas pupils and teachers helped in other ways. It gave to British teachers and pupils alike a new dimension to geographical and racial studies. Teachers have had to change their views about black immigrant schoolchildren. Their knowledge of life and people in the Caribbean, Africa, and Asia was scant. So the children were, in their way, educating the teachers just as the teachers were educating them! Teachers were learning, too, that the state of education varies from island to island in the West Indies and from country to country in Africa and that generalizations as to standards of education for certain age groups could not be made. Although the basic pattern of education in all British or former British colonial territories was the same, there were variations and immigrant pupils did not cause such major setbacks in standards as has been claimed. It should again be emphasized here that, on the contrary, they added something. A. Roy Truman made this observation:

> Their song and dance have enriched the customary repertoires. In secondary schools, pupils of many nationalities are found serving as prefects, leading orchestras and performing in plays and operas. But echoes in the adult world are occasionally heard.

The Commonwealth Immigrants Advisory Council recommended the formation of The National Committee for Commonwealth Immigrants, whose advisory officer was appointed in 1964. By that time the Council had realized that the local authorities and voluntary bodies interested in the welfare of Commonwealth immigrants were inadequate and were very often unaware of the work being done in other areas. Thus arose the need for an officer who collected and circulated all the relevant information and who became familiar with experiments and methods that were being tried in areas where Commonwealth immigrants had settled. This officer was also available to advise local authorities and others on measures to improve relations between immigrants and the community.

The National Committee for Commonwealth Immigrants was a small voluntary committee of non-official persons, some nominated by the Commonwealth Immigrants Advisory Council, some by the Institute of Race Relations which had already been formed since 1958, and some by the National Council of Social Service, with other members co-opted. Most blacks in Britain and those whites whose consciences were not clouded by hypocrisy admitted that these quasi-government, semi-voluntary, and voluntary bodies were set up to cushion the blow of the Commonwealth Immigrants Act. There was much justification for this line of thought. One can hardly claim that they have made any great inroads into the problem of racial integration. Consequently, it surprised no one when in April, 1965, a Race Relations Bill was introduced by the British government. By then white liberals and black leaders in Britain realised that the machinery of British law would have to be used if the immigrant population was going to receive any measure of recognition as citizens. Up to that time all forms of racial discrimination could be practiced and the immigrant had no protection under the law.

This first Race Relations bill dealt with restrictive clauses in leases and sales agreements for houses, apartments, etc., discrimination in public places and racial incitement. A government-sponsored amendment further proposed the establishment of conciliation machinery for the investigation of complaints, instead of resorting to criminal prosecutions. Before that, there was absolutely nothing to prevent clauses being inserted into leases and sales agreements to prevent purchase or rent by blacks and others. This bill was designed to make such discriminatory clauses invalid and unenforceable in law. It was of particular interest and assistance to skilled and professionally qualified immigrants who wished to purchase or rent accommodation in middle-class areas from which they had been excluded in the past. However, this bill, as it was originally drafted, specifically excluded private lodgings, hotels, and clubs. It applied to places "of public resort" and was of negligible use to students or immigrant workers seeking lodgings. The bill did outlaw racial discrimination in theatres, movie theatres, dance-halls, sports grounds, swimming pools, and other places of public entertainment or recreation.

This Race Relations bill met considerable opposition before it was accepted and passed. Members of Parliament had shown persistent reluctance to pass legislation outlawing racial discrimination. By January,

1964, the bill, a private members' bill, had been presented to Parliament for the ninth time by Fenner Brockway, a prominent figure in the fight for African and West Indian rights. Selwyn Lloyd, Leader of the House, made the excuse that the legislative program for that session was full to capacity and that he could not hold out any hope of it receiving the special facilities it would need to become law in the present parliament. The Conservatives had practiced these delaying tactics at every turn when Mr. Brockway turned up with his hardy perennial. However, Harold Wilson, leader of the opposition Labour party in the House of Commons said in support of the bill:

> We, the Labour Party, support Mr. Fenner Brockway's private members' bill. If that bill does not become law before the election—and if a Labour Government be elected—we would legislate on the lines of this bill as a Government measure against racial discrimination and incitement to racial hatred. . . . In relation to the problem of immigration and the integration of races in this country, we regard the implementation of this bill as specially important.

The bill still had to weather a stormy time even after decades of indecision, disagreements, rifts and arguments. However, the Race Relations Act which was eventually passed several months later in April, 1965, left many loopholes and much to be desired. One thing the bill did, though, was to create a new offense of "incitement to racial hatred in a public meeting or public place by spoken or written words." The maximum penalties proposed on summary conviction were imprisonment for not more than six months, or a fine of £200, or both, and, on indictment, two years' imprisonment or a fine of £1,000, or both. Ironically, the first person to be indicted and imprisoned under this clause of the Race Relations Act was not a white man, but a black man! He was Michael De Freitas of Trinidad who went to Britain in 1950. When arrested in 1967 for having delivered what the police called "an inflammatory speech against white people" in Reading, he was known as Michael X, Britain's leading Black Muslim leader. He had become interested in the Black Muslims three years earlier, after meeting the late American Muslim leader, Malcolm X. Michael X, also known as Michael Abdul Malik, was found guilty under the Race Relations bill and jailed for the maximum term. As was expected, this galled the black population in Britain—even those who did not agree with Michael X's black power preachings. For there were worse offenders who were white and got off scot free. Some right-wing race-hating members of Parliament have made much more inflammatory statements than Michael X and have not been prosecuted. It should not surprise anyone when Britain thus stands accused by black Africans and West Indians of operating two sets of standards in law: one for her white first-class citizens; and the other for black second-class immigrants. Confidence in British justice and fair play has now become a derisory matter among black people.

The scope of the bill was further widened a few years later to cover other fields where discrimination was being practiced. These areas of discrimination were detailed by Roy Jenkins, the Labour home secretary, in the House of Commons on July 16, 1967:

> The Government has decided in principle that the Race Relations Act should be extended to deal with discrimination on grounds of colour, race or ethnic or national origins in employment, housing, insurance and credit facilities. In addition public places will be given a wider definition than under the present Act. . . . We propose that, in relation to employment, the new legislation should provide the fullest possible opportunity for industry to use its own machinery for conciliation.

Mr. Jenkins sincerely believed that "legislation on these lines will strengthen the position of all those who are anxious to co-operate in removing racial discrimination from our national life and will provide a necessary sanction against the few who are determined not to do so."

His sincerity and hopes were not to be realized that year; for it was not until the following year, on November 26, 1968, that the new Race Relations bill became law. Included in the provisions of the new act were places where members of the public gathered—entertainment, recreation and refreshment centers—as well as transport, travel, education, training, banking, and insurance facilities. People in business, the professions and trades, in addition to local and public authorities were covered by the new law. This provision included organizations making grants, loans, credits, or generally providing finance. The act defined discrimination as treating a person less favorably than another person—on grounds of color, race, or ethnic or national origins—in the provisions of goods, facilities, and services and in employment and housing. The definition included segregating people on grounds of color, race or ethnic or national origins.

But the primary motive for the bill was not immediate or wholesale prosecution of any act of discrimination brought to the notice of the law. Its purpose was to declare discrimination wrong in principle and to throw the weight of legislation behind voluntary bodies. The bill placed emphasis on conciliation through an enlarged and strengthened Race Relations Board. Industry was, however, given the first opportunity to deal with complaints in employment through its own voluntary machinery.

The Race Relations Board, its conciliation committees, and the voluntary machinery in industry were under an obligation to try to arrange settlements and seek assurances that there would be no repetition of discrimination against black workers. Only when this course failed could there be recourse to the courts. These were specially designated county courts sitting with assessors with special knowledge and experience in problems of community relations.

Discrimination was not viewed legally as a criminal offense under the 1968 bill. The courts were given power to grant injunctions restraining discrimination; to award damages for material loss or for loss of opportunity. This last statement meant loss of any benefit which might reasonably have been secured but for discrimination, or to make a declaratory judgment. These damages were not to be restricted to the county court limit of £500. Recognizing that legislation of itself could not solve all the problems of racial discrimination, the architects of this new Race Relations bill reconstituted the National Committee for Commonwealth Immigrants as a statutory body to be known as the Community Relations Commission. Its task was to continue the work of the committee in encouraging harmonious relationships between different racial groups.

The commission did not seem to be aware of the growing restlessness and impatience among the black immigrants who had long been disenchanted with the soft-pedalling, the alleged diplomacy and tact of the British government and their superficial attempts to integrate all races of the population into one harmonious whole. They were beginning to read hypocrisy and humbug into these "integration" moves. They wanted stronger action from the few leaders in their own ranks. The cry was for toughness, aggression, militancy. The mood of the American Black Power movement had crossed the Atlantic and was entering the mind of the black man in Britain. At the forefront of this wave of feeling was Michael

Malik. The black population was split in two factions over the Malik affair. There were those like Barbadian Eric Brant, a thirty-three-year-old property dealer and former seaman settled in London, leader of the sixty-thousand strong Barbados Overseas Community and Friends Association, who did not want violence of any sort, and described a speech of Michael Malik's in which he said that English people were "nasty and vicious" as "imbecilic," adding: "This man is saying that his views are a reflection of what the majority of coloured people in this country think. I rather believe that it represents one opinion only—his own."

Michael Malik's views were, however, shared by other blacks in Britain. Sympathy was shown by the young St. Lucian artist Winston Branch of the Slade School of Art. He painted an abstract portrait of Malik called "Alas Poor Michael!" Describing the portrait Branch declared:

> "Alas, poor Michael" amply sums up my belief that he was sent to jail because he simply said things the British Government didn't like. In my painting I try to convey the fact that Michael's ideology of black power will live on, despite his removal from the scene.

Even the staid and at one time rather conservative-minded West Indian Standing Conference was in 1968 predicting "Race war in Britain is inevitable." Spokesman for the Standing Conference Jeff Crawford, known for his level-headed and sober approach to problems of racial discrimination in the formative years of the Standing Conference, had changed. In a speech he warned that the black community in Britain was already conquered and therefore a war could only be aimed at liquidating or repatriating the blacks.

He went on: "In my opinion the stage has been reached when it is imperative that every black person in this country prepares himself for the inevitable offensive."

Mr. Crawford claimed that the offensive had been predicted not only by Enoch Powell—the Conservative rightwinger who wants black immigrants sent back home—but by more than 90 percent of the nation as a whole. Mr. Crawford claimed: "Cynics would say that a counter-offensive was unnecessary. But I contend that once again, history shows that the police inevitably side not with the oppressed but with the oppressors."

This warning did not come from an extremist. Crawford's views are shared by others in positions of responsibility. Dermott de Trafford, chairman of the employment panel of the National Committee for Commonwealth Immigrants, said: "Unless steps are taken now to right the wrongs we shall have ourselves to blame if in ten years there are race riots on the scale of those in Watts County, California."

Consequently it was not at all surprising when on Sunday, January 12, 1969, some five thousand largely nonwhite demonstrators sloshed through rainswept streets and battled with the British police to protest against racism in Britain and Rhodesia's white minority government. This march was described as London's first major "black power" march. Clusters of white sidewalk spectators replied "go back home" to marchers' chants of "black people unite and fight" and "long live black power." Double police cordons pushed back two attempts by protesters to enter and occupy Rhodesia House, the London office of the Salisbury Government.

Demonstrators threw bottles, pennies, and banner poles at the police during two charges. Two policemen were hurt and several protesters reeled away with bloody faces. Some twenty demonstrators fell under police horses in the scramble, but escaped unhurt. After the Rhodesia House confrontation had quietened down, about five hundred demonstrators attacked nearby South Africa House in Trafalgar Square, breaking more than fifty panes of glass with bricks and garbage cans. Barricades inside foiled attempts to enter by side doors. A police sergeant prevented some of the crowd from entering until reinforcements arrived. One man smashed window after window using a motorcycle crash helmet. Another followed suit with an umbrella. Some demonstrators picked up a news vendor's wooden stand and hurled it through the remaining panes. A litter bin was wrenched off a lamp post and stuffed with paper and cloth before being set alight and hurled into the midst of some policemen. The officers scattered, then waded into the demonstrators. Police smashed abandoned banners and staves which marchers later set afire. Dozens of shoes were lost in the scuffles. Less than half the marchers were white. There were strong contingents of Africans, West Indians, Indians, and Pakistanis. Arms linked, the protesters had set off, at the beginning of the demonstration, from Hyde Park speakers' corner shouting "Arm the African workers," and "Hang Ian Smith" (Rhodesia's rebel premier).

There were loud cries of "Disembowel Enoch Powell," and marchers later produced a black and white coffin with "common" written on the black part and "wealth" written on the white. Protesters pulled from it an effigy of Powell and set it on fire. The head was wrenched off the blazing dummy and tossed about like a ball.

Many of the white protesters represented branches of the Young Communists League. About half the total demonstrators strode behind the banner of the Zimbabwe Solidarity Committee during the two and a half hour march. That group had claimed that it would take over Rhodesia House for the people of Zimbabwe—the African name for Rhodesia. The rest lined up behind the Birmingham-based Black People's Alliance, which sent ten busloads of supporters to protest "living in a state which has gone racist." Organizers ordered a nonviolent march, with the stipulation, "Retaliate if necessary." One declared at the beginning of the march: "This is the start—the first time that black people have marched in London streets together. It is a start for next summer." Civil rights sources said the Black People's Alliance, which includes fifty-five organizations of minority groups, was unique in incorporating both moderate and militant black power advocates.

This is most significant and shows clearly the mood of the black population of Britain. It conjures up a picture of a future of racial disturbances if the British government and others in authority continue to allow racial feelings to be further aggravated by Negrophobe members of Parliament and other white racists.

The British government's policy on the question of its immigrant population appears to be one of pacification—of the whites. For although the Race Relations bill has been broadened in scope, its effect has been weakened by conciliation rather than by direct effect through the courts. While it is true that legislation will not stop race prejudice, yet it can ease the condition, which is worsening as the government's integration policies fail to show fruitful results. At the same time, the government, at every opportunity, has been curtailing the numbers of black immigrants allowed into Britain. The state of the black man in Britain in 1969 and after was still a parlous, insecure one.

BIBLIOGRAPHY TO CHAPTER SIXTEEN

"Artist Paints 'Poor Michael X' " *Advocate-News* (Barbados: March 20, 1968).

"The Church and Race Prejudice." *Flamingo Magazine* (London: December, 1962).

Commonwealth Immigrants Advisory Council. *Second Report.* London: H.M.S.O. (February, 1964).

"Five Thousand in First U.K. Black Power Show." *Advocate-News* (Barbados: January 15, 1969).

"How British Police Arrested Michael X." *Advocate-News* (Barbados: March 20, 1968).

"The Immigrant and the Church." *Flamingo Magazine* (London: January, 1962).

"Immigration: What Now?" *Flamingo Magazine* (London: January, 1965).

Institute of Race Relations. *News Letter.* London: 1963.

"McAlpine's Travels." *Flamingo Magazine* (London: February, 1965).

"Migrants disillusioned by white morals." *Maypole News* (Birmingham: Mid-September, 1961).

"Race hate bill in but out." *West Indies Observer* (January 18, 1964).

Nicholson, Rev. G. H. *Some Problems of Race.* Burghfield, Nr. Reading: privately printed. n.d.

Rickards, Colin. "Ban immigration . . ." *Advocate-News* (Barbados: July 17, 1966).

Smithers, David. "Sir Learie hits 'No Blacks' Tory M.P." *Daily Mirror* (Trinidad: May 20, 1965).

Truman, A. Roy. "School" in *Colour in Britain.* Ed. Richard Hooper. London: 1965.

"United Kingdom." *The Parliamentarian* (London: July, 1968).

Wilson, Peter. "West Indians and the Trade Unions." *Flamingo Magazine* (London: January, 1962).

CHAPTER XVII

SELF-IMPROVEMENT AT ALL COSTS

Black immigrants "come hell or high water" had come to Britain to better themselves, and, in spite of increasing odds against them, they *were* bettering themselves: hanging on to their jobs under great strain, saving money, educating their children, buying houses, and acquiring the modern conveniences enjoyed by white British workers. Socially and economically they were gradually, and without being outwardly conscious of it, becoming carbon copies of their white workmates. In race-conscious Wolverhampton, West Indian and other blacks have been getting on reasonably well in their jobs in spite of increasing pressures. Apart from the Transport Commission, the major employing source of black labor in Wolverhampton has been Goodyear, the tire manufacturers. On a much smaller scale blacks are employed in other industrial factories in and around the area where wages are fair by British standards.

From 1961, Birmingham presented a different picture. Blacks did not meet with the kind of concentrated prejudice found in Wolverhampton. Firms like B.S.A., big drug manufacturers, and some small factories employed several West Indians purely because they were supposed to be good cricketers. In fact, like many other English cities, Birmingham depended on immigrant labor to man the essential services—hospitals and transport. Many blacks worked in the building trade and in semiskilled jobs at the Austin car factory. The pattern is pretty much the same in Sheffield, Yorkshire. West Indians and other immigrants work in factories and foundries, on the railways and buses in this city of steel. Most of these workers said they lived a fairly quiet life and could save money.

A Sheffield employer said: "The coloured men I have on my books are good men, but very few of them who apply are able to do more than unskilled labouring jobs and there are only so many of those."

This began to change by 1964, as more and more black workers were learning skills. On the question of obtaining employment in Sheffield, blacks experienced little or no discrimination. Trouble began, as in most other British towns, when black men would try to mix with white girls after work. By the middle and late sixties a wedge of separation had grown between black and white.

However, as far as employment was concerned, the picture was relatively encouraging. For instance, the Vauxhall factory at Luton, Bedforshire first started to take West Indian workers in 1956, when more and more began to make their home there. In 1962 there were three thousand in Luton. During that period Jack Manton, then Welfare Officer at Vauxhall's, said: "When West Indians first came to us we put them on any jobs that were available; not necessarily labouring jobs. Some of them have proved themselves to be quite good mechanics." There are more West Indians working at Vauxhall than at any other factory in Luton. They work in all departments, the majority in skilled jobs, having learnt their trade at the factory itself. There are welders, sprayers, assemblers, fitters, machinists, trimmers, and metal finishers. Pay has always been good at Vauxhall, as at most automobile factories, and there has been no distinction between English and West Indian workers there on the question of rates of pay.

The majority of blacks who migrated to Britain "job-hunting" settled in London in specific areas, primarily working class. By far the heaviest concentration of blacks is to be found in the Paddington and Brixton districts. However, there are sizable pockets of them in no fewer than twenty-six London districts. Like blacks elsewhere in Britain they do shift work in public transport, hospitals, and factories. It has been no coincidence that in London, immigrants have moved into areas which, between the wars, had become centres of fairly large but poor Jewish communities. As a result, ghettos sprang up and racial antagonism and ostracism found fertile soil. These are now well ingrained in the fabric of life in those areas. Meanwhile blacks have learnt skills, are bus conductors, factory foremen, charge hands and supervisors. Many have whites working under them, which can be another source of conflict. Blacks experienced most difficulty in getting London employment as department store assistants and in white-collar jobs. Much the same can be said of blacks in other British towns.

In one of the Fine employment agency windows in Praed Street, near Paddington Station, there were, directly after the passing of the Commonwealth Immigrants Act, seventy job cards posted. Sixty-nine of them had typed at the bottom: "Regret no overseas applicants for the post." Those cards and other more subtle evidence of the color bar in British industry and commerce offered a clear warning. Many of the blacks in London and in other cities were born and educated in Britain and wanted something better than shift work on buses. Since 1964 there has been growing resentment against a system which, with sleek good manners, ignored their GCE "O" Level passes (high-school graduation equivalent) and treated blacks as something less than human. It was a system that had a measure of government authority; because from 1954 employment offices had been instructed to accept orders from employers who wanted to run all-white offices and factories, though they were first expected to try to make the employer change his mind.

London department stores at one time developed their own way of dealing with black applicants for employment. Inquiries about prospects for an eighteen-year-old black girl (with shorthand and typing) were made of several stores, including Marks & Spencer in Catford, and Woolworths, the British Home Stores, and the Co-operative in Lewisham, an area of South London with a big black population. More direct approaches were made to Harrods, which caters for the more upper-crust society of Knightsbridge, and to another big London store whose public relations man admitted, off the record: "We've got a damned touchy personnel department, allergic to the press."

The results of these inquiries were quite revealing. Marks & Spencer had "no objections to an employment interview"; Woolworth's was taking only fifteen-year-old girls straight from school, "because of the wages"; the British Home Stores personnel office in Lewisham said: "Oh, she's coloured, is she. I'm sorry, dear, I'm afraid we don't take coloured people at all." The headquarters of that store tried unconvincingly to deny this policy.

A salesman at the Co-operative store in Lewisham said he understood black sales staff were not employed there, though the superintendent said such a bar was against all Co-operative principles. At head office they gave the familiar story of support for a new black employee, but the staff objected. The public relations man at the big London store said black workers were employed but "more behind the scenes." He gave the usual explanation for this: "Suppose you put a nice coloured chap behind the counter and an American from the wrong part of America came in and started being rude about it. One thinks of the coloured chap, you know. . . ." Harrods' personnel manager said: "We've many coloured workers but it's quite true that we haven't yet got them as sales assistants. The management's views on the sales side is, I believe, rather like that of the Commissioner of the Metropolitan Police—anyone in direct contact with all customers must be acceptable to all customers." Discrimination was rampant in employment up to 1964. An oil executive said: "Once I had a coloured boy apply for a chauffeur's job. And, well, between ourselves, I didn't particularly want a coloured chauffeur. But at the same time it was easy to find a perfectly logical reason for not taking him. There usually is. He didn't know his London." This state of affairs simply could not be allowed to go unchallenged indefinitely; hence, after much pressure from the press and from fairminded people in and out of Parliament, the second Race Relations bill was passed in 1968. It was designed to stop this type of discrimination in employment. There are still white employers who try devious ways to get around the bill so as to avoid prosecution. But it is a long tedious process before a victim of such discrimination can reach the courts with his case; and not all blacks bother to bring cases of discrimination before the public. They prefer to shrug off the matter and let it drop.

While the British government had been pursuing its policy of reducing the numbers of black immigrants to Britain, it was allowing another type of black immigrant to enter rather easily. For in the very year that the Commonwealth Immigrants Act was passed, black recruits were being welcomed into the British Army with open arms. In 1962, there were black recruits from the Seychelles, Fiji, and the West Indies: 593 West Indians were serving in the British Army; there were 80 from British Guiana, 71 from Barbados, 273 from Jamaica, 35 from the Leeward Islands, 61 from Trinidad, 42 from the Windward Islands and 25 from elsewhere. This drive to attract black recruits stemmed from the fact that there were serious shortages in the British army; since black soldiers had already proved their value in the British army during the war years, it was felt that they could do so again. As a result the war office began a vast overseas recruiting drive that attracted thousands. The success of this form of black immigration was summed up by one British commanding officer, who said: "West Indians take trouble with their appearance and make naturally smart soldiers. They are often splendid athletes and are a great asset to regimental sports—particularly boxing, cricket and running."

These recruits could sign up for either six or nine years. The British press initially gave much publicity—sometimes adverse—to the government's plan for recruiting black volunteers from the Commonwealth, especially after imposing the Immigrants Act. The fact that recruits had to pay £80 towards their passage to Britain (refunded two years later) was another bone of contention. More important was how black soldiers would react when asked to go to quell uprisings in black territories. When asked, all replied that they would go anywhere and carry out whatever orders their regiments issued. Political implications, they said, were no concern of theirs. Black men serving in the army, navy and air force were, in fact, involved in British actions in the Caribbean, Africa, and parts of the Middle East.

Another type of immigrant who was more fortunate than the majority was the student who came to Britain to study for a profession and then return home. The kind of discrimination he experienced was not as malignant as that accorded to the black immigrant worker. This pattern has remained unchanged. It was the same before World War II and even earlier. Students, it was felt, were only passing through and would not remain permanently and cause competition in jobs, etc. Nevertheless, they still had to suffer indignities because of their race. They took the memory of these indignities back home with them. If the British are unpopular today in their former colonial possessions they have only themselves to blame.

Black students from Commonwealth countries still come in increasing numbers to Britain to study for professions. It was recorded in 1966–67 that over seventy-three thousand people from other countries were studying full-time there, the highest number ever recorded. Of these, 11,722 were from Commonwealth countries of the Caribbean. The annual survey by the British Council Cultural Organisation in London stated that this showed an increase of two thousand over the total for the previous academic year 1965–66. Of this latest total, over seventeen thousand were studying at universities—more than half of them as postgraduates. A similar number were at technical colleges and there were eighteen hundred studying law in London's Inns of Court, five hundred at colleges of education, sixteen thousand in hospital nursing training, twelve thousand undertaking various forms of practical nursing, and six thousand in private colleges and other institutions. Over forty-six thousand students came from Commonwealth countries, the six thousand from Nigeria being the largest number from any one state. Within Britain, half of all the visiting students were in London, the six thousand at London University—the country's largest—representing the biggest single concentration, of whom nine hundred were at the London School of Economics and Political Science.

Another black minority group in Britain which escapes the kind of violent prejudice met by the mass of black workers is the artistic sector. Included in this group are singers, musicians, actors, actresses, painters, and sculptors. They move and operate within a society which, by its very nature, does not place undue emphasis on the limitations of convention and conformity. Hence blacks in the artistic and entertainment world are accepted; but there are frustrations and prejudices, nonetheless. The black actor up to the early years of the sixties was never given "a fair crack of the whip." Opportunities were very narrow and in order to eat he had to accept the broad-smiling "Yes, b'wana, Yes massa boss," parts.

After a long time black actors could stomach no more of these Uncle Tom roles and they began to refuse to accept them. Many attempts had been made by black actor-producers to get a black theatre group going—by Pearl Connor, wife of the late Edric Connor, the famous singer-actor, by Jamaican Lloyd Reckord, himself an actor-playwright-producer, and Jamaican actor Clifton Jones who started the New Negro Theatre Company in mid-1960. Jones stated a fact which had been ignored by English producers: "Good Negro actors abound in this country. They deserve good theatre. It is our aim to get together really first-class actors who will appear in a variety of plays, preferably written by Negroes."

This Jones did. He showed, too, that black actors could perform plays written by whites and for whites. He chose two one-act plays for the company's first venture at the Theatre Workshop at Stratford, London: Paul Green's *No Count Boy* and William Saroyan's *Hello Out There*. Both played to full houses and were very successful. But Jones's success had a bitter taste, as he said: "The actors were seen doing good work, and they were promptly swallowed up and given tatty jobs on television. But I shall persevere."

Others persevered, too, and by 1969 the position of the black actor and actress had improved considerably. They were being accepted more as humans than as stereotypes in the theatre and on the motion picture and television screens. This change in status has been largely due to the fact that black writers have sprung up and have been writing plays of high standard for black actors and actresses. But blacks, as Clifton Jones had remarked, had shown that their talent was not restricted merely to black parts. British theatre producer Joan Clarke also wrote a few years ago:

> I have as producer of the West Indian Drama Group, presented plays by George Bernard Shaw, William Saroyan and Eugene O'Neill with entirely West Indian casts. My experience has convinced me that in emotional range and flexibility, the Negro actor is second to none. Our West Indian version of Eugene O'Neill's classic play, *Anna Christie* ran for five weeks in London, and a very high level of excellence was sustained throughout the entire run. The national press gave very encouraging reviews, and the company played to large and enthusiastic audiences throughout.

The position of the black musician, pop singer, dancer and bandleader has been much better. For many decades they have been accepted as "naturals" and reached the top, commanding star positions and fat fees. Even before the turn of this century when black American artists settled in Britain, black musicians and singers gained top billing. In the years just before and during World War II the most popular big band in Britain was that of West Indian leader Ken "Snakehips" Johnson. It played in the most exclusive clubs until a Luftwaffe bomb fell on the Café de Paris in Piccadilly one night, killing Snakehips Johnson outright while the band was actually playing.

Black boxers, too, have always been in a favored position and excelled in a craft at which it was conceded that they were masters. The same claim can be made for athletes.

Up to the end of World War II African or West Indian writers were almost nonexistent in Britain. Then in the decade that followed, something fresh and exciting happened to English literature when an avant-garde of West Indian writers began to make a name for themselves. One of the first critics to bring this phenomenon to the notice of the literary world was English critic Robert Robinson who wrote: "I think the West Indian idiom is about to undergo a literary commercialisation." Writers like the late Edgar Mittelholzer, George Lamming, Samuel Selvon, John Hearne, Vidia Naipaul, Jan Carew, Andrew Salkey, Peter Kempadoo, Orlando Patterson, Garth St. Omer, Michael Anthony, Dennis Williams, Namba Roy, Merrill Ferguson, Lindsey Barrett were all from the Caribbean—and were enjoying success along with Cyprien Ekwensi, Amos Tutuola, Ellis Komey, Wole Soyanke, Chinua Achebe, Bloke Modisane, from Africa, and some Asians.

Like other black immigrants, black writers went to Britain to earn a living. The fact of their blackness made them outsiders in English literature. They have been operating from the perimeter of the world of letters and this has given them a uniqueness and exoticism along with a feeling of isolation. Edgar Mittelholzer, the doyen of Caribbean writers in the two decades after World War II, wrote over a score of books, some of them concerned with English characters and themes based in Britain. The same can be said of the Trinidad Indian Vidia Naipaul, and a few other black writers.

These black writers all differ in everything except the fact that they are writing in the English language. Themes, styles, dialect, all reflect the individuality of the writers and their backgrounds. Yet, it is still fashionable, in certain quarters, for regional tags to be placed on their books. In the main, however, their work is judged by the same literary standards as that of the white writers. No longer do the English critics regard them as colorful novelties and give them the "noble savage" treatment, which was typical of the pioneering years of the last two decades, as Barbadian writer George Lamming explained:

> The British West Indian writer occasions surprise and creates a certain confusion. He confuses because, for a variety of reasons, he seems so perilously near to the English whose judgement begins with the conscious premise that he is, in fact different. His conception of what a novel is seems to be the same. He does really speak English. It is not his second language. And even when it makes embarrassing demands on his tongue, or emerges in strangely hybrid forms, it does not seem to cause any surprise. It confuses because he is African or

> Indian descent, or what-have-you, yet it seems to belong to a wholly different pattern of calculations and ambitions. For this very reason he will be grouped together as a separate entity within the body of English literature.

The fact that black writers, be they West Indian, African, or Asian refuse to be type cast by the critics does not mean that they are trying to run away from themselves and their roots. On the contrary. For it has been from those very roots that black writers had to draw their motive power, their material. In 1960 George Lamming made this clear observation:

> The West Indian novel, by which I mean the novel written by the West Indian about the West Indian reality, is hardly twenty years old. And here is the fascination of the situation. The education of all these writers is more or less middle-class Western culture, and particularly English culture. But the substance of their books, the general motives and directions, are peasant. One of the most popular complaints made by West Indians against their novelists is the absence of novels about the West Indian middle-class.
>
> Why is it that Reid, Mittelholzer in his early work, Selvon, Neville Dawes, Roger Mais, Andrew Salkey, Jan Carew—why is it that their work is shot through and through with the urgency of peasant life? And how has it come about that their colonial education should not have made them pursue the general ambitions of nonprovincial writers. . . Unlike the previous governments and departments of educators, unlike the businessman importing commodities, the West Indian novelist did not look out across the sea to another source. He looked in and down at what had traditionally been ignored. For the first time the West Indian peasant became other than a cheap source of of labour. He became, through the novelist's eye, a living existence, living in silence and joy and fear, involved in riot and carnival. It is the West Indian novel that has restored the West Indian peasant to his true and original status of personality.

The peasant and the soil have been brought back to literature by West Indian writers. The West Indian who came nearest to being an exception to the present idiom was John Hearne. His main obsession was with an agricultural middle-class Jamaica. To quote Lamming: "He is not an example of that instinct and root impulse which return the better West Indian writers back to the soil." Yet most West Indian novelists have preferred to remain in Britain "living in a state of chosen exile." They fear a return to the Caribbean. They will not return in any permanent sense, "because they feel that at some time they will be ignored in and by a

This is Lamming's contention and a valid one. He added: "In spite of all that has happened in the last ten years I doubt that he [the West Indian writer] would be happy to go back. Some have tried; some would like to try. But no one would feel secure in his decision to return. It could be worse than arriving in England for the first time."

Three or four at most have gone back home and have managed to stick it out in their island territories in the Caribbean. One has since returned to Britain. New writers are constantly joining the ranks of the majority of other black immigrants who will never return home. Racial attitudes have been growing worse, tension is mounting yet the majority of the one and a half million black immigrants will remain. They face the possibility of race riots, a host population which is showing open hostility, and a climate that is never friendly and inviting. But they stick it out. They have bettered themselves and their growing children. They went to Britain to improve their fortunes and then sail or fly back to their sunny shores. "But," writes Donald Hinds, "in the majority of cases intention seldom becomes reality."

For those who have remained, integration has been made increasingly difficult by persistent racial animosity. That this animosity has come not only from the "lunatic fringe" but also from right-wing Conservative members of Parliament, immigration and customs officers, dockworkers and housewives shows that no sector of the white population is immune from race hate. That racial bigots like Enoch Powell, Duncan Sandys, and Cyril Osborne have a majority following among the white population is frightening.

But Britain's blacks are not taking this with passive indifference. Powell's anti-black speeches have caused an awakening among them. They have now arrived at the bitter truth that all blacks are in the same racial boat. As one of them put it: "Every black person has a problem, and they've all started to see how it ties on to others' problems."

BIBLIOGRAPHY TO CHAPTER SEVENTEEN

Clark, Joan. "The Negro on the 'White' Stage." *Tropic Magazine* (London: April, 1960).

Dunn, Peter. "The Black List of Jobs." *The Observer Weekend Review.* (London: May 3, 1964).

Hiro, Dilip. "The Young Are Ready to Hit Back." *The Observer* (London: July 14, 1968).

"Negro Theatre Company." *Tropic Magazine* (London: June, 1960).

Scobie, Edward. "Men of Steel." *Flamingo Magazine* (London: May, 1964).

———. "The New Brummies." *Flamingo Magazine* (London: November, 1961).

———. "Soldiers of the Queen." *Flamingo Magazine,* London: 1962.

———. "Vauxhall's West Indians." *Flamingo Magazine* Vol. 2, No. 12 (1963).

CHAPTER XVIII

THE GRADUAL PROCESS OF ASSIMILATION

"Here they stayed, and in time vanished as completely as a conjuror's rabbit—biologically absorbed into the mainstream of Anglo-Saxon pallor."

Elspeth Huxley in Blacks Next Door

The way things stood in Britain in the latter half of 1969, the black man faced four alternatives: integration, assimilation, separation, or repatriation. The birth of the new decade—the seventies—has not shown any change. The black man is under the same stresses. On the one hand attempts have been and are being made to integrate him while on the other he is meeting hostility and suggestions have been made from responsible quarters for his repatriation. There is the growing black militancy which would not mind if black and white lived separate parallel lives, side by side. But by far the most widespread movement among black people in Britain is for total equality of economic and social rights now. This presupposes first class citizenship. The mood is not one of compromise and blacks will accept nothing less. This is something with which both Labour and Conservative governments have refused to come to grips; for, as Lord Byers, chairman of the Liberal party, noted, "There is a bit of Powellism in every Englishman." However, these anti-black signs have not stopped, what one writer termed "the gradual process of assimilation."

The acceptance of three blacks as Metropolitan policemen in London does not add up to full employment equality. Nor does one black radio or television announcer mean that all avenues of opportunity are open wide for all blacks in Britain. A couple of black magistrates and justices of the peace, a few borough councillors, a life peer in the House of Lords are merely pebbles on the vast shore of acceptance and assimilation. These morsels of success which blacks have been allowed to achieve in Britain after generations of settling there are certainly nothing to sing hosannas about. Blacks have not traveled far since those years after the Mansfield decision in 1772 when all blacks in Britain were freed and could move about the streets of English towns and cities as free men and women. The successes of a handful of blacks in the eighteenth century did not open doors or bring acceptance for the forty-five thousand blacks who lived in Britain in those years. In the words of the English proverb: "One swallow doesn't make a summer."

The position, if anything, became worse after emancipation and moved ahead much too slowly and in too meagre a fashion to have any profound significance in race relations in the last quarter of this century. It is because of this snail's pace progress that the mood of the black man is one of urgency, and of anger. Blacks are not prepared to wait on the white man's compassion and charity. They are not disposed any longer to turn the other cheek. They have done that for too long and have not achieved equality. For the black man in Britain and elsewhere, "Uncle Tom" has been well and truly dead and buried. There will be no resurrection.

But there was a period in Britain, particularly in the nineteen fifties and early sixties, when the attitude of the black man was far different from what it is today. He felt then that his only hope of acceptance by the host population was to get lost and metaphorically "whitewashed." In other words, he was deliberately setting out to become a "black Englishman." He was discarding—as much as he could—all that was black. He wanted to forget his "blackness," to cast it aside and become one of the white herd in dress, speech, eating and drinking habits, and all the other social trivia. He was putting milk in his coffee in other ways, too, for what he considered sound reasons. Deep down he knew that he could not call himself a first-class citizen even if he wanted to. His passport might claim that he is a "British subject" and "a citizen of the United Kingdom and Colonies"; as Jamaican author, Andrew Salkey, once remarked, he may have "been fed on the Mother Country myth" to the extent of believing implicitly and passionately that Britain is his matriarchal home, yet the truth was that he was allowed to exist only on the perimeter of British life. He was not "accepted" in either social or political institutions of his mother country.

Economically, too, blacks were fully aware that they did not receive equal pay for equal work, unless they belonged to a union; and it was well known that unions tended to operate a closed door policy when it came to black workers. This was shown on many occasions, and once, quite glaringly, when 591 members of the General Municipal Workers' Union employed at an aluminum works at Banbury in Oxfordshire, voted "No" in a ratio of three to one on the question: "Should coloured workers be admitted to the factory?" There were several other barriers of non-acceptance, some of them put up even by the very young: by the cockney schoolboy, for instance, who told a black boy born in London, "Go back to Africa." From this unformed age, the English begin to "keep out" the black man living in Britain. Little wonder that black American writer Roi Ottley commented several years ago after a visit to Britain that "Blacks meet formidable obstacles in obtaining white-collar and skilled employment. Few Negroes hold Government positions." He was perfectly right, for no black man would be considered qualified for a foreign office appointment. There were no top black executives in big business, no black judges, no practicing Queen's Counsels. To the claim that there are several popular and successful doctors working in English hospitals, a curious yet valid explanation has been offered, and one which black doctors have been heard to repeat: they maintain that some superstition underlies this popularity, based on the English belief that black doctors have, allied to their professional skill, the powers of the medicine man who uses obeah, voodoo or ju-ju. "Black brings luck" is a favorite saying of the English. For instance, many a shopkeeper will feel that good luck will be his for the day if a black man is the first person to buy something in his shop when he opens. To usher in the New Year Scottish people try to get a black man to walk in through the front door to guarantee them a lucky year.

In Britain, black may bring luck to whites but not to blacks seeking equality for which they decided to undergo a nearly complete transformation of identity, background and, indeed, personality. It was this which prompted Dr. Harold Moody way back to remark: "By far too many of us are lacking in pride of race and are quite content to be thought English." Roi Ottley, too, observed this tendency when he visited Britain during World War II and after. He noted: "In deportment, speech and habits they [blacks] are Englishmen distinguished from their white countrymen only by color . . . Negro Englishmen consequently are able to develop a culture and sophistication and acquire a refinement rarely found among Negroes in the United States." In other words, blacks in Britain had become black Englishmen. This transformation was a gradual, studied and deliberate process; one which took years to polish. The tendency to smooth out rough edges of the sing-song West Indian accent, in fact to drop it altogether for one which, even when used by the English, sounded cultivated, was common among immigrants from these colonies; from the educated middle-class to the man working as a kitchen hand.

The portrait of the black Englishman took fuller shape with mode of dress, and ways of behavior. Depending on his social background in the Caribbean, the West Indian fell in automatically with the habits of the English class to which he felt an affinity. The man who held a white-collar position in Trinidad, Jamaica, Barbados or any of the other islands would aim to resemble his English counterpart. The West Indian porter or barrow boy would dress in the manner of the English version.

Weaned on rum as they were, West Indians at first had no palate for English beer. Before long they became regulars at their local pubs, and could knock back their pints of mild and bitter with the ease of custom. Even their swear words changed and became English in flavor.

The desire to equalize, to get closer in looks and behavior to those who were once masters in colonial lands had very early beginnings. Kenneth Little explained how this came about:

> The colonies from which West Indians come, Jamaica and Barbados in particular, have been Europeanised, or rather "anglicised," for several hundreds of years. As the descendants of Africans who were torn away from their native culture, present and preceding generations of coloured West Indians have never known any recognised culture other than an English one. English is the native and universal language of the West Indies and English customs, notions of etiquette and social behaviour have been accepted and followed in good class West Indian houses for nearly a century.

African slaves who were brought to the Caribbean were not only "torn away from their native culture," they were forced out of their tribal groupings. The result was that slaves banded together could not communicate in their native tongue. They had to learn a common language, and this was primarily English. Dr. Little elaborated on this similarity between West Indian and British:

> Education, too, in West Indian schools is entirely on English lines, and the school curricula show few if any, divergences from those of an English secondary school. West Indians are not only taught to regard themselevs as members of one of the oldest of British colonies, but are proud to think of themselves as British citizens.

Hundreds of thousands of West Indians were "anglicized" from birth. They sang English hymns in Church of England choirs, and gave forth with patriotic fervor such flag-waving songs as "Land of Hope and Glory" and "Rule Britannia"; they were acquainted at an early age with Shakespeare, Pope, Milton, Cowper, Dryden, Byron, Wordsworth, Keats, Dickens, among other English men of letters. They had no heroes of their own, they thought. In fact, they were taught to believe that. So when West Indians read in the British press that they were lowering the standard of life in Britain, they felt hurt and discarded. Bewilderment took hold of them because they had always considered themselves as British as the British themselves. They were to learn differently in the years ahead.

The desire to emulate the English was especially true of people from the island of Barbados, known as "Little England." Barbadians in Britain formed the bulk of the bus drivers and bus conductors. They have been described as "more English than the English," but the same thing applied in perhaps a slightly lesser degree to all West Indians. V. S. Naipaul, the Trinidad novelist and critic stressed the fact that "It is not fully realised how completely the West Indian Negro identified himself with England. Africa has been forgotten; films about African tribesmen excite derisive West Indian laughter." (This was a valid observation of the black man in Britain in the fifties and early sixties—the period under examination at this stage.) Naipaul himself at that time objected to being labelled "a West Indian writer," even though he was born in Trinidad, and in spite of the fact that several of his books dealt primarily with life in Trinidad. George Lamming thought that Naipaul's desire to be classed as a West Indian writer had been "wiped out of his guts with the diabolical help of Oxford" which he attended. Certain other writers from the Caribbean shared that feeling, though it went deeper, right to the roots of race. It was, in fact, a discarding of Africa—the Africa blacks had been seen in films and read about in the white man's history and geography books. This was most noticeable in Guyanese-born Edward Braithwaite whose best-selling *To Sir with Love* was published in 1959. Braithwaite, a former RAF fighter pilot, had been based in Britain for several years after demobilization at the end of World War II. Writing about this quality in the two authors, Frank Biralsingh, a Guyanese graduate from the University of the West Indies noted:

> These writers fail to establish strong kinship with India and Africa, and although they do not openly say so, imply that they are more British than Indian or African. In fact, both Mr. Naipaul and Mr. Braithwaite seem a little ashamed of their racial ties with India and Africa respectively, and the disillusionment of the Guyanese, when faced by a colour bar in Britain, is all the more painful because of his genuine admiration for British customs and manners.

It was precisely for this reason that blacks felt deeply hurt when they were treated as though they were outsiders by a country they chose to regard as "Mother." A new mood began to stir among the blacks in Britain. They no longer wanted to be considered "carbon copy" Englishmen. The race riots and the increasing race hatred were destroying the ideal of the black Englishman. There was a feeling, too, as Donald Hinds put it, that "people lose respect for us when we let them think that we want to be black Englishmen." G. A. Morron, a Jamaican living in Wolverhampton in 1962 wrote: "I am a Jamaican and I believe we should all join hands and hearts in establishing a firm relationship with the REAL Mother Country—Africa." Curiously enough, this reversion was predicted by a Martinique poet-politician, writer Aimé Césaire, as far back as 1956. He was then a delegate at the First International Congress of black writers and artists held in Paris at the Sorbonne's Amphithéatre Descartes under the auspices of the French-African institution, Présence Africaine. Talking about white imperialism Césaire contended that "any political and social régime which destroys the self-determination of a people also destroys the creative power of that people."

He examined what had been done by the metropolitan powers to the subject races in the colonies and argued:

> The situation, therefore, in the colonial countries, is tragic. Wherever colonisation is a fact the indigenous culture begins to rot. And, among these ruins, something begins to be born which is not a culture but a kind of sub-culture, a sub-culture which is condemned to exist on the margin allowed it by European culture. This sub-culture has no chance whatever of growing into an active living culture.

This subculture the black man took with his few personal belongings to Britain. That was why it had been easy for him to become a black Englishman and live on borrowed ways and customs until he was persistently discarded and forced to abandon all hope of pleasing. Césaire had contended that the only solution was for African peoples to regain their racial dignity and historical initiative. He was referring to black people everywhere, particularly those living in Western countries like America, France, and Britain. He prophesied:

> In the culture to be born there will no doubt be old and new elements. How these elements will be mixed is not a question to which any individual can respond. The response must be given by the community. But we can say this: that the response will be given, and not verbally, but in tangible facts, and by action.

"And by action." This prophecy was to become reality in the middle sixties and to reach a high point in 1969 and 1970 with the Black Power and other militant movements. Attempts at integration at government and other levels had seemed pathetic and half-hearted. It was as though white integrationists went about this exercise in two minds: they did not oppose integration, because there was nothing else to be done; and at the same time deep down in their subconscious they did not want it. Blacks were tolerated, but not accepted. There were those who believed that integration would come slowly. Organizations, groups, bodies were set up in order to get West Indians and other immigrants in Britain to integrate into their local communities. But the race solution was receding as the years moved ahead. A few years ago the struggle was against hypocrisy and apathy. Now it is against open and unashamed racialism. The black man was being forced to resort to self-imposed segregation and develop services geared to his own tastes. "The average immigrant," said one, "no longer feels like integrating into English society as he might. Friendship is a two-way thing, and the English won't play." Undoubtedly the English like it that way. One of the black leaders said:

"By the act of leaving home, blacks exposed themselves to change. They were prepared before to do what was necessary to fit into the new society. But the English were at home. Most of them refused to change even a little and make some adjustment. Blacks are no longer bending over backwards to please. In fact, they don't care very much what the English think about integration." In 1967 the position was clearly stated by British writer Colin MacInnes:

> In our dealings with black Britons, two alternatives now face us. One is to recognise that they are Britons just as we are, and entitled to (not "granted") total equality of economic and social rights—not next year, sometime, never, but at once. The other is to continue politely to reject them, and create hostile black ghettos in our country—which will certainly result in, what we call, "disturbances" or "incidents."

The British chose to take the latter alternative until bigots like former Colonial Secretary Duncan Sandys and Enoch Powell appeared on the scene, preaching open removal of blacks from Britain (something advocated from the beginning of the postwar immigration of blacks by fascist leaders Colin Jordan and Sir Oswald Mosley).

With the Conservatives in power it has become more and more difficult for blacks to come and live in Britain. As Commonwealth immigrants coming into Britain to work, blacks now have to obtain a work permit for a specific job in a specific place. Permits will be granted only where local (white) labor is not available and for a maximum of twelve months. Extensions to those permits will be considered "on merit" and will be granted only to immigrants who remain in approved employment or obtain other employment. In other words, black immigrants were being treated as foreigners with no right of permanent settlement. Applications for permanent settlement would be considered at the end of four years of approved employment, as in the case of foreigners. Dependents of immigrants under this new plan would have the chance to join them in Britain; not as a right but in the same way as people who immigrate to Britain from outside the Commonwealth. As though to soften the blow, the Conservative government declared that it would aim to improve conditions for those blacks already there, and to ensure that everyone was equal under the law. It promised that it would seek to see that there would not be first-class and second-class citizens but one class.

In spite of the promise of the Conservatives their tough line on blacks is not at all surprising, in view of the heavy racial bias under which the British General Election of June 18, 1970, was fought; and at which race-touting Enoch Powell doubled his majority in his Wolverhampton constituency. Lord Byers was stung to remark that this victory "was bad for the country." And indeed it was; for already the position for blacks in the first six months of 1970 had been threatening. "Skinheads"—white youths with clean-shaven heads—were out in packs attacking Pakistanis and other blacks. These assaults were on the increase. Members of the Black Power movement were facing more police brutality. There had been large-scale race riots in Leeds in July, 1969, when over one thousand white men and youths roamed the streets breaking windows and assaulting blacks. This trouble had been organized by an extreme right wing group —the National Front Movement—whose members kept chanting in the streets of the busy northern industrial city of Leeds "Send the Blacks home," and "Let's get the Paks" (Pakistanis).

This ugly mood brought back the memory of the horrors of Nottingham and Notting Hill over twelve years earlier. The reaction among blacks in Britain today is far different from what it was in 1958. They will not take violence lying down; they will not hide or run away. It is the British attitude which could cause serious trouble; for the British feel that any trouble that can be caused by one black man among fifty whites could be quickly silenced. And there lies the danger. Whites will never again silence blacks. Colin MacInnes views this situation with some foreboding but a little hope:

> There may be no exact parallel with conditions here in Britain, and in the U.S. In America it is, alas, too late—here we still have time, if only just. . . . We still have a last chance, but we had better hurry.

The English do not seem to want to hurry. On the contrary, the signs indicate that they are taking backward steps and retreating into the troubled mood of 1958. George Lamming had warned, as far back as 1962, "I don't think we have heard the last word from Notting Hill." The state of black-white relations in Britain in 1972 may prove him right. Headlines back in August 1970 were reminiscent of 1958, when tension was building up: WARNING OF MORE UK RACIAL CLASHES, CHANGE TOWARDS MIGRANTS FELT, FIGHT AGAINST BRU-

TALITY PROMISED, and POLICE CLASH WITH BLACK PROTESTERS.

The police were accused of discrimination and brutality against blacks. On Sunday, August 9, 1970 police clashed with black demonstrators as they tried to re-route a Black Power march through the West London districts of Notting Hill and Paddington. The disturbance started when police sealed off a street ahead of the two hundred flag-waving demonstrators, protesting police hostility to the black residents of the two areas. The marchers hurled bottles and beer cans at the police. Demonstrators sent police helmets flying in the scuffle that followed. Seventeen policemen were injured in the clashes, six of them having to go to hospital for treatment of injuries. A total of nineteen persons were arrested and charged with offenses including assault on a police officer, possessing an offensive weapon, assault and threatening behavior.

Jeff Crawford, secretary of the ten thousand-strong West Indian Standing Conference, said that the march was called because local authorities and the police had been threatening to close The Mangrove Club, owned by West Indians. Speaking after the demonstration, Michael X warned: "The battle for the true liberation of all our territories will have to be fought on the streets of London." This clash was the second in two weeks involving London police and blacks. The marchers chanted "Kill the pigs," and carried a pig's head on a pole.

Britain's security police were alerted and were investigating a document being circulated in London threatening police and newspapers in the name of black power. This document stated:

> Today it is police stations which are raided. Tomorrow it will be your racialist newspapers. In other words we shall do unto the police what they do unto us. In accordance with this determination and resolve we have issued an ultimatum to the Commissioner of Police giving him fair and due warning so the pigs would come to their senses before it is too late. We are also giving your white press vultures warning not to print false and biased reports about black people. The black man is not going to tolerate any nonsense from any white quarter, police or Press. Hope you cats will bear that in mind.

Even one-time moderates like Jeff Crawford have reached the point of exasperation. Referring to the clash between blacks and police when seventeen policemen were hurt, he said:

> If you hurt an animal and it becomes cornered and trapped, and can no longer escape, it hits back in desperation and fear to get out. This is the feeling of the black community. All hope has been lost.

Leaders of black activist groups, loosely connected as a Black Power movement, warned of more violence. They said their followers would use "any means you care to mention. . . . I think you have seen quite a few manifestations of these in the past few weeks, and I think you will see a lot more."

Repeating the mood of anger, Vince Hines, information officer of the militant Racial Action Adjustment Society (RAAS) stated: "The black youth of this country is growing more angry and frustrated. The present situation is leading towards an atmosphere of total hate."

Jeff Crawford summed up the situation with words of despair:

> Unless something is done right now to try and resolve the situation which is rapidly deteriorating, it is almost certain that there might be one or two killings in these clashes with the police. It is possible that a policeman or policemen will be killed. As far as I am concerned, most of the magistrates' courts are protection rackets for the police.

This condition is explosive. Again the British government is showing a lack of interest in this worsening situation. It is as if government is in accord with what is happening. Little wonder that Mr. Waldo Ramsey, Barbados' High Commissioner in London, observed at that time:

> Some British people seemed to think that they had a mandate in some cases to be as hostile as possible to West Indians. Nowadays one got the feeling as one walked along the road in Britain that there was a greater propensity to open hostility.

If allowed to continue, with police brutality going unnoticed, unchecked by government authorities, then the situation for blacks will be totally unbearable. It bears repeating that blacks are reacting differently today. They are answering back in kind and taking steps to protect themselves, prepared to meet violence with violence. They will no longer accept bad treatment but feel they are more entrenched in the fabric of English life and must stand up for their rights.

That relations between blacks and whites in Britain in 1970, the beginning of a new and more enlightened decade, were at their worst is an indictment of the British as racists. After four and a half centuries of closer and closer contact, the black man is still unwanted in Britain. The new Immigration Bill which was passed in March, 1971, has further strengthened the barrier and the influx of immigrant workers has been reduced to a trickle of about four thousand a year, half of whom are professional people, mostly doctors and nurses. In this new bill, Enoch Powell's views can be clearly seen; particularly in three aspects. One of these concerns the necessity for immigrants who are admitted to Britain for a limited time to register with the police. This necessity to bring the police into the lives of black people where already friction and mistrust exist is an omen of disaster. The second deals with applicants for permanent residence who have lived in Britain for five years. Apart from having a good character, the applicant must possess "a sufficient knowledge of English." This, of course, will leave much power in the hands of those whose job it will be to decide on this "sufficient knowledge." The third point involves the clause in the bill which gives the government new powers to provide financial aid for voluntary repatriation. Many people believe that this is the British government's first step towards compulsory repatriation. Enoch Powell, jubilant over the government's immigration measures, which are coming closer in line with his own, took occasion when controversy over this new bill was raging to renew his call for massive voluntary repatriation. He claimed that Britain's blacks will total at least four million by 1985, declaring:

> There is only one way to avert the prospects staring us in the face in the next decade—that is, massive, albeit voluntary repatriation. It is in the time of the rising generation that the harvest will be reaped from the dragon's teeth that have been sown and are being sown still. The British people and Parliament are apparently oblivious of the catastrophe which broods above them.

Immigrant organizations en masse attacked the new bill, holding meetings, staging protest marches and strikes. A campaign of civil disobedience was planned as soon as the bill was passed. A West Indian immigrant leader in London called on all West Indian doctors and nurses in Britain to go on strike for a week—to show how much the country depends on immigrants. Rudy Narayan, a barrister, told a 250-strong meeting of the West Indian Standing Conference on March 26, 1971: "The people of this country will only realise how they need us through suffering and pain. If they die in their beds because there is no one to look after them they will realise our importance to this country." Mr. Narayan went on to say that the clause in the Immigration Bill on voluntary repatriation was the most dangerous. It would inevitably lead to compulsory repatriation. Peter Hain, twenty-one-year-old chairman of the Action Committee against Racialism said: "The Immigration Bill is a declaration of war on Britain's black community. It is an ultimately racialist measure."

Commenting on Powell's inflammatory speech at the time the new bill was being debated, Mr. David Oldham, secretary of Surrey county's anti-apartheid movement stated:

> Powell's scheme is entirely racialist as we understand it. I think that it must have a very detrimental effect indeed on all coloured people in this country and on Britain's relations with the Commonwealth and the United Nations. Powell wants to send home only coloured people. He is saying nothing about the Americans, the Canadians, the Australians and other white immigrants who come here.

A Swedish newspaper, *Aftonbladet*, described the new bill as the first set of racial laws introduced in Western Europe since Nazi legislation against the Jews in the thirties. Universal opinion is that there will be serious and far-reaching repercussions. Sydney Bidwell, a Labour member of Parliament from the racially mixed West London areas of Hanwell and Southwall has said: "Already there is fear stalking the land among coloured people as a result of the Bill's proposals." On March 21, 1971, a party of 178 Jamaicans had returned home from Britain with complaints that racial discrimination was one of the main problems they had to face there. A spokesman for the group said that most of them returned to Jamaica to settle because life in Britain was very rough and getting worse daily. However, nearly two million blacks have remained to try and ride out the storm.

By now, the British should know, understand and accept the blacks in their midst. Their refusal to do so mars their reputation as moral leaders, which wears very thin when their attitude to blacks is examined. Time has almost run out, and if they do not act they will have only themselves to blame for the troubles that lie ahead. Britain will be the laughing stock of countries like Rhodesia, South Africa, and America and her hypocrisy will be exposed. Millions of blacks the world over will despise Britons more than they now hate them for the sins of their colonial past. It will be several generations before black people will, in all humanity, be able to pardon Britons for the race hatred embedded in their lives. This sin, one of the sins of their slave-trading fathers, as British writer James Pope-Hennessey once wrote, will first have to be washed clean away from their system.

However, in the face of all these dangers, the fact of assimilation remains. It is biologically more likely that the minority two million blacks in Britain will assimilate rather than integrate with the fifty million white majority, providing there is no compulsory mass repatriation. Several years ago in his study *Nature Knows No Color-Line*, J. A. Rogers observed:

> The present Negro strain in Britain is disappearing into the white one precisely as the past. The descendants of Daniel Taylor, father of Coleridge-Taylor, for instance, are now almost indistinguishable from white. There is no reason to believe that what I myself, saw in England as regarding racial inter-mixture was essentially different from that in the many centuries preceding.

History has proved J. A. Rogers right. Blacks in Britain are now gradually being "biologically absorbed in the mainstream of Anglo-Saxon pallor," as they have been from the very first time they settled on the shores of Britain. This is unfortunate for the black man, for as V. S. Naipaul wrote "to accept assimilation is in a way to accept a permanent inferiority." Ironically, the black man has no other alternative, as long as he remains on the British scene.

It is in these conflicting circumstances that the black man in Britain finds himself. Time will never be able to improve his condition. It can only lighten his darkness.

Therein lies the tragedy.

BIBLIOGRAPHY TO CHAPTER EIGHTEEN

Biralsingh, F. M. "To John Bull With Hate." *Caribbean Quarterly* 14 (December, 1968).

"Change Towards Migrant Felt." *Advocate-News* (Barbados: August 29, 1970).

Hinds, Donald. *Journey to an Illusion.* London: 1966.

MacInnes, Colin. "Through a Glass Darkly." *New Statesman* (London: August 18, 1967).

Morran, G. A. "Mother Africa." *Flamingo* (London: October, 1962).

Naipaul, V. S. *The Middle Passage* London: 1962.

"Police Clash with Black Protesters." *Advocate-News* (Barbados: August 10, 1970).

"Probe Into Threat to Police, Press." *Advocate-News* (Barbados: August 14, 1970).

Rogers, J. A. *Nature Knows No Color-Line.* New York: 1952.

Scobie, Edward. "Black Englishmen." *Flamingo* (London: November, 1962).

"U.K. Immigration Clampdown." *Advocate-News* (Barbados: July 4, 1970).

"Warning of More U.K. Racial Clashes." *Advocate-News* (Barbados: August 11, 1970).

"West Indian Leader Tells What It's Like in Britain." *Advocate-News* (Barbados: August 12, 1970).

"Youth Gangs Attacking Immigrants." *Advocate-News* (Barbados: April 12, 1970).

INDEX

Index

Index

Index

Index